THE MEANING OF *RUAḤ* AT QUMRAN

SOCIETY
OF BIBLICAL
LITERATURE

DISSERTATION SERIES

Number 110

THE MEANING OF *RUAḤ* AT QUMRAN

by
Arthur Everett Sekki

Arthur Everett Sekki

THE MEANING OF *RUAḤ* AT QUMRAN

Scholars Press
Atlanta, Georgia

THE MEANING OF *RUAḤ* AT QUMRAN

Arthur Everett Sekki

Ph.D., 1987
University of Wisconsin
(Madison)

Advisor:
Keith N. Schoville

Library of Congress Cataloging in Publication Data

Sekki, Arthur Everett.
The meaning of ruach at Qumran / Arthur Everett Sekki.
p. cm. -- (Dissertation series / Society of Biblical Literature ; no. 115)
Bibliography: p.
ISBN 1-55540-351-4 (alk. paper). -- ISBN 1-55540-352-2 (alk. paper)
1. Dead Sea scrolls--Criticism, interpretation, etc. 2. Ruaḥ (The Hebrew word) I. Title. II. Series: Dissertation series (Society of Biblical Literature) ; no. 115.
BM487.S44 1989
296.1'55--dc20 89-6280
CIP

Printed in the United States of America
on acid-free paper

TABLE OF CONTENTS

Chapter Page

ACKNOWLEDGMENTS

I would like to thank the faculty of the Department of Hebrew and Semitic Studies of the University of Wisconsin-Madison and especially my advisor, Professor Keith N. Schoville, for making this study possible. I would also like to thank Professor Emeritus Menahem Mansoor for the years of guidance and encouragement he has given to me in the study of Hebrew and semitics and particularly of the sectarians of Qumran. Finally, I would like to thank my family and friends for their constant support.

CHAPTER 1

INTRODUCTION

A basic problem from the beginning of the study of the Dead Sea Scrolls and continuing to the present[1] has been in determining when *ruaḥ* in the sectarian literature refers to God's Spirit, man's spirit, angel/demon, wind or breath. The kinds of determinations scholars make in this regard will influence not only their views of sectarian pneumatology in general but also their views on the beliefs of the Qumran community in other areas. For example, scholars who view *ruaḥ* in the Scrolls predominately in terms of the two spirits of 1QS 3:13-4:26 (usually defined as psychological/cosmic in nature and as involving an Iranian, cosmic dualism) tend to understand it as a predestined good or evil spirit/spirituality dominating men and forming the basis for Qumran's religious exclusiveness with its corresponding doctrines of double predestination and righteous hatred for those outside the community.[2] Other scholars, how-

---

[1]*Cf.* F. Manns, *Le symbole Eau-Esprit dans le Judaisme Ancien,* (Jerusalem: Franciscan Printing Press, 1983), p. 83. Manns disagrees with P. Guilbert's definition of *ruaḥ* in 1QS 3:7 as simply man's spirit. *Cf.* also M. Delcor, "V. Doctrines des Esseniens," *Supplement au Dictionnaire de la Bible,* Fasc. 51, (Paris, 1978), col. 963: "chercheurs. . . se divisent en deux camps à propos de l'interpretation des deux esprits: ceux qui donnent à *rwh* le sens de 'puissance angélique cosmique', et ceux qui comprennent ce terme dans le sens d'un 'instinct moral intérieur à l'homme'."

[2]*Cf.* D. Dombkowski Hopkins, "The Qumran Community and 1QH Hodayot: a Reassessment," *Revue de Qumrân* 10 (1981), pp. 338-9: "We have said above that Qumran's self-understanding in relation to the rest of the world usually emerges as a by-product of the discussion of the two spirits in 1QS 3:17-4:26; in this passage dualism presents itself in two aspects: the human (psychological) and the cosmic (cosmological) . . . . As a consequence of this cosmological and psycho-

ever, who view *ruaḥ* more in terms of its Old Testament background, tend to understand its use in the Scrolls in its more biblical sense as God's Spirit [3] or as a simple disposition in man[4] and therefore tend to see less of a strict cosmic dualism with its harsh boundaries between the sect member and those outside the community.[5] The definition of *ruaḥ* in the Scrolls, then, is a matter of importance. It tends to affect our view of Qumranian religion as a whole and its place within intertestamental Judaism.

The basic goal of this study, then, is to clarify the meaning and use of the Hebrew word *ruaḥ* among the Qumran Sectarians through an analysis of this word as it appears in the non-biblical writings (both "sectarian" and "non-sectarian") which have been found in the eleven caves associated with this community. It seems reasonable to investigate the meaning of *ruaḥ* in all the non-biblical writings found at Qumran and not just those regarded as "sectarian" for the following reasons: 1) expressions of *ruaḥ* in non-sectarian documents can be helpful in understanding corresponding sectarian expressions since they often share the same Hasidic background (*cf.* the analysis of 4Q504, 1-2, V 15 in chapter three below), and 2) there is some

---

logical dualism of the two spirit doctrine in 1QS, the Qumran community emerges as the predistined 'lot' of the rightreous elect standing in a mutually exclusive relationship with those outside of the community who have been predestined to the 'lot' of the wicked; in other words the Qumran sect takes its stand over against the rest of the human race in a context of double predestination. This gap between Qumran and the rest of the world is reinforced by the demand for 'eternal hatred' of all 'men of perdition'."

[3] *E.g.*, Peter von der Osten-Sacken, *Gott und Belial, traditionsgeschichtlichliche Untersuchungen zum Dualismus in den Texten aus Qumran* in Studien zur Umwelt des Neuen Testaments 6, (Göttingen: Vandenhoeck & Ruprecht, 1969), pp. 131-7 and 165ff.

[4] P. Wernberg-Møller, "A Reconsideration of the Two Spirits in the Rule of the Community (1Q Serek III,13 - IV,26)," *Revue de Qumran* ,11 (1961), pp. 413-441.

[5] *Cf.* Dombkowski Hopkins, "Community," p. 341 and nn. 58 & 59.

uncertainty as to what the sectarians did or did not compose.[6] Some fragments found at Qumran, for example, are parts of apocryphal and pseudepigraphical works already known, parts of which could have arisen in the Qumran community.[7] But more importantly, some of the unknown works discovered may not be sectarian compositions (*e.g.*, 11Q Ps^a Plea, cf. chapter three, n. 65) although most of them probably are.[8] The primary area of our investigation, then, will be the non-biblical, Hebrew Scrolls as a whole, and as the study progresses, possible non-sectarian sources of *ruaḥ* will be identified and handled on the basis of their individual character. We should note also that Old Testament expressions and concepts of *ruaḥ* have often had a strong impact on sectarian usage (*e.g.*, Ezk. 36-37, cf. chapter three, section 2d); these will be compared to sectarian expressions whenever this is helpful.

The basic methodology of this study is to compare the contextual meanings of *ruaḥ* in the non-biblical, Hebrew Scrolls with its linguistic patterns (usually syntactical in nature, but not limited to this) to see if any of these patterns has a semantic value independent of its particular context. If a semantic value can be discovered for a given pattern of *ruaḥ* as seen in less ambiguous contexts, the same pattern may be able to shed light on the meaning and use of *ruaḥ* in a disputed or ambiguous context. In working with a given meaning of *ruaḥ*, then (*e.g.*, "angel"), the most basic syntactical patterns (*e.g.*, number, gen-

---

[6]*Cf.* the most recent discussion of this issue in Hermann Lichtenberger, *Studien zum Menschenbild in Texten der Qumrangemeine*, Studien zur Umwelt des Neuen Testaments, 15 (Göttingen: Vandenhoeck & Ruprecht, 1980), pp. 13-45.

[7]*Cf.* chapter 4, n. 177 below. Fragments identified with certainty at Qumran are from *1 Enoch, Jubilees, Ben Sira, Tobit, Epistle of Jeremy* and parts of the *Testaments of the XII Patriarchs* (Levi and Naphtali); some think that fragments of *Test. of Judah, Test. of Joseph* and *Test. of Benjamin* may also be present at Qumran, but *cf.* J. J. Collins, *Jewish Writings of the Second Temple Period*, ed. by M. E. Stone (Philadelphia: Fortress, 1984), p. 333, who notes that the identification of these fragments at Qumran is as yet "quite uncertain."

[8]*E.g.*, 1QS, 1QSb, 1QH, 1QM and CD.

der, qualifiers) associated with its meaning are first separated into categories and then arranged in the analysis according to their frequency, but the search for meaningful patterns is not limited simply to syntax. The goal of the study is to uncover any pattern of *ruaḥ* which might have its own semantic value. Thus, for example, there seems to be no special meaning attached to the singular of *ruaḥ* as the object of the preposition ב, but in association with the verb נתן (with God as the subject), it becomes a clear reference to the Spirit of God (*cf.* the analysis of ברוח אשר נתתה בי in chapter 3 below).

A study using a methodology similar to that described above was done by D. Lys in his examination of the development of the meaning of *ruaḥ* in the Old Testament.[9] He found that the most important linguistic patterns for understanding the meaning of *ruaḥ* in a given context were its gender and its use or non-use of the definite article.[10] He noted that the masculine gender and the article each tend toward a personification of *ruaḥ*, and when used together (as in 1 Kings 22:21) they are able to give this word a "*personnalisation plus accentuée;*"[11] conversely, the feminine gender and lack of an article each tend toward depersonalization, and when used together (*e.g.*, in reference to God's *ruaḥ*) they are able to avoid any tendency toward personification.[12] As Lys traced the development of *ruaḥ* from the earliest texts of the Old Testament to the latest,[13] he also found (with only a few exceptions) that the fundamental semantic significance of the gender of *ruaḥ* and the use of the

---

[9]Daniel Lys, "*Ruaḥ*", *Le Souffle dans L'Ancient Testament* (Paris: Presses Universitaires de France, 1962).

[10]*Ibid.*, p. 32 n. 2 and p. 336 n. 2. The gender and use of the article with *ruaḥ* is a constant theme in Lys' analysis of this word as a means for understanding its meaning in disputed or ambiguous contexts; *cf. ibid.*, pp. 48 & 56 n. 1; pp. 79, 127-130, 172, 195 & 227-8 n. 1; pp. 269, 276-7, 283-5, & 299 n. 2; p. 306 n. 2; p. 322 n. 3; and p. 344 n. 1.

[11]*Ibid.*, p. 32.

[12]*Ibid.*, p. 130.

[13]*Cf. ibid.*, pp. 16ff. in which Lys offers a statistical and chronological outline of the occurrences of *ruaḥ* in the Old Testament as the basis for his subsequent analysis.

article as outlined above remained essentially unchanged.[14] The relevance of these results for our study is that the same, basic semantic value Lys saw for the gender of *ruaḥ* in the Old Testament can also be seen for *ruaḥ* in the Scrolls. This is less true for Lys' observations on the article.[15] The presence of a masculine or feminine gender, however, seems to have at least as much semantic value in the Scrolls for distinguishing between possible meanings of *ruaḥ* as it has in the Old Testament.[16] The evidence suggests, in fact, that the basic function of the gender of *ruaḥ* in the Old Testament as Lys describes it was clearly recognized by the sectarians and consciously used by them in their own writings. This should become especially apparent, for example, when we note that in the non-biblical, Hebrew sectarian writings every contextually unambiguous use of *ruaḥ* as an angel or demon is syntactically masculine, whereas every contextually unambiguous use of *ruaḥ* as the spirit of man (with one exception) is feminine.

In the second chapter, then, this study will trace the development of research into the meaning of *ruaḥ* in sectarian pneumatology from 1950 to the present. This will serve as a background for chapters 3 - 7 in which the patterns and contextual meanings of *ruaḥ* in most of the non-biblical Hebrew Scrolls will be analyzed (ch. 3, God's Spirit; ch. 4, man's spirit; ch. 5, angel/demon; ch. 6, wind and breath; and ch. 7, analysis

---

[14]*Ibid.*, *cf.* p. 32 n. 2 and p. 56 n. 1.

[15]The article appears with *ruaḥ* only six times in the approximately 234 published occurrences of this word in the Scrolls. In some pointed texts (*e.g.*, Eduard Lohse, *Die Texte aus Qumran, Hebräisch und Deutsch mit masoretischer Punktation, Übersetzung, Einführung und Anmerkungen* (2nd; München: Kösel Verlag, 1971), *cf.* 1QH 12:11 & 13:19 *in loco*) the editors will indicate an article on *ruaḥ* with an attached preposition, but this is probably a mistake. *ruaḥ* in 1QH 12-11 & 13:19 probably refers to God's Spirit (*cf.* chapter 3 below), and in the 35 cases in which *ruaḥ* is used with this meaning it has the article only one time, and even in this case the article does not define *ruaḥ* as such but rather the construct phrase in which *ruaḥ* is the genitive (*cf.* the analysis of משיח הרוח in chapter 3 below).

[16]This is especially true for 1QS 3:13-4:26; *cf.* chapter 8 below.

and comparison of the results of chapters 3-6). Most of the occurrences of *ruaḥ* in 1QS 3:13-4:26, however,will not be treated in chapters 3-7 but in chapter 8; these occurrences will require special treatment because of their relationship to the "two-spirit" teaching of 1QS 3:18ff. and the involved discussion which has arisen on the nature and extent of this pneumatology in sectarian thought. Our contribution to the interpretation of *ruaḥ* in 1QS 3:13-4:26, in fact, will be based primarily on the results of chapters 3-7. The general conclusions of this study will be found in chapter 9.

CHAPTER 2

A CHRONOLOGICAL SURVEY OF THE LITERATURE

1. From 1950 through 1955: initial questions about *ruaḥ*.

a. Understanding *ruaḥ* as God's Spirit,[1] man's spirit or an angel.

The first scholar to attempt a definition of *ruaḥ* within the basic theological thought of Qumran was K. G. Kuhn in 1950.[2] When he wrote, only sections of the Cave I scrolls were available, chiefly from 1QH, 1QM and 1QpHab with most of the important lQS scroll (especially columns 3 and 4) still unpublished.[3] On the basis of this evidence, however, Kuhn felt that there was at least one passage, 1QH 4:31, which clearly taught that a person at his entrance into the sect underwent an inward religious change or *Neuschöpfung* through the spirit formed for that person by God. Kuhn compared this teaching to the Spirit/flesh theology of Paul in 1 Cor. 3:1 and Gal. 6:1 and his "earthly/heavenly" dichotomy of 1 Cor. 15.[4] The central idea is that man's way is not established כי אם ברוח יצר אל לו "ausser in dem *Geist*, den *Gott* ihm gebildet hat;" this is in contrast to man's natural spiritual condition as a יצר החמר "Gebilde aus Ton," (*cf.* 1QH 4:29). The meaning of יצר as a spiritual

---

[1]There are various practices among scholars in capitalizing the translation of *ruaḥ* as "spirit"; in this dissertation "spirit" will be capitalized only when it refers to the Spirit of God.

[2]K. G. Kuhn, "Die in Palästina gefundenen hebräischen Texte und das Neue Testament," *Zeitschrift für Theologie und Kirche*, 47 (1950), pp. 192-211.

[3]*Cf.* Dupont-Sommer, "L'instruction sur les deux Esprits dans le 'Manuel de Discipline'," *Revue de l'histoire des religions*, cxlii (1952), 6 n. 3.

[4]K. G. Kuhn, "Texte," p. 201.

Neuschöpfung in 1QH 4:31 was confirmed for Kuhn by the use of יצר in 1QH 3:21, which he translates as follows:

> . . . und ich weiss, dass eine Hoffnung ist für den, den Du gebildet hast (יצר) heraus aus dem Staub zur ewigen Gemeinschaft (סוד עולם) und dass Du den verkehrten Geist (רוח נעוה) gereinigt hast von grosser Sünde, so daß er (nun) steht in der Standmannschaft des Volkes. . . .

Here (and by implication in 1QH 4:31)[5] it was clear to Kuhn that "mit dem wort יצר nicht von der Schöpfung des Menschen die Rede ist, sondern gewissermaßen von einer Neuschöpfung, nämlich der Zugehörigkeit zu der Gemeinde."[6] It is possible at this point that Kuhn may have seen in 1QH 4:31 a relationship to God's Spirit or some other spirit external to man as the origin of man's new spirituality, but this is unclear. In the following years he would maintain that passages like this involve no more than man's spirit which he receives at birth,[7] and in doing so he also departs from his emphasis on *ruaḥ* as a spiritual *Neuschöpfung* as experienced at one's entrance into the Qumran community. We will investigate the nature of this change in more detail later.

Soon after Kuhn published his article, E. Sjöberg published a dissenting opinion as part of a broader topic he had developed on Palestinian Judaism.[8] His general conclusion was that the evidence of the scrolls available at that time was not sufficient to demonstrate that the concept of *Neuschöpfung* as Kuhn

---

[5]*Cf.* E. Sjöberg, "Wiedergeburt und Neuschöpfung im palästinischen Judentum," *Studia Theologica,* 4 (1950), p. 78. This is also how Sjöberg understands Kuhn's argument at this point: "Durch den von gott gebildeten Geist kann der Mensch also die sonst unmögliche Gerechtigkeit gewinnen. Das könnte sich auf eine Neuschöpfung des Menschen beim Eintritt in die Sekte beziehen."

[6]K. G. Kuhn, "Texte," p. 201 n. 7.

[7]*Cf.* R. Jewett, *Paul's Anthropological Terms* (Leiden: Brill, 1971), pp. 82-3. Jewett notices no change in Kuhn's new view of *ruaḥ* (since 1952), but see in this chapter below.

[8]Sjöberg, "Wiedergeburt," pp. 44-85.

described it existed among the sectarians.[9] A *Neuschöpfung* of this type would be unique in Palestinian Judaism.[10] This does not mean that Judaism did not look for a transformation of man's character at the *eschaton*,[11] but such changes were not to be expected in man's basic nature in the present era, nor were they thought to be necessary or desirable. Man had an inclination to the bad (יצר הרע) and an inclination to the good (יצר טוב), and he had a free responsibility to follow the latter.[12] In view, therefore, of the absence of *Neuschöpfung* theology in Palestinian Judaism in general, alternative explanations of Kuhn's evidence seemed preferable to Sjöberg. For Kuhn's view that יצר in 1QH 4:31 refers to a *Neuschöpfung* at one's entrance into the sect, Sjöberg provided an alternative parallel from bBer. 60b, which refers to God's activity of forming (יצר) man's spirit or soul (נשמה) at his birth.[13] Seen in this light, it becomes clear that *ruaḥ* in 1QH 4:31 is "der von Gott gebildete Geist . . . der jedem Menschen bei seiner Schöpfung gegebene Geist."[14] And as to the meaning of יצר in 1QH 3:21, it cannot be proven that the sect member is speaking about being rescued from the sinfulness of his natural condition through a process of *Neuschöpfung* at his entrance into the sect. It is possible the sect thought that a man's character is determined at his creation.[15]

---

[9]*Ibid.*, p. 78-81. Note also on p. 85 (korrekturzusatz zu S. 79) that 1QS 3:13-4:26 came to late for use in the body of Sjöberg's article.

[10]*Ibid.*, p. 78: "In den neuentdeckten Sectenrollen aus der Höhle am Toten Meer finden wir nach K. G. Kuhn auch ein Beispiel des Neuschöpfungsgedankens, und zwar in einer sonst im Judentum nicht belegten Form: der Eintritt in die Sekte sei als Neuschöpfung verstanden worden."

[11]*Ibid.*, p. 70.

[12]*Ibid.*, pp. 68-9.

[13]*Ibid.*, p. 79. Sjöberg translates bBer. 60b as follows: "Mein Gott, die Seele (נשמה), die du mir gegeben haṣt, ist rein; du hast sie in mir gebildet (יצרתה), du hast sie mir eingehaucht und du bewahrst sie in mir und du wirst sie einst von mir nehmen und du wirst sie mir in der Zukunft wiedergeben."

[14]*Ibid.*

[15]*Ibid.*, p. 81.

With the full publication of 1QS in 1951,[16] most scholars including Kuhn became convinced on the basis of 3:13-4:26 that a major theme in the sectarians' teaching about *ruaḥ* had to do with two spirits, one good and the other evil, which determine a person's spirituality from birth. As noted above (*cf.* pp. 7-8), Kuhn (on the basis of 1QH) initially described the sectarian concept of *ruaḥ* as a spiritual *Neuschöpfung* which occurred at a person's entrance into the community, and he compared this to similar ideas of Paul in the New Testament. After the publication of 1QS, however, Kuhn no longer saw a similarity between Paul and the Scrolls but rather a *contrast*: the "spirit" as the basis of sectarian piety is not God's Spirit (as in Paul) nor any other spirit external to man, but it is the human spirit itself,[17] and it is not a regenerated human spirit given to the sect member at his entrance into the community but a static, predestined *habitus* given to the pious person at creation or birth (*Schöpfungsmäßig*).[18] Most scholars during the 1950's followed

---

[16]M. Burrows, (ed. with the assistance of J. C. Trever and W. H. Brownlee), *The Dead Sea Scrolls of St. Mark's Monastery*, vol. II, fasc., 2 (New Haven, 1951). *Cf.* also W. H. Brownlee, "The Dead Sea Manual of Discipline, Translation and Notes," *Bulletin of the American Schools of Oriental Research, Supplementary Studies*, nos. 10-12, (1951).

[17]K. G. Kuhn, " Πειρασμός - ἁμαρτία - σάρξ im Neuen Testament und die damit Zusammenhangenden Vorstellungen," *Zeitschrift für Theologie und Kirche*, 49 (1952), p. 214.

[18]*Ibid.*, p. 215. Although most scholars have understood the two spirits of 1QS 3-4 as angelic beings as well as spiritual forces in men, it is clear that at this time, at least, Kuhn viewed them as no more than human, religious dispositions; *cf. ibid.*, p. 205 n. 1: "Der erste Johannesbrief gibt also hier in der Sache wie im Wortlaut völlig die Begrifflichkeit dieser jüdisch-palästinischen Sekte wieder. *Daraus* erklärt es sich, daß hier πνεῦμα τῆς ἀληθείας eigentlich als anthropologischer Begriff erscheint." Note also *ibid.*, p. 209, "Wirkt hier noch die alttestamentliche Gegenüberstellung nach, wo der Mensch as 'Fleisch' charakterisiert wird gegenüber den 'Geist Jahwes'. . . so wird doch auch der große Unterschied zur alttestamentlichen Redeweise deutlich, weil in den Texten dieser Sekte, 'Fleisch' ja nicht einfach zum Geist *Gottes* in Gegenstatz steht, sondern zum 'Geist der Wahrheit',

Kuhn in this view of sectarian pneumatology except that they tended to understand the two spirits of 1QS 3-4 not only as spiritual forces or dispositions in man but also as angelic beings (usually further identified with the Prince of Lights and Angel of Darkness).[19] It appears that Kuhn later agreed with the

---

den der *Gläubige* gemäß seiner Vorherbestimmung *hat*. So ist der Mensch als 'Fleisch' Gottes unwürdig und anfällig für das Böse, oder besser... für den Bösen, während der Geist des Frommen als der 'Geist der Wahrheit' ihn in die Kampffront auf seiten Gottes gegen den Bösen stelt." See also *ibid.*, p. 214 n. 2; in James 4:2, Kuhn says that πνεῦμα here is "nicht der Geist im christlichen Sinne, sondern der Menschengeist, d.h. der-- gewiß von Gott gegebene, aber schöpfungsmäßig gegebene-- gute Geist, den der Mensch *hat*, '*sein gutes Ich*, das sich gegen ein böses Ich behaupten muß'. . . . Das entspricht also genau der Anschauung der neuen Palästinatexte von dem prädestinierten, schöpfungsmäßig dem Frommen eignenden 'Geist der Wahrheit' als 'seinem, des Frommen, Geist', der im kampf steht mit dem 'Giest des Frevels'."

[19]*Cf.* M. Burrows, *More Light on the Dead Sea Scrolls* (New York: Viking Press, 1958), pp. 280-1: "The spirits of light and darkness which struggle in man's soul and in the universe are sometimes called angels. Thus it is made clear that they are both God's creatures and subject to him . . . . It is equally clear, however, that the two spirits or angels are powers outside of man. . . ." Burrows notes only one scholar, E. Schweizer (*ibid.*, p. 293), who questioned the angelic status of the two spirits; *cf.* E. Schweizer, "Gegenwart des Geistes und eschatologische Hoffnung bei Zarathustra, spätjüdischen Gruppen, Gnostikern und den Zeugen des Neuen Testaments," *The Background of the New Testament and its Eschatology*, (Festschrift for C. H. Dodd, Cambridge, 1956), p. 490 in which he compares the two spirits of 1QS 3-4 to the two impulses of rabbinic theology. Schweizer finally concludes, however, that the two spirits should be understood as "Mächte. . . die außerhalb des Menschen stehen, ihn verführen oder ihm helfen," *cf. ibid.*, p. 492. For other scholars at this time beside Kuhn who did not understand the two spirits as having a personal, angelic status, *cf.* F. M. Braun, "L'arrière-fond judaïque du quatrieme evangile et la Communaute de l'Alliance," *Revue Biblique*, 62 (1955), p. 13 and Goeffrey Graystone, "The Dead Sea Scrolls and the New Testament," *Irish Theological Quarterly*, 22 (1955), pp. 227.

majority on this point,[20] but the most significant change in his position would be his return to the view in "Texte" (*cf.* pp. 7-8 above) that 1QH teaches a spiritual *Neuschöpfung* analogous to that of early Christianity,[21] a view later developed by his students.[22] By the early 1960's, in fact, a key issue among scholars was how to relate the sectarian understanding of their spirituality as a *Neuschöpfung* to their understandinging of it as an inherited, spiritual *habitus* since both meanings of *ruaḥ* seemed to be clearly present in Qumran literature (*cf.* sections 2 and 3 of this chapter below).

From 1952 through 1955, however, scholars were generally not aware of possible tensions in sectarian pneumatology. Their basic goal was to develop an integrated definition of *ruaḥ* in sectarian thought as this relates to God, man, and the angelic figures which mediate between them. From this point in our analysis to the end of this subsection (*1a*), then, we will describe the basic views of these scholars (*viz.*, A. Dupont-Sommer, B. Otzen, H. Wildberger, Y. Yadin and E. Sjöberg). At times the possibility of Persian or Christian influence on the Scrolls played a dominant role in the scholarly formulation of an understanding of sectarian pneumatology: these approaches

---

[20]*Cf.* K. G. Kuhn, "Qumran," *Religion in Geschichte und Gegenwart*, 3rd ed., V. (1961), col. 747; Kuhn notes that there is not only an alternation between "spirit" and "angel" in 1QS 3:18ff. but also that the two spirits are called "the Prince of Lights" and "Angel of Darkness."

[21]*Cf.* K. G. Kuhn, "Der Epheserbrief im Licht der Qumrantexte," *New Testament Studies*, 7 (July, 1961), p. 344. Kuhn compares 1QH 3:19-22 with Eph. 5:14 and concludes that 1QH 3:19-22 reflects "der Gedanke eines völligen Neuanfangs gegenüber dem bisherigen Sündenschlaf und Sündentod durch die *Aufnahme in eine exklusive Heilsgemeinde*, so wie hier in die christliche Gemeinde durch die Taufe" [emphasis his].

[22]*Cf.* especially H. W. Kuhn , *Enderwartung und gegenwärtiges Heil. Untersuchungen zu den Gemeindeliedern von Qumran mit einem Anhang über Eschatologie und Gegenwart in der Verkundigung Jesu*, Studien zur Umwelt des Neuen Testaments, 4 (Göttingen: Vandenhoeck & Rupricht, 1966), pp. 120ff. *Cf.* also section three of this chapter below.

will receive special attention in this chapter below in sections *1b* and *1c*.

In an article published in 1952 Dupont-Sommer suggested that the sectarians thought of man's soul as being a "mixture" of the two spirits, which in turn were identical with the Prince of Lights and Angel of Darkness.[23] The proportions of each spirit differ in each individual, and this creates the variety of spiritual dispositions within humanity. In this way he explained the close connection between the inwardly experienced presence of the two spirits in men and the angelic powers of 1QS 3:20ff. He did not make clear, however, precisely how the sectarian viewed this mixture of angelic forces making up his inner and outer world. Did the sectarian view them as *conditioning* his spirit or as actually *being* his spirit, *i.e.*, as making up its constituent elements? In writing about the soul as a "mixture" of the two angelic spirits, it would seem that Dupont-Sommer intended the latter. But in doing so he needed to show that an identification of man's spirit with transcendent and (partially) divine cosmic powers is not contrary to other themes in sectarian theology which seem to *contrast* man and his spirit to the heavenly world of God and His angels.[24] Later, however, Dupont-Sommer seems to have moved away from this identification. In an article in 1955, for example, he sees a close connection between Philo's account of two "powers" (good and bad) entering man's soul at birth and the two-spirit doctrine of the sectarians.[25] Here it is clear that man's soul is regarded as sepa-

---

[23]Dupont-Sommer, "instruction," pp. 18 and 28-9.

[24]*Cf.* 1QH 1:21-27; 3:19-24; 11:10-14; 13:13ff. and also the comments of Schweizer, "Gegenwart des Geistes," p. 491 on the relationship of man's spirit to the two spirits of 1QS 3:18ff.: "Darin setzt sich das alttestamentliche Wissen darum, daß der Geist Jahwes nicht der Geist des Menschen ist, fort. Die griechische Konzeption von der Identität des Geistes im Menschen mit dem kosmischen göttlichen Geist ist hier noch nicht eingedrungen."

[25]A. Dupont-Sommer, "Le problème des influences étrangères sur la secte juive de Qoumrân," *Revue d'histoire et de philosophie religieuses*, 35 (1955), p. 85 (citing Philo): "'Dans toutes les âmes, au mo-

rate from the two invasive powers which struggle with each other for domination over it. And in his major 1959 commentary on the Scrolls he no longer describes man's soul as a "mixture" of the two spirits; rather, man's soul or spirit "participates" in them[26] and they, in turn, struggle within him.[27] The two spirits, then, are seen perhaps more as conditioning man's spirit than as constituting it or as forming the basic elements of its nature.[28]

Another approach to the anthropological/cosmological nature of the two spirits was suggested by B. Otzen. This involved a late Jewish way of thinking in which man as a "microcosm" reflects everything that happens in the "macrocosm" (the world). As applied to 1QS 3:13-4:26, the two spirits are regarded non-mythically as two opposing principles or impulses, which in turn are a reflection of cosmic forces understood mythically as dominating the world.[29] A problem in Otzen's approach, however, is that he does not show evidence of this kind of thinking in the Scrolls themselves. He presents no more than a working hypothesis. His hypothesis, furthermore, does not adequately explain the *dominant* nature of the cosmic forces in

---

ment même de la naissance, pénètrent en même tempts deux Puissances, l'une salutaire et l'autre malfaisante'."

[26]*Idem*, *Les écrits Esséniens découverts près de la mer Morte* (Paris: Payot, 1959), p. 93 n. 4.

[27]*Ibid.*, p. 94 n. 6.

[28]Dupont-Sommer's position here seems to have remained basically unchanged; *cf. idem*, "Deux documents horoscopiques esséniens découverts à Qoumrân, près de la Mer Morte," *Comptes Rendus de L'Académie des Inscriptions et Belles-Lettres* (Paris, 1965), pp. 244-5. It is true that Dupont-Sommer describes man's spirit here as comprising (*comprendre*) a "mixture" of the two spirits (*les deux esprits*) in greater or lesser amounts of each, but he does not capitolize *esprit* at this point as he usually does when referring to the two spirits in a cosmic sense; when he does refer to them in this sense, he speaks of man's spirit as "participating" in them (*ibid.*, p. 245).

[29]Benedikt Otzen, "Die neugefundenen hebräischen Sektenschriften und die Testamente zwölf Patriarchen," *Studia Theologica*, 7 (1953), pp. 135-6.

man as described in 1QS 3:13-4:26. Men here not only *reflect* the activity of the two spirits and the two angels in the cosmos but are dominated by them.[30] It is perhaps for these and similar reasons that very few scholars have followed Otzen's lead here.[31]

In 1954 H. Wildberger did a short study on the dualism of the Scrolls.[32] His basic position was that the Scrolls teach both an anthropological and a metaphysical dualism and that this teaching has its origin ultimately in Zoroastrianism.[33] His analysis of this dualism was much the same as Kuhn's[34] but with one exception: he identified the "spirit of perversion" with Belial as a personal, angelic figure, and on the basis of 1QS 10:21 he described Belial as being kept "in the heart" of his adherents.[35] How Wildberger understood the corresponding "spirit of truth" is unclear, but logically it would seem that

---

[30]*Cf.* the comment of Millar Borrows in *More Light*, p. 281: "The connection between these two types of dualism is seen by Otzen in the idea that the division of mankind to which each individual will belong is determined by the outcome of the struggle in his own soul. This, it seems to me does not accurately represent the thought of the Manual of Discipline. No doubt the element of personal decision and effort was recognized in practice, but little room is left for it in the passage in question. Schweizer's judgement, that the outcome both in the universe and in the individual soul is determined not by the spirit of man but by the power of God, is more in accord with the implications of the text."

[31]I have found only one such scholar: *cf.* Josef Schreiner, "Geistbegabung in der Gemeinde von Qumran," *Biblische Zeitschrift*, 9 (1965), p. 135.

[32]Hans Wildberger, "Der Dualismus in den Qumranschriften," *Asiatische Studien*, 8 (1954), pp. 163-177.

[33]*Ibid.*, pp. 166 and 177.

[34]*Ibid.*, p. 177 n. 35: Wildberger writes, "Erst nach Abschluß meiner Arbeit bin ich aufmerksam geworden auf den Artikel von K. G. Kuhn: 'Die Sektenschrift und die iranische Religion,' in *Zschr. f. Th. und K.* 49, 1952, S. 296. Daß er zu ähnlichen Ergebnissen kommt wie ich, ist mir eine wertvolle Bestätigung meiner Sicht."

[35]*Ibid.*, p. 167.

this spirit would also have an angelic status and be capable of being kept "in the heart" of those devoted to him. If so, this puts him in tension with Kuhn's definition (at the time) of the spirits of truth and perversion as no more than predestined, spiritual dispositions within men.[36]

After the first edition of 1QM was published by E. L. Sukenik in 1954,[37] a number of commentaries on it appeared in the following year, the most detailed and extensive of which was a book by his son, Yigael Yadin.[38] Yadin regarded 1QS 3:13-25 as presenting a deterministic and dualistic doctrinal viewpoint, and he believed that the author of 1QM had made frequent use of it.[39] Now Yadin's analysis of 1QM clearly showed that its author envisioned more than just a conflict between human armies. God Himself, assisted by the "Angel of Light," would carry on a simultaneous battle with the sectarians' supernatural enemies, *i.e.*, Belial, the spirits (devils) of his lot and the angels of destruction.[40] Yadin's view that 1QM is an application of 1QS 3:13-25, then, would tend to support the idea that the sectarians (or at least the author of 1QM) understood the two spirits of lQS 3:13-25 as part of a supernatural, *cosmic* conflict, *i.e.*, as involving more than simply a psychological battle within the human heart.[41]

---

[36]*Cf.* n. 18 above.

[37]E. L. Sukenik, *אוצר המגילות הגנוזות בידי האוניברסיטה העברית*, ("The Dead Sea Scrolls of the Hebrew University") (Jerusalem: Bialik Foundation and Hebrew University, 1954), pp. 16-34, plates 16-34.

[38]Yigael Yadin, *מגילת מלחמת בני אור בבני חושך ממגילות מדבר יהודה*, ("The Scroll of the War of the Sons of Light against the Sons of Darkness") (Jerusalem: Goldberg's Press, 1955).

[39]*Ibid.*, pp. 220-1.

[40]*Ibid.*, p. 221.

[41]*Cf.* Wernberg-Møller, "Reconsideration," p. 428 n. 30, who believes that the two angels of lQS 3-4 (as personifications of the two spirits) are no more than psychological dispositions in men; *cf.* also Herbert May,"Cosmological Reference in the Qumran Doctrine of the Two Spirits and in Old Testament Imagery," *Journal of Biblical Literature*, 82 (1963). p. 5, who disagrees with Wernberg-Møller on this point and cites the work of Yadin in 1QM as support for the view that both

A final contribution to be considered here is a short article by E. Sjöberg[42] which, despite its length of only six pages, was a major contribution to the study of *ruaḥ* in the Scrolls. This was the first artricle to make an attempt to define in a comprehensive manner references to God's Spirit in 1QH in relationship to man, and given the consensus of subsequent scholarship, it was largely successful.[43] Sjöberg's position here is that K. G. Kuhn in his initial article in 1950[44] was, after all, correct when he described sectarian theology as teaching a spiritual transformation or *Neuschöpfung* of a person at his entrance into the Qumran community. Sjöberg had originally doubted this and had interpreted the evidence offered by Kuhn in 1950 as referring to a spiritual status given to the sectarian at birth.[45] After the publication of 1QS, Kuhn then moved toward the views of Sjöberg; he no longer described the sectarians' spiritual life in terms of a *Neuschöpfung* but as a static, predestined *habitus* given at birth.[46] By 1955, however, most of the major scrolls were available, and the analysis of these scrolls led Sjöberg to evalutate the question once more in this present article. His conclusions were that 1QH clearly taught "die Neuschöpfung beim Eintritt in die Sekte, nicht um die ursprunglich Schöpfung des Menschen"[47] and that its proper theme was "die Schwachheit des natürlichen Menschen und die Erneuerung durch die Gnade

---

the two spirits and the two angels are cosmic beings. However, it is not necessary to identify the two spirits with the two angels to do justice to the cosmic scope of 1QS 3-4 (as can be seen especially in K. G. Kuhn's work previous to 1960; *cf.* pp. 3-4 above).

[42]Eric Sjöberg, "Neuschöpfung in den Toten-Meer-Rollen," *Studia Theologica*, 9 (1955), pp. 131-6.

[43]Sjöberg has the support of a strong consensus in sixteen of his seventeen definitions of *ruaḥ* in 1QH: man's spirit in 3:21 and 11:12; God's Spirit in 4:31; 7:6f.; 9:32; 12:11; 12:12; 13:18f.; 14:25; 16:7; 16:11; 16:12; 17:26; f 2:9; 2:13; and 3:14.

[44]K. G. Kuhn, "Texte."

[45]Sjöberg, "Wiedergeburt," pp. 79ff.

[46]K. G. Kuhn, "Πειρασμός," pp. 214-5.

[47]Sjöberg, "Neuschöpfung," p. 133.

Gottes."[48] This spiritual renewal is to be characterized above all by the granting of knowledge and the Spirit of God.[49] A primary evidence upon which Sjöberg based this revaluation of *ruaḥ* was a comparison of 1QH 3:19-23 and 11:10-14. It is interesting to note that one of the strongest supporters of Sjöberg's analysis of these passages (although without mentioning Sjöberg's article) is H. W. Kuhn, a student of K. G. Kuhn and author of one of the most definitive studies in this area do date.[50]

b. Iranian influence of the concept of *ruaḥ* in sectarian thought.

Almost from the beginning of Qumran research and even before the publication of the "two spirit" passages of 1QS, some scholars felt that there was definite evidence of Iranian influence on sectarian thinking.[51] After the full publication of 1QS with its dualistic, two-spirit teaching in 3:13-4:26, this impression was strengthened primarily because it was difficult to show how the Old Testament alone could have given rise to a belief in two spirits closely associated with two angels of cosmic proportions, who ruled over the conduct of all men.[52] Not

---

[48] *Ibid.*, p. 135.

[49] *Ibid.*: "Die grosse Rolle der Erkenntnis der göttlichen Geheimnisse war uns schon in der Gemeindeordnung der Sekte (DSD [*i.e.* 1QS]) entgegengetreten, auch kam die Bedeutung der Führung durch den Geist Gottes dort zum Vorschein. Beides wird immer wieder in den Lobleidern betont."

[50] *Cf.* H. W. Kuhn, *Enderwartung*, pp. 80-5 and 113. Note also the comment of S. F. Noll, "Angelology in the Qumran Texts" (unpublished dissertation, U. of Manchester, 1979), p. 93: "H. W. Kuhn in his detailed study of the two hymns in 1QH iii 19-36 and xi 1-14 has put subsequent interpreters in his debt."

[51] *Cf.* K. G. Kuhn, "Texte," p. 211 and Dupont-Sommer, "L'instruction," p. 16.

[52] *Cf.* Dupont-Sommer, "instruction," p. 16: "Cette conception des deux Esprits est absente de l'Ancien Testament. Elle est, au contraire, essentielle dans les Gâthâ. Par exemple, Yasna, XLV, 2:

Je vais discourir des deux Esprits,

everybody at that time, however, agreed that Zoroastrianism (or some form of it) was the primary source of this two-spirit dualism. G. Molin, for example, sought to find its source the the Old Testament, especially as this is viewed against the wider backgound of the Ancient Near East,[53] and K. Schubert sought its source in early Jewish Gnosticism.[54] Strong positions against Iranian influences were later developed by F. Nötscher[55] and P. Wernberg-Møller.[56] At present, scholars seem to be undecided about the strength of Iranian influence at Qumran.[57] It is impor-

---

Dont le plus saint, au commencement de l'existence, a dit au destructeur:

'Ni nos pensées ni nos doctrines ni nos forces mentales,
ni nos choix ni nos paroles ni nos actes,
ni nos consciences ni nos âmes ne sont d'accord.'

Et encore *Yasna*, XXX, 3:

Or, à l'origine, les deux Esprits que sont connus (. . .)
comme jumeaux
sont l'un le mieux, l'autre le mal
en pensée, parole, action. Et entre eux deux,
les intelligents choisissent bien, non les sots."

[53]Georg Molin, *Die Söhne des Lichtes, Zeit und Stellung der Handschriften vom Toten Meer*, (Wien: Verlag Herold, 1954), p. 129.

[54]Kurt Schubert, "Der Sektenkanon von En Feshcha und die Anfänge der jüdischen Gnosis," *Theologische Literaturzeitung*, 78 (1953), col. 504. In this article Schubert sees the origin of the two spirits in the Gnostic *syzygy* concept, but no one seems to have followed him on this.

[55]Freidrich Nötscher, *Zur theologischen Terminologie der Qumran Texte*, Bonner Biblische Beiträge, 10 (Bonn: Peter Hanstein, 1956), pp. 86-92.

[56]Wernberg-Møller, "Reconsideration," pp. 413-441.

[57]*Cf*. Shaul Shaked, "Qumran and Iran: further considerations," *Israel Oriental Studies*, 2 (Tel Aviv University, 1972) , 433: "There exists by now [1972] a fairly large body of literature around the subject of possible Iranian influences in the writings found at Qumran. It is fair, I believe, to summarize the position of the debate on the subject by stating that the issue is undecided, and that the views are more or less balanced whether to accept or reject the possibility of strong Iranian components in the theology and literature of the sectarians whose

tant to note, however, that the relationship between sectarian dualism and Persian thought has had, in fact, only an indirect bearing on the definition of *ruaḥ* in the Scrolls. It is generally true that those who deny Iranian influence tend to interpret *ruaḥ* in 1QS 3:13ff. as a psychological concept and those who affirm this influence tend to view *ruaḥ* here as a cosmic entity,[58] but this is not always or necessarily the case.[59] We have already seen, for example, that K. G. Kuhn, a strong advocate of Iranian influence, regarded the two spirits of truth and perversion in 1QS 3-4 as essentially anthropomorphic concepts.[60] H. May , on the other hand, while not denying Iranian influence, defended the cosmic status of the two spirits on the basis of Old Testament conceptions alone.[61] The interpretation of *ruaḥ*, then, has tended to depend not so much on a direct appeal to Iranian writings as on its actual context in the Scrolls themselves as these are interpreted in the light of related intertestamental and Old Testament sources.[62]

If the above observation is valid, however, this does not mean that possible connections to Iranian thought are com-

---

center was at Qumran." The situation seems to be about the same today; cf. Noll, "Angelology," pp. 201-2 n. 90.

[58] *Cf.* Wernberg-Møller, "Reconsideration," pp. 417-8.

[59] *Cf. ibid.*, p. 441: this assumption has apparently led Wernberg-Møller to lump K. G. Kuhn with Dupont-Sommer in the view that the two spirits are angelic beings. By 1961 Kuhn had, in fact, adopted this view (*cf.* n. 20 above), but it is not present in Kuhn's writings as reviewed by Wernberg-Møller (*cf.* n. 18 above).

[60] *Cf.* n. 18 above; *cf.* also Henri Michaud,"Un mythe Zervanite dans un des manuscrits de Qumrân," *Vetus Testramentum*, 5 (1955), 137-147. Although Michaud see a strong influence of Zervanism on 1QS 3:13-4:26, he seems to distinguish between the two spirits and the two angels of this section (*ibid.*, pp. 140-1) and to regard the two spirits as essentially dispositions within men (*ibid.*, p. 145 sec. 2).

[61] May, "Cosmological Reference," pp. 1-14.

[62] *Cf.* K. G. Kuhn, "Die Sektenschrift und die iranische Religion," *Zeitschrift für Theologie und Kriche*, 49 (1952), p. 10 n. 3; Kuhn notes that the author of 1QS 3-4 had probably not even heard of the name Zarathustra.

pletely irrelevant. Some sort of contact with Iran seems to be reasonable, and this may be especially true in cases in which the supposition of Iranian influence may help to explain apparent tensions within the sectarian view of *ruaḥ* which are difficult to understand on the basis of the Scrolls and related Jewish literature alone. One case involves the relationship of God's Spirit (as presented in the Old Testament) to the two spirits of 1QS 3-4. Is the "spirit of truth" here the same as God's Spirit in Qumranian belief[63] or is it essentially different?[64] If an exegetical analysis indicates not only that they differ but are also in fundamental tension with each other in their place and function in sectarian thought, the possibility of Iranian influence within an otherwise biblical concept of *ruaḥ* may help to explain how this uneasy relationship developed.[65] Similar cases may also exist in sectarian passages outside of 1QS 3-4 in which *ruaḥ* (as man's spirit) seems to have a status and function different from its characteristic use in the Old Testament to describe a simple disposition or spiritual condition in man.[66] If this is the case, Iranian influence may help to explain this development[67] to alert the scholar to the possibil-

---

[63]So Frank M. Cross, Jr., *The Ancient Library of Qumran and Modern Biblical Studies* (2nd ed.; Garden City: Doubleday, 1961), p. 213.

[64]So Otto Betz, *Offenbarung und Schriftforschung in der Qumransekte*, Wissenschaftliche Untersuchungen zum Neuen Testament, 6 (Tübingen: Mohr, 1960), pp. 143ff.

[65]The possibility of foreign ideas, incompletely assimilated, may be a factor in much of the disagreement and uncertainty about the meaning of *ruaḥ* in the Scrolls. After referring to seven of the most contested occurrences of *ruaḥ* in CD and 1QS, Burrows in *More Light*, p. 292 writes, "From these and the many other passages that might be cited, it seems impossible to derive a clear, consistent meaning for the word 'spirit'."

[66]Perhaps in some of these cases (*cf.* especially 1QH 15) it refers to a "predestined being" of man which totally determines the course of his religious life, leaving no room for the freedom of the will; *cf.* H. W. Kuhn, *Enderwartung*, pp. 120-130.

[67]*Ibid.*, p. 130.

ity of parallel and even conflicting views of man and his spirit in the Scrolls.[68]

In summary, then, it seems fair to say that for most scholars the actual use of Iranian sources to define *ruaḥ* in the Scrolls has remained more on the fringes of Qumranian research than at its center. Most would likely agree with Wernberg-Møller's view that the Scrolls should be interpreted first of all as Jewish writings within a literary tradition rooted in the Old Testament,[69] although they would not perhaps agree with all of his conclusions.[70]

c. The meaning of *ruaḥ* in the Scrolls and its relationship to early Christianity.

A major issue during the early years of Scroll research was the relationship between the sectarian concept of *ruaḥ* and its counterpart (πνεῦμα) in the New Testament. This issue was an important part of the work of a number of scholars, some of whom tended to identify key sectarian and New Testament concepts of spirit (especially in relationship to God)[71] and others who denied these identifications and emphasized the differences.[72] For some of these scholars, at least, it seems that their identification of *ruaḥ* in the Scrolls with πνεῦμα in the New Testament was more the result of a previous identification of the Scrolls as Christian writings than a result of an exegetical analysis of *ruaḥ* itself.[73]

---

[68]*Cf.* especially Lichtenberger, *Studien*, p. 174.

[69]Wernberg-Møller, "Reconsideration" p. 416.

[70]*Cf.* section *3d* of this chapter below.

[71]*E.g.*, J. L. Teicher, " The Teaching of the Pre-Pauline Church in the Dead Sea Scrolls," *The Journal of Jewish Studies*, 4 (1953), pp. 9-13.

[72]*E.g.*, Joseph Coppens, "Les Documents du Désert de Juda et les Origines du Christianisme," *Analecta Lovaniensia Biblica et Orientalia*, Sér. II, fasc. 39 (1953), 32-33 and 39.

[73]*Cf.* the comments of Jean Carmignac, *Christ and the Teacher of Righteousness*, trans. by K. Pedley (Baltimore: Helicon Press, 1962), pp. 32-42 regarding Dupont-Sommer's initial suggestion that there was Trinitarian teaching evident in the Scrolls.

As outlined already in section *1a* of this chapter, some of the first comparisons of the Qumran and New Testament concepts of "spirit" were done by K. G. Kuhn in 1950[74] and 1952.[75] In 1953 two more studies appeared which came to mutually opposing conclusions, one by J. L Teicher and the other by J. Coppens.[76] Teicher believed that that Qumran community was really a pre-Pauline form of early Christianity as reflected primarily in Acts[77] and that the "Spirit of Truth" (identified as the Angel of Truth)[78] was identical to the "Holy Spirit" of the Jerusalem Church.[79] This identity is especially apparent in their similar functions of giving birth to their communities (*cf.* Acts 2:1, 4 & 44; 4:31-2; with 1QS 1:11-13),[80] in "helping" their members against the "Spirit of Iniquity" (*cf.* John 14:16-18 with 1QS 3:24),[81] and in their mutual opposition to Paul's view that a cleansing from sin though the Spirit takes place in the present (*cf.* 1 Cor. 6:11) rather than in the eschatological future (*cf.* 1QS 4:20-1).[82] Coppens, on the other hand, without ever mentioning Teicher's work on Qumran as a pre-Pauline Christian group (available since 1951), saw no essential difference between Paul and primitive Christianity in their pneumatology[83] nor did he see a special relationship in this respect between Acts (Teicher's primary source for pre-Pauline Christianity) and the Scrolls; there was, in fact, a strong contrast between them since the Scrolls know of no present outpouring of the

---

[74]K. G. Kuhn, "Texte," pp. 192-211.

[75]*Idem*, "Πειρασμός," pp. 200-222.

[76]*Cf.* nn. 71 and 72 above.

[77]Teicher, "Teaching," pp. 1ff.

[78]*Ibid.*, vol. 3 (1952), p. 112 n. 4.

[79]*Ibid.*, vol. 4 (1953), p. 10.

[80]*Ibid.*, pp. 1-2 and 9-10.

[81]*Ibid.*, pp. 1-10.

[82]*Ibid.*, p. 10: "(Acts) lacks any reference to the Charismatic gifts of sanctifying man and cleansing him from sin"; but *cf.* Acts 11:9 and also 1QH 16:12.

[83]Coppens, "Documents," pp. 23-39.

Spirit while Acts does.[84] Coppens finally concludes that the sectarians knew only of a "holy spirit," *i.e.*, "l'esprit que tout homme possède, mais que les membres de la secte sont parvenus à sanctifier progressivement par l'élimination des penchants mauvais et de tout esprit impure"[85] and that they expected God's Spirit, as such, to be communicated to them only at the end of time.[86] A final key difference between Teicher and Coppens may be in their views of how the Scrolls relate God's "Holy Spirit" (whether present or future) to God Himself. It seems clear that Coppens regards this Spirit as God's own Spirit in a more traditional, Christian sense,[87] whereas Teicher seems to regard it as ultimately no more than an angelic, created figure.[88]

In subsequent scholarship, R. Brown emphasized the basic difference between the Spirit of Truth in John's Gospel as the "third Person of the Trinity" and the corresponding spirit of truth at Qumran as essentially a non-Trinitarian concept.[89] A key principle in evaluating terminological parallels like this is to appreciate the "tremendous chasm between Qumran thought and Christianity. . . . The Essene sectarians were not Christians, and the recognition of this will prevent many misinterpretations."[90] At this time G. Graystone also made the same point in a series of articles comparing Qumran to early Christianity,[91] and in his analysis of "spirit" in the Scrolls and

---

[84]*Ibid.*, pp. 36-7.

[85]*Ibid.*, p. 36 n. 46.

[86]*Ibid.*, p. 37 n. 46.

[87]*Ibid.*: "Il existe cependant à côte dé cet 'esprit saint' qui indique la qualité morale et religieuse des hommes fidèles à la loi, un Esprit saint qui est à Dieu, l'Esprit de Dieu. . . . Cet 'Esprit de Dieu' ressemble beaucoup plus à l' Esprit saint de la foi chrétienne."

[88]Teicher, "Teaching," vol. 3, p. 112 n. 4: "The 'Angel of Truth' is identical with the 'Spirit of Truth'."

[89]Raymond Brown, "The Qumran Scrolls and the Johannine Gospel and Epistles," *The Catholic Biblical Quarterly*, 17 (1955), p. 559.

[90]*Ibid.*, p. 571.

[91]Graystone, "Scrolls," vol. 22 (1955), 214-230, & 329-346 and vol. 23 (1956), pp. 25-48.

in the New Testament he basically reflected the views of Coppens as outlined above. He goes beyond Coppens, however, in two basic respects: he believes that the eschatologically awaited Holy Spirit at Qumran should not be regarded as "personal" in a Christian sense[92] and he makes it clear that the two spirits should not be regarded as angelic beings but rather as "two spiritual currents or tendencies."[93]

In summary, then, the theory that the Scrolls should be read as early Christian documents has found little acceptance among scholars.[94] There are, of course, parallels between the New Testament and the Scrolls in various areas including pneumatology,[95] but this does not necessarily imply a direct or close dependence in either direction.[96]

d. Conclusion to section 1, chapter 2.

During this initial stage of research (1950 through 1955), it became evident that a major problem in the study of sectarian theology would be to determine when *ruaḥ* referred to the human spirit and when it referred to a spirit beyond man such as God's Spirit or an angel. This was a period marked by fundamental shifts of opinion on this issue among leading scholars. It culminated in a small article by E. Sjöberg in which he reversed his former opinion and concluded (primarily on the basis of 1QH) that the Scrolls did, in fact, contain the idea of a *Neuschöpfung* or inner spiritual transformation through God's Spirit in the sectarian at his entrance into the Qumran community. Despite its size of only six pages, this article was an im-

---

[92]*Ibid.*, vol. 23, 33-4. *Cf.* the same opinion at this time in Nötscher, *Terminology*, p. 42.

[93]Graystone, "Scrolls," vol. 22, p. 227; *cf.* also n. 19 above.

[94]*Cf.* Burrows, *More Light*, p. 269 and Geza Vermes, *The Dead Sea Scrolls, Qumran in Perspective* (Cleveland: Collins & World, 1978), p. 117.

[95]*E.g.*, as pointed out by W. D. Davies, "Paul and the Dead Sea Scrolls: Flesh and Spirit," *The Scrolls and the New Testament* (ed. by K. Stendahl; New York: Harper and Brothers, 1957), p. 177.

[96]*Ibid.*, pp. 180ff. *Cf.* also the assessment of Vermes, *Perspective*, pp. 211-221.

portant contribution to the meaning of *ruaḥ* in the Scrolls, which anticipated much of the work of later scholarship.

In section *1b* of this chapter we dealt with the impact of Persian thought on Qumran and found no *necessary* connection between views on this and one's definition of *ruaḥ* in the Scrolls. We noted, however, that the supposition of Persian influence of some sort might help to explain instances in which an exegesis of *ruaḥ* in the Scrolls may lead to seemingly contradictory or ambiguous results, i.e., cases in which Persian concepts of "spirit" may have been inadequately integrated into Qumran's more traditional and biblical definitions.

In section *1c* of this chapter we considered the relationship of the Scrolls to early Christianity. Our conclusion was that the pneumatology of the Scrolls should not be understood uncritically against the background of early Christian thought or expression.

2. From 1956 through 1961: conflicting solutions to the problem of *ruaḥ* in the Scrolls.

a. Preliminary observations.

After the publication of Sjöberg's article in 1955 in which he defined *ruaḥ* in 1QH as God's Spirit given to the sectarian at his entrance into the community,[97] it became increasingly apparent that K. G. Kuhn's definition of *ruaḥ* as simply a static, predestined *habitus* in man from birth might not be sufficient as a complete view of Qumran's pneumatology.[98] Also, the precise relationship between these two definitions (*i.e.*, God's Spirit *vs.* man's static, predestined spirit) was unclear. Did the sectarian believe that he was *born* with a spiritual disposition purer than that of the non-sectarian which qualified him to be a "son of righteousness," or did he think of his spirituality as something beyond his own natural capacities, *i.e.* as a transformation (*Neuschöpfung*) of his spirit through the work of God's Spirit as part of his membership in the sect?

---

[97]Sjöberg, "Neuschöpfung," pp. 131-6.

[98]Kuhn himself apparently recognized this; *cf.* n. 21 above.

Under Kuhn's previous definition of *ruaḥ* as a predestined *habitus* in man, the view of the sectarians seemed to be clear and consistent. *ruaḥ* in their inner religious experience was always essentially man's *ruaḥ* in contrast to that of God or an angel.[99] Kuhn certainly recognized that the sectarians could think of *ruaḥ* in a traditional, biblical way as "God's Spirit" (*e.g.*, in 1QS 4:20ff. as the Holy Spirit given to the believer by God above and beyond man's predestined, spiritual condition), but he thought that they expected this Spirit only in the eschatological future.[100] Spirituality at Qumran, then, never really involved any divine or angelic powers beyond man himself. This is why, in Kuhn's opinion, 1QS 3:15ff. (which describes the two spirits as dividing mankind into two exclusive groups) is not necessarily inconsistent with 1QS 4:20-23 (which describes the two spirits as carrying on a struggle within the individual). In both cases this treatise is describing good and evil *dispositions* within the individual sectarian;[101] the difference is simply that the evil disposition is given a name in 1QS 4:20-23 (*viz.* the "spirit of iniquity"), whereas in 1QS 3:15ff. the sectarian's evil disposition is understood implicitly

---

[99]K. G. Kuhn, "Πειρασμός," pp. 214-5.

[100]*Idem,* "Sektenschrift," p. 302 n. 4: "der. . . Dualismus der beiden Urgeister der Wahrheit und des Frevels in Sekt. 4, 20ff. verbunden ist mit den alttestamentlichen Gedanken von dem 'neuen Geist', dem 'Heiligen Giest'. . . den Gott dem Frommen ins Herz geben wird. . . ."

[101]*Cf.* Wernberg-Møller, "Reconsideration," p.432 n. 46, who feels that Kuhn has incorrectly minimized the true tension between 1QS 3:15ff. and 4:20-23 when 3:13-4:26 is interpreted dualistically. He would be correct if Kuhn at this time viewed the two spirits as cosmic entities or identified them with the Prince of Lights or Angel of Darkness (as Wernberg-Møller aparently believes, *cf.* n. 59 above) since the "spirit of iniquity" in 4:20-23 would then not be conceptually parallel to the "flesh" implicit in 3:15ff. and other logical problems would arise (*cf.* chapter 8 below). Kuhn's own position, however, could have been made less ambiguous if he would have made it more clear that the *sharp,* dualistic division of humanity into realms of darkness and light depends more on the function of the two angels (3:20ff.) than on the two spirits (*cf.* chapter 8, n. 86 below).

as his "flesh," *i.e.* "die Sphäre des Widergöttlichen" which he shares with all men (*cf.* 1QS 11:12ff. with 3:21ff. which together show that the sectarian's "flesh" makes him vulnerable to sin, although "flesh" is not mentioned in 3:21ff.). What we have here, then, is no more than a matter of terminology: in 3:15ff. the "spirit of iniquity" is used exclusively to describe a dominantly evil disposition of the non-sectarian, whereas in 4:20-23 it is also used to describe an evil (but not dominant) disposition of the sectarian.[102] The author of this treatise could be regarded as ambiguous (*e.g.*, he could have used בשׂר or a completely new term to describe the sinful aspect of the sectarian's character in 1QS 4:22-23), but in Kuhn's view he should not be regarded as being inconsistent or contradictory.

With Sjöberg's 1955 article,[103] however, the internal consistency of sectarian pneumatology as outlined by Kuhn was open to question. How could the sectarians understand their spirituality both as an inheritied disposition *and* as a gift of God's Spirit at their entrance in the community? Some years later Kuhn's students, H. W. Kuhn and H. Lichtenberger would wrestle with the problem and conclude that the two-spirit theology of 1QS 3:13-4:26 was not successfully integrated into the rest of sectarian thought.[104]

---

[102]K. G. Kuhn, "Sektenshrift," p. 302 n. 4; cf, also n. 1.

[103]Sjöberg, "Neuschöpfung."

[104]*Cf.* H. W. Kuhn, *Enderwartung*, pp. 120-1: "Neben den Aussagen über die durch den Eintritt in die Gemeinde vermittelte Gabe des Geistes kann in den Gemeindeliedern auf grund einer dualistischen Geist-/Geisterverstellung auch von der *ruaḥ* gesprochen werden, die dem Menschen schöpfungsmäßig gegeben ist und sein Handeln von vornherein festlegt. . . . Von daher muß die Möglichkeit offengelassen werden, daß auch die Qumrantexte bzw. die Gemeindelieder eine fremde Vorstellung zum teil essenischem Glauben angepaßt haben." *Cf.* also Lichtenberger, *Studien*, p. 174: "Ein wichtiges Ergebnis unserer Analysen war gewesen, daß das Reden vom Menschen in den Qumrantexten nicht einheitlich ist. . . . Das Ergebnis ist also eigentlich ein negatives, nämlich die Infragestellung einer einheitlichen 'qumranischen' Sicht des Menschen, wie sie häufig angenommen wird, wobie man meist 1QS 3-4 zur Richtschnur macht."

But Sjöberg's work affected not only K.G. Kuhn's position. It affected also the "majority" position of this time, but in a more indirect and less visible way.[105] This position went beyond Kuhn in viewing the two spirits of 1QS 3-4 as cosmic, angelic creatures as well as forces immanent in men,[106] and it interpreted 1QH and other sectarian literature in the light of this pneumatology.[107] As a result, most scholars tended to equate the spirit of truth in 1QS (understood as an angel) with God's holy Spirit in 1QH and elsewhere.[108] But Sjöberg's work challenged this simple equation. The basic message of 1QH for him had to do with the weakness and spiritual perversity of man by nature as a contrast to God's grace and ability to renew and cleanse man through His holy Spirit.[109] This is in contrast to the two-spirit theology of 1QS 3-4 as understood by most scholars at this time in terms of Iranian, cosmic dualism and divine

---

Lichtenberger then quotes with approval the observation of A. L. Irwin, "Conflict Spirit-Dualism in the Qumran Writings and the New Testament," unpublished dissertation, Hartford Theological Seminary, 1960, pp. 1-2: "The Two-Spirit theology which comes to overt and extended expression in a well-known section of the Manual of Discipline (. . .) is *not* as has been widely assumed the dominant pneumatology of the other writings, or even of the remainder of the manual."

[105]It is relatively easy to trace Sjöberg's effect on K. G. Kuhn and his students since Sjöberg related his work directly to Kuhn (*cf.* Sjöberg, "Wiedergeburt," p. 78 and *idem*, "Neuschöpfung," p. 131), and its effects can be seen in the later work of Kuhn and his students. Nevertheless, in their later work there is supprisingly little reference to Sjöberg's significant 1955 article, "Neuschöpfung." The same is true in the work of those in the majority position; also, since Sjöberg did not relate his work explicitly to this position, his actual effect on it is much more a matter of inference.

[106]*Cf.* n. 19 above.

[107]*Cf.* the comments of Lichtenberger and Irwin in n. 104 above.

[108]*Cf.* E. L. Beaven, "Ruah Hakodesh in some Early Jewish Literature," unpublished dissertation, Vanderbilt University, 1961, p. 90: "The point at issue is whether רוח קודש and רוח אמת are synonymous as most interpreters suppose."

[109]Sjöberg, "Neuschöpfung," pp. 134-5.

predestination.[110] Here the emphasis is not so much on the contrast between man's sinfulness and God's grace, as Sjöberg showed in 1QH;[111] the primary contrast in 1QS 3-4, rather, is between two angelic powers, good against evil, and their respective angelic and human followings. Furthermore, there is no real ethical contrast between the sectarian's spirit and the good spiritual power of 1QS 3-4; the two, in fact seem to merge together with the description of the sectarian's spiritual nature as a natural, foreordained "inheritance" in the spirit of truth.[112]

During this period (1956-1961) it became increasingly evident that it would be difficult to integrate the pneumatology of 1QS 3-4 into the predominant pneumatology of 1QH,[113] and a

---

[110]Wernberg-Møller, "Reconsideration," p. 428: "[1QS 3:13-4:26] is widely interpreted along the lines of Iranian, cosmic dualism and divine predestination."

[111]Sjöberg, "Neuschöpfung," pp. 134-5: "Ihr eigentliches Thema ist die Schwachheit des natürlichen Menschen und die Erneuerung durch die Gnade Gottes."

[112]*Cf.* W. D. Davies, "Paul," p. 172: "[The two spirits] are regarded as a kind of permanent element in every man, since creation, until the 'End' decreed by God." *Cf.* also Friedrich Nötscher, "Geist und Geister in den Texten von Qumran," *Mélanges Bibliques,* rédigées en l'honneur de A. Robert, Paris, 1957), p. 306: "Geist kommt ebenso *Gott wie Menschen* zu. Zwischen beiden Arten besteht kein absoluter Gegensatz, ja nicht einmal ein grundsätzlicher Unterschied." In what follows Nötscher offers an analysis of *ruaḥ* which mixes together evidence from 1QH, and 1QS 3-4. Contrast this view with Sjöberg's analysis of 1QH in "Neuschöpfung," pp. 134-5: "Kein Mensch kann vor Gott gerecht sein. Voll von Sünde und schuld steht er vor Gott. . . . Aus dieser schwacken und sündigen Existenze wird der Mensch durch den Eintritt in die Sekt und die dadurch geschehene Neuschöpfung erlöst. . . . Den verkehrten Geist des Menschen hat Gott gereinigt. . . . Er hat seinen heiligen Geist auf ihn gesprengt, um ihn zu reinigen und die schuld zu sühnen."

[113]*Cf.* Irwin, "Spirit-Dualism," pp. 50ff. in which he compares the work of two scholars, A. Dupont-Sommer and T. H. Gaster, who believe that the two-spirit dualism of 1QS 3-4 can be seen in 1QH: "Places where Dupont-Sommer sees this doctrine [*i.e.,* the two-spirit teaching

growing number of scholars began to consider the possibility that the basic presuppositions underlying the approach of the majority position might be flawed. By 1961 two mutually exclusive positions had evolved, both of which were critical of the majority. The one agreed with the majority that there were both biblical and dualistic/Iranian elements in sectarian pneumatology, but strongly disagreed that these elements were successfully integrated into a single consistent system of thought;[114] the second agreed that the Scrolls had a consistent pneumatology, but disagreed that cosmic dualism (Iranian or otherwise) had ever been a part of this.[115] In the following two sub-sections of this chapter (*2b* and *2c*) we will outline these two positions.

b. The position that the Scrolls do not contain a single consistent pneumatology.

According to O. Betz, the scholarship of his time had not considered the possibility that the pneumatology of the Scrolls might contain conflicting and contradictory elements,[116] and in general this observation seems to be true. However, scholarship had been steadily moving in that direction. We noted above (section *2a*), for example, that the findings of Sjöberg's article, "Neuschöpfung," tended to clash with the pneumatology of

---

of 1QS 3-4] are frequently found to be reconstructions. Dupont-Sommer finds the doctrine where Gaster does not recognize it; Gaster assumes it where Dupont-Sommer has another interpretation; and at no point do they clearly agree upon its presence." *Cf.* also Jacob Licht, "The Doctrine of the Thanksgiving Scroll," *Israel Exploration Journal*, 6 (1956), pp. 3-6, who believes that the doctrine of the two spirits underlies the thought of 1QH but also notes that these two spirits are never mentioned in it.

[114]*E.g.*, Betz, *Offenbarung*, and Irwin, "Spirit-Dualism."

[115]*Cf.* especially Wernberg-Møller, "Reconsideration,"; *cf.* also Nötscher, *Terminologie*, pp. 79-92 and Marco Treves,, "The Two Spirits of the Rule of the Community," *Revue de Qumrân*, 3 (1961), pp. 449-452, who minimize the effects of Iranian influence and the presence of a strict cosmic dualism at Qumran.

[116]Betz, *Offenbarung*, p. 143.

1QS 3-4 as generally understood at that time, and this is true of other studies which followed. A. Dietzel[117] and R. Schnackenburg,[118] for example, both recognized with Sjöberg the essential contrast between the lost, spiritual condition of man by nature and the transforming power of God's Spirit given to the Qumran community and its members as an eschatological (rather than an inherited) gift.[119] But perhaps the most important study of this time was a work by H. W. Huppenbauer in which he analyzed the dualistic patterns of the Scrolls and found that the type present in 1QS 3:13-4:26 was not representative of the kind of dualism present in the Scrolls as a whole.[120] He saw five basic types of dualism, four of which were relatively prevalent in the texts: these are ethical,[121] physical-metaphysical,[122] cosmic,[123] and eschatological dualism.[124] A fifth type, mythological, deals with the two-spirit teaching of 1QS, with its two contending angelic princes--mythological figures present also in 1QM and CD. Huppenbauer notes that the other dualisms presumably should be considered in the light of this mythological dualism (as was the opinion of most scholars then) but he also

[117]Armin Dietzel, "Beten im Geist. Eine religionsgeschichtliche Parallele aus den Hodajot zum paulinischen Beten im Geist," *Theologische Zeitschrift*, 13 (1957), pp. 12-32.

[118]Rudolf Schnackenburg, "Die 'Anbetung in Geist und Wahrheit' (John 45:23) im Licht von Qumran-Texten," *Biblische Zeitschrift*, 3 (1959), pp. 88-94.

[119]*Cf.* Sjöberg, "Neuschöpfung," p. 136 n. 2: "Bei dieser eschatologisch eingestellten Sekte ist es nicht überraschend, dass die Neuschöpfung auch mit dem eschatologischen Ausblick verbunden wird."

[120]Hans Walter Huppenbauer, *Der Mensch zwischen zwei Welten. Der Dualismus der Texte von Qumran (Höhle I) und der Damaskusfragmente. Ein Beitrag zur Vorgeschichte des Evangeliums*, Abhandlungen zur Theologie des Alten und Neuen Testaments, 34 (Zürich: Zwingli Verlag, 1959), pp. 103-114.

[121]*Ibid.*, p. 104.

[122]*Ibid.*, pp. 104-8.

[123]*Ibid.*, pp. 108-110.

[124]*Ibid.*, p. 111.

notes that this dualism, in fact, is an extreme form used with caution by the sectarians and found relatively rarely in their writings.[125]

About a year after Huppenbauer's study, two major works appeared which energetically stated the case for the presence of conflicting pneumatologies in the Scrolls, one by O. Betz (mentioned above) and the other by A. L. Irwin.[126] Betz analyzed sectarian pneumatology primarily in relationship to the concept of revelation in the Scrolls and concluded that two conflicting doctrines of *ruaḥ* could be discerned through careful analysis: one deals with the Spirit of God, which Betz called *Geistlehre*, and the other with the two spirits of 1QS 3-4, which he called *Geisterlehre*.[127] The *Geistlehre* teaches that men by nature have a *ruaḥ* which is similar in "*Substanz*" to God's own Spirit (since it comes from Him) and therefore can be regarded as "*heiliger Geist*."[128] This is God's initial granting of His Spirit which calls men into life. But through their fleshly nature men defile God's "spirit" (which now belongs to them as their own spirit) and therefore must be granted a second gift of God's Spirit at their entrance into the sect in order to transform them from "Menschen des Verderbens" to "Kinder der Wahrheit." This is a process which takes place throughout life, but in the eschatological future a third, definitive granting of God's Spirit is to take place in which the sectarians are

---

[125]*Ibid.*, p. 110: "Wir haben gesehen, dass die DSS von solch extremen Formen des Dualismus sehr vorsichtig machen. Es ist ja kaum von ungefahr, dass die Unterweisung über die zwei Geister im bisher veröffentlichten Material einmalig ist. Und der mythologische Gegensatz Gott (Engel des Lichts)-- Belial (Engel der Finsternis o.ä.) liegt ausserdem mit Sicherheit nur in der Kriegsrolle und in der Damaskus-Schrift vor."

[126]*Cf.* n. 114 above. It is interesting to note that neither Irwin or Betz make use of Huppenbauer in *Der Mensch* or Sjöberg in "Neuschöpfung."

[127]Betz, *Offenbarung*, p. 143.

[128]*Ibid.*, pp. 129 and 140.

so transformed that they become like angels and attain to angelic wisdom.[129]

In comparing the above *Geistlehre* to the *Geisterlehre* of 1QS 3-4, Betz found the following differences: 1) the *Geistlehre* is closely related to God's revelational activity in the present, whereas for a consistent *Geisterlehre* God has no real contact with men, and revelation (together with the historical process this implies) is utimately unnecessary since everything is already predestined and man's fate is sealed;[130] 2) the essential contrast in the *Geistlehre* is between the spirit of man (originally holy but now defiled) and the Holy Spirit of God, whereas in the *Geisterlehre* the contrast is carried into the supernatural realm of the two spirits in their cosmic opposition to each other;[131] 3) the *Geistlehre* directly relates man to God, whereas the *Geisterlehre* places angelic intermediaries between them;[132] 4) the *Geistlehre* conceives of men (even the opponents of the community)[133] as receiving a "holy spirit" at birth which undergoes a defilement through the influence of the flesh and eventually has to be cleansed by God's Spirit at one's entrance into the community,[134] whereas the *Geisterlehre* views men as being essentially different from the beginning[135] and as having a spirit created by God appropriate to one's predestined lot under either the spirit of truth or spirit of darkness (understood as angels);[136] finally, the *Geistlehre* looks forward

---

[129] *Ibid.*, pp. 140-1.

[130] *Ibid.*, p. 149.

[131] *Ibid.*, pp. 143.

[132] *Ibid.*, p. 144.

[133] *Ibid.*, pp. 126 and 141.

[134] *Ibid.*, pp. 140-1.

[135] *Ibid.*, p. 146

[136] *Ibid.*, p. 147; *cf.* also pp. 58 & 129 n. 3 and pp. 143-4. Note that Betz later came to the conclusion that the two spirits were not angels but rather that they "stellen das sittliche Prinzip, die Kraft des Handelns dar;" *cf.* Otto Betz, *Der Paraklet: Fürsprecher im häretischen Spätjudentum, im Johannesevangelium und in neu gefundenen gnostischen Schriften* (Leiden: Brill, 1963), p. 67.

to earthly leaders anointed with the Spirit who will lead a victory over earthly enemies with the attainment of earthly blessings, whereas the *Geisterlehre* looks forward to a heavenly leader (the angel Michael), who will lead a victory over cosmic enemies with the attainment of heavenly blessings envisioned as a transformed heavenly existence among the angels.[137]

Generally speaking, scholarship has not followed Betz in his description of the spirits of men and angels as being of the same "*Substanz*" as God's Spirit,[138] nor have many adopted his view that there are three stages in which men receive the gift of God's Spirit.[139] Betz' main contention, however, that the two-spirit teaching of 1QS is in tension with the doctrine of

---

[137]*Ibid.*, pp. 151-2.

[138]It is difficult to know exactly what Betz means when he says that the Spirit of God and the spirits of men and angels are all of a like *Substanz*. Perhaps a more representative opinion of sectarian pneumatology on this issue can be seen in Schweizer, "Gegenwart des Geistes," p. 491: "Darin setzt sich das alttestamentliche Wissen darum, daß der Geist Jahwes nicht der Geist des Menschen ist, fort. Die griechische Konzeption von der Identität des Geistes im Menschen mit dem kosmischen göttlischen Geist ist hier nicht eingedrungen." It is not until the later rise of Gnosticism, as such, that man in his spirit feels an identity between himself and God; *cf.* Eduard Schweizer,"πνεῦμα, πνευματικός," *Theological Dictionary of the New Testament*, 6 (trans. and ed. by G. W. Bromily; Grand Rapids, 1961), p. 392: "More and more the soul is felt to be alien, though of the same substance as God."

[139]*Cf.* Herbert Braun, *Qumran und das Neue Testament*, band II (Tübingen: Mohr,1966), p. 253: Braun mentions only Betz as holding this opinion and remarks, "In jedem falle aber wird in Qumran nicht von einer Geistgabe bei der Geburt, sondern nur von einer solchen bei der Bekehrung und im Eschaton, also, von einer zweifachen, nicht von einer dreifachen Geistgabe zu sprechen sein. . . ." For a defence of Betz' position, *cf.* Wolf-Dieter Hauschild, *Gottes Geist und der Menschen. Studien zur frühchristlichen Pneumatologie*, Beiträge zur evangelischen Theologie, 63 (München: Kaiser Verlag, 1972), pp. 248ff.

God's Spirit (especially as seen in 1QH) has found support among later investigators.[140]

In the second work mentioned above,[141] A. L. Irwin analyzed the major types of dualism present in the Scrolls and found that the dualism underlying 1QS 3:13-4:26 is relatively rare[142] and unrepresentative[143] of the Scrolls as a whole and at times inconsistent with the more characteristic aspects of their teaching.[144] The general dualism characteristic of all the Scrolls Irwin called conflict spirit-dualism, *i.e.* a general pattern of conflict which always involves a concept of *ruaḥ*,[145] and within this basic type he isolated four subtypes: 1) community dualism, which divides the Qumran community from non-members[146] and is the most basic subtype in the Scrolls,[147] 2) cosmic-metaphysical dualism, which has to do with the two-spirit teaching of 1QS 3-4,[148] 3) eschatological dualism, which anticipates the future as imminent or actually inaugurated (*cf.* especially 1QM),[149] and finally 4) soteriological dualism, which distinguishes man's natural, perverted spirit from God's "saving spirit" (*i.e.* the sectarian's new spirit from God--found only in 1QH).[150] Elements of these dualisms appear in various

---

[140]*Cf.* n. 104 above.

[141]*Cf.* n. 114 above.

[142]Irwin, *Spirit-Dualism,* p. 8: ". . . nor should we be amazed if we discover its pneumatology [*i.e.*, of 1QS 3-4] to be a distinctive one which is not shared by the Manual as a whole and which indeed can be positively identified only in one other scroll [*i.e.*, 1QM] and in only particular parts of that writing."

[143]*Ibid.*, p. 12: "We shall see in succeeding chapters that this pneumatology [*i.e.*, of 1QS 3-4] is not nearly so pervasive in, nor so basic to the Qumran writings as has been generally supposed."

[144]*Ibid.*, pp. 32 and 82-3; *cf.* Irwin's remarks on both cosmic-metaphysical and eschatological dualism in the second reference.

[145]*Ibid.*, p. 76.

[146]*Ibid.*, p. 23.

[147]*Ibid.*, p. 78.

[148]*Ibid.*, pp. 78-9.

[149]*Ibid.*, pp. 79-80.

[150]*Ibid.*, pp. 80-1.

combinations in the Scrolls and for the most part form a harmonious whole much like musical variations "linked to each other in a persistent over-all theme."[151] An exception to this, however, is the cosmic-metaphysical dualism of 1QS 3-4 with its emphasis on the "Angelic Intermediary." Here a definite tension can be seen between the view that this angel defeats Belial (and so is exalted) and the view that God Himself accomplished this.[152]

In summary, then, the view that the Scrolls contain conflicting pneumatologies is indirectly traceable to Sjöberg's 1955 article, "Neuschöpfung," in which his description of *ruaḥ* in 1QH tended at that time to conflict with the general understanding of *ruaḥ* in 1QS 3-4. His interpretation of 1QH anticipated much of the work of later scholars. Finally, the work of Huppenbauer in *Der Mensch,* Betz in *Offenbarung,* and Irwin in *Conflict Spirit-Dualism* independently questioned the prevailing consensus that 1QS 3-4 contained the dominant pneumatology of the Scrolls while, in addition, Betz and Irwin felt that this pneumatology was in conflict with other sectarian pneumatologies and dualistic elements.

c. The position that the Scrolls contain a consistent pneumatology but do not contain cosmic dualism (Iranian or otherwise).

For a number of years scholars had been questioning the majority concensus which tended to view sectarian dualism as strongly cosmic in nature due to a significant Iranian influence,[153] but the most extensive questioning of this view came in Wernberg-Møller's 1961 article, "Reconsideration." In this article Wernberg-Møller strongly questioned the consensus that 1QS 3:13-4:26 reflects an Iranian, cosmic dualism and sought to interpret this passage in a more biblical light. Given his alternative approach to 1QS 3-4, the tension between *ruaḥ* in this passage (as generally understood at that time) and *ruaḥ* in 1QH

---

[151] *Ibid.,* p. 77.

[152] *Ibid.,* p. 80.

[153] *Cf.* Molin, *Söhne,* pp. 129-130 and Nötscher, *Terminologie,* pp. 79-92.

(as understood by Sjöberg and a growing number of scholars) might seem to be less. The two spirits of 1QS would be seen as two good and evil dispositions much like the two *yetzers* of rabbinic theology, and the presence of God's Spirit against this background would seem to be similar to that in later Jewish throught. Nevertheless, not all the tension would be resolved. As Sjöberg has noted, rabbinic *yetzer* theology in principle has no place for a spiritual "Neuschöpfung,"[154] and if Sjöberg is also correct that 1QH teaches the necessity of a "*Neuschöpfung*" as a basic element in sectarian piety, a definite contrast between 1QS 3-4 (as Wernberg-Møller interprets it) and 1QH would still exist.[155] It is not clear, however, that Wernberg-Møller's purpose was to resolve this tension as such or even that he saw it as a general problem in sectarian pneumatology--although it is clear that he regarded teachings of 1QS and 1QH as an integrated whole[156] and thought that scholars produced unnecessary tensions within 1QS itself (*e.g.*, between 3:13ff. and 4:20ff.)

---

[154]Sjöberg, "Wiedergeburt," p. 68: "In keinem Falle bedeutet die Neuschöpfung eine Veränderung der natürlichen ethische und religiösen Ausrüstung des Menschen. . . . Eine Neuschöpfung, um den Menschen zu einem vollwertigen ethisch-religiösen Leben fähig zu machen, ist nicht nötig."

[155]Compare the following: Sjöberg in "Neuschöpfung," p. 134 notes that the spiritual weakness of man by nature in 1QH "macht es für ihn unmöglich, das richtige Gotteserkenntnis zu gewinnen und nach Gottes Willen zu Leben" until he enters the sect and experiences an "Erneuerung" though God's Spirit, which "bei ihm ein neues Leben ermöglicht," (*ibid.*, p. 136); in contrast, Wernberg-Møller in "Reconsideration," p. 422 n. 19 sees 1QS 3-4 as teaching that "man was created fit to rule, not only the earth, but over his inclinations" and when he does not succeed, it is because he himself allows his "perverse and sinful propensities to determine his behaviour," (*ibid.*, p. 422). The sectarians, then, felt a spiritual "solidarity" (*ibid.*, p. 428) with mankind and "are not separated from the rest of humanity by a radical constitutional difference due to opposed metaphysical principles, but entirely to God's election." (*ibid.*, p. 424).

[156]*E.g.*, *ibid.*, p. 415 n. 5: "The present writer is inclined to believe that the theology of 1QH is not basically different from that of 1QS."

by interpreting it in terms of Iranian, cosmic dualism.[157] He believed that these and other tensions within 1QS could be eliminated if the two spirits of columns 3 and 4 were understood in a more biblical sense as two balanced dispositions within man rather than as two cosmic beings.[158] His interpretation of the two spirits of 1QS 3-4 in this article is perhaps the strongest and most detailed statement of its kind to date.[159]

Before entering into a fuller discussion of Wernberg-Møller's article, however, we should assess the scholarship preceding it and most directly related to its thesis.[160] In the concluding statement of his article, Wernberg-Møller notes that much of what he had written was not new but that he had simply made a more thorough application than others to the interpretation of 1QS 3-4 of views which were already present in scholarship.[161] This does not seem to be entirely accurate, however. There are at least two fundamentally important views in his article which seem to be original with him: these are 1) that there is no cosmic dualism at all in 1QS 3-4[162] and 2) that

---

[157]*Ibid.*, p. 432 n. 46.

[158]*E.g.*, *ibid.*, p. 433 n. 47.

[159]In any discussion of the "anthropological" interpretation of *ruaḥ* in 1QS, Wernberg-Møller's work is always at the forefront. In the 1981 article by Dombkowski Hopkins, "Community," for example, the only scholar she discusses at any length as representative of this interpretation of *ruaḥ* in the Scrolls is Wernberg-Møller.

[160]For a general perspective on the relationship of Persian thought to the meaning of *ruaḥ* in the Scrolls, see section *1b* of this chapter.

[161]Wernberg-Møller, "Reconsideration," p. 441.

[162]*Cf.* May, "Cosmological Reference," p. 1, who notes that Wernberg-Møller finds "no evidence of cosmic dualism and no Zoroastrian influence;" *cf.* also Domkowski Hopkins, "Community," p. 342.

It is difficult to know exactly what Wernberg-Møller means by the term "dualism" in his interpretation of 1QS 3-4 or what he means when he talks about the dualistic views of others since he does not define the various possible meanings of this term; *cf.* John G. Gammie, "Spatial and Ethical Dualism in Jewish Wisdom and Apocalyptic Literature," *Journal of Biblical Literature*, 93, (1974), pp. 356-7, who notes

1QS 3-4 does not divide mankind into two distinct, spiritual groups.[163] Conversely, however, he would be able to show

---

that scholars in general have shown "a lamentable lack of precision in defining and distinguishing between types of dualism." If, however, we adopt Licht's definition of "cosmic" dualism (*cf.* Jacob Licht, "An Analysis of the Treatise of the Two Spirits in DSD," *Scripta Hierosolymitana*, 4 (1958), p. 92: "These camps [the two opposing groups of mankind] are conceived as the realms of two supernatural rulers: the Prince of Lights and the Angel of Darkness. Thus the dualistic principle is extended beyond humanity into the cosmic spheres."), it will be seen that on this basis no scholar cited by Wernberg-Møller denies the presence of some element of cosmic dualism in 1QS 3-4. To do so would mean that the "angels" of this section would have to be regarded as no more than personifications of spiritual forces within men's hearts (as does Wernberg-Møller, "Reconsideration," p. 426 n. 30) and neither Schubert or Wolverton, cited by Wernberg-Møller as denying the presence of any cosmic dualism in 1QS (*ibid.*, p. 413 n. 1 and p. 418 n. 8, respectively), hold this position; *cf.* Schubert, "Sektenkanon," col. 506 and Wallace I. Wolverton, "The Double-Minded Man in Light of Essene Psychology," *Anglican Theological Review*, 38 (1956), p. 169. It is true that Wolverton, citing Molin, says that Essene dualism is chiefly a "heart dualism" and that ultimately even this does not appear as a "true duality," but he no more than Molin, (*cf.* Molin, *Söhne*, pp. 126-7) questions the cosmic status of the angelic powers: "The two spirits or angels, the Prince of Lights and Belial, are continually at war, but the transcendent God who is over all will in the end dispose of Belial," (Wolverton, "Double-Minded Man," p. 169). Wernberg-Møller also gives the impression that O. Seitz regards the two angels of 1QS 3-4 as no more than personifications in man (*cf.* Wernberg-Møller, "Reconsideration," p. 426 n. 30), but see n. 164 below.

[163] *Viz.*, that there is no evidence of a community dualism based on the idea that that community members are fundamentally different from non-members in their spiritual constitution due to opposed metaphysical principles; *cf. ibid.*, p. 424; *cf.* also *ibid.*, p. 431, "But then we have arrived at the thesis of the present article, namely that the dichotomy of our 'essay' [1QS 3:13-4:26] does not lie in the distinction between pious and impious ruled by conflicting spirits respectively, but in the opposed mental dispositions of every human being," and *ibid.*, pp. 428, "The sons of righteousness are, in a way, regarded as a section

precedence in earlier writings for at least four other views basic to his thesis: these are 1) that the two spirits of 1QS 3-4 have only an anthropological significance,[164] 2) that Iran is not the

---

within the larger whole, the sons of perversion, and as belonging to them."

The question of community dualism is closely tied to that of cosmic dualism treated above in n. 162 since it is difficult to maintain that the sectarians saw themselves as having the same spiritual potential for obeying the law as non-sectarians if they also believed that they were under the good spiritual influence of a cosmic Prince of Lights while the outside world was under a cosmic Angel of Darkness with a host of evil spirits doing his bidding. In this situation it is difficult to talk about a balance between the good and evil impulse in man with man's choice operating in a free manner. Rather, there are conflicting angelic figures, each ruling over his own "dominion" (ממשלה) and externally influencing man's spiritual life in either a good or evil direction. Wernberg-Møller, then, is able to cite only one scholar as denying any true dualism (and therefore community dualism) in the Scrolls, *viz.*, W. I. Wolverton (*cf. ibid.*, p. 418 n. 8). But as we saw in n. 162 above, this seems to be a misunderstanding of Wolverton in respect to cosmic dualism, and the same seems to be true in respect to his views on community dualism; *cf.* Wolverton, "Double-Minded Man," p. 168: "As we have suggested, the word *dipsychos* hints at a dualism of some kind. It may have evoked in the minds of St. James' hearers the picture of the opposing realms of good and evil, an idea that Judaism generally, it is believed, had incorporated from contacts with Persian thought. Whatever its provenance the Essenes certainly had a pronounced and distinctive dualism."

[164]I have found only four scholars previous to Wernberg-Møller's article, "Reconsideration," who regarded the two spirits as no more than forces within men. In every case, however, they distinguish between the two spirits and the two angels of 1QS 3-4 and regard the two angels as cosmic beings exercising dominion over the two opposed societies of sectarians and non-sectarians: *cf.* F. M. Braun, "L'arrière-fond," pp. 12-14, K. G. Kuhn, "Sektenschrift," pp. 301-2 n. 4, Graystone, "Scrolls," vol. 22, 227-8 and Nötscher, "Geist," pp. 310 & 413-4. Wernberg-Møller, however, never mentions either F. M. Braun or Graystone in "Reconsideration," and he appears to regard Kuhn (at that time) as holding to a cosmic view of the two spirits (*cf.* n. 59 above).

source of the two-spirit theology of 1QS 3-4,[165] 3) that the majority approach involves conceptual tensions between 1QS 3:13ff. and 4:20ff.,[166] and 4) that the concept of predestination

---

Wernberg-Møller does cite a number of scholars who he says have a "psychological" interpretation of the two spirits in 1QS 3-4 (*viz.*, Oscar J. F. Seitz, *ibid.*, p. 416 n. 6; W. D. Davies, *ibid.*, p. 418 n. 8; Friedrich Nötscher, *ibid.*, p. 419 n. 13; and E. Schweizer, *ibid.*, p. 423 n. 22), but it is difficult to know what he means by "psychological." He probably does not mean that these authors recognize a psychological as well as a cosmic dimension to the function of the two spirits since this has never been an issue; *cf.* James H. Charlesworth, "A Critical Comparison of the Dualism in 1QS 3: 13-4:26 and the 'Dualism' Contained in the Gosple of John, " *John and Qumran* (London, 1972), p. 82, who notes that the consensus of scholarly opinion readily concedes that "cosmic dualism does break into the so-called 'psychological' arena of each man." Wernberg-Møller must mean that the authors he cites recognize with him only the psychological aspect of the two spirits, but this is not the case with most of them. For example, Oscar Seitz in "Two Spirits in Man: An essay in Biblical Exegesis," *New Testament Studies*, 6 (1959/60), p. 91, likens the pneumatology of 1QS and the *Testaments of the Patriarchs* to that of *Hermas*, whose concept of "spirit" he describes as "invasive" (in Mandate five) and as coming upon man "from without"; W. D. Davies in "Paul," pp. 172-3 notes that the two spirits are not merely inherent properties in man since they are described as angels, thus preserving the "otherness" of the two spirits "even when they appear to be merely immanent;" finally, for Schweizer in "Gegenwart des Geist," *cf.* n. 19 above. Only Nötscher in "Geist," p. 310 described the two spirits in 1QS 3:18-19 as essentially no more than "gegenstzliche Geisterrichtung" in man, but in a later work he seems to have given up this position; *cf.* Freidrich Nötscher, *Gotteswege und Menschenwege in der Bibel und Qumran* (Bonn: Hanstein Verlag, 1958), p. 92, in which he describes the spirits of 1QS 3:18 as a *plurality* of good and evil angelic beings.

[165]*E.g.*, Molin, *Söhne*, p. 129 and especially Nötscher, *Terminologie*, pp. 86-92. We should note that Molin and Nötscher do not believe that cosmic dualism is entirely absent in the Scrolls (they both accept the presence of the two cosmic angels) but only that this dualism has its roots in the Old Testament rather than in Persia.

[166]*E. g.*, K. G. Kuhn and Licht (*cf.* Wernberg-Møller, "Reconsideration," p. 432 n. 46) have both dealt with the apparent ten-

is not basic to the teaching of *ruaḥ* in 1QS 3-4 (or in the rest of the Scrolls).[167] It would seem, however, that these general views in themselves, if correct, would not sustain the basic thesis of his article, *viz.*, that the two-spirit "dualism" of 1QS 3-4 does not extend beyond the dichotomy of two perfectly balanced *yetzers* in the individual man over which *he* has control.[168] We will see that in order to sustain this thesis, Wernberg-Møller must rely primarily on the views unique to him (as outlined above) by systematically contesting the presence of any cosmic dualism (*i.e.*, as this relates not only to the two spirits but also to the two angels) or any community dualism (*i.e.*, any significant spiritual distinctions between community and non-community members).

What will follow, then, is a basic outline of Wernberg-Møller's interpretation of 1QS 3:13-4:26 as this pertains primarily to the nature of the dualism in these passages.

He begins by noting that 1QS should be interpreted not as an isolated unit but rather in the light of sectarian literature as a whole[169] and especially in the light of 1QH and 1QS 11.[170] In this way it would be seen that 1QS 3-4 contains no dualistic or deterministic teachings. He notes that some scholars see these teachings also in 1QH, but he believes that this is because they have been influenced by a false dualistic and deterministic in-

---

sion between 1QS 3:13ff. and 4:20ff. but in different ways. Kuhn felt that the problem was only one of terminology (*cf.* K. G. Kuhn, "Sektenschrift," pp. 301-2 n. 4 and section *2a* of this chapter above); Licht, however, who unlike Kuhn (*cf.* n. 18 above) believed that the two spirits were cosmic in nature (*cf.* Licht, "Analysis," p. 93), could not accept his view but offered a new translation of 1QS 4:23-24 which he felt solved the problem (*ibid.*, p. 98 and p. 91 n. 13). See also Delcor, "Doctrines," cols. 963-4 for still another more recent approach.

[167] *E.g.*, Schubert, "Sektenkanon," col 506, who believes that men by their good and evil deeds place themselves under good or evil angelic influence; *cf.* especially Nötscher, *Terminology*, pp. 79-80, 84, 185 and 180.

[168] *Ibid.*, pp. 422 and 433.

[169] *Ibid.*, p. 416.

[170] *Ibid.*, p. 415 n. 5.

terpretation of 1QS 3-4 which they have then applied to 1QH.[171] Furthermore, 1QS should be interpreted against the backgound of the Old Testament and intertestamental literature rather than that of Iranian origins.[172]

In 1QS 3:18 Wernberg-Møller notes that the verb וישם corresponds to ויפח in Gen. 2:7 and refers to God creating two dispositions (like the rabbinic good and evil *yetzers*) in man.[173] רוחות here, then, has nothing to do with metaphysical beings; the implication of this passage is not that the "spirits" rule over man, but that man was created to rule over them.[174]

In 3:20 the two angels should not be regarded as cosmic beings but as personifications of the two opposing dispositions in each individual.[175]

---

[171]*Ibid.*, "in some cases he [Licht] imposes. . . a wrong interpretation on a 1QH passage in order to fit it into its supposed parallel in 1QS. For example. . . he understands 1QH 4:38. . . both dualistically and deterministically on the basis of 1QS 3:17-19." It should be noted, however, that Wernberg-Møller tends to assume rather than demonstrate that there are no significant dualistic or deterministic elements in 1QH.

[172]*Ibid.*, pp. 416-18.

[173]*Ibid.*, p. 422.

[174]*Ibid.*, p. 422 n. 19.

[175]*Ibid.*, p. 423 n. 30. Wernberg-Møller appears to indicate that Oscar Seitz in "Two Spirits," pp. 89ff. shares this view. It may be true that Seitz regards the two spirits as only human dispositions (he is unclear on this point), but this is not so with regard to the two angels; *cf. ibid.*, pp. 92-3: "According, the *Manual* divides mankind into two categories. Those who are under the dominion of the prince of light and walk in the way of light, are called the sons of righteousness, or sons of light. Those under the dominion of the angel of darkness, who walk in the ways of darkness, are known as sons of perversion, or sons of darkness. Even the sons of righteousness may be led astray by the angel of darkness. This angel has other spirits assigned to him, who strive to overthrow the sons of light, and are therefore probably to be identified with the angels of destruction. However, the God of Israel and the angel of his truth have helped all the sons of light." Wernberg-Møller mentions no other scholars who view the two angels as simply personifications of human dispositions.

The basic intent of 4:2-8 and 4:9-14 is not to describe two opposite groups of mankind with their separate life-styles and rewards, but rather both sections are addressed to the sectarians, who in their basic spiritual constitution had a feeling of solidarity with the rest of mankind. The phrase כול הולכי בה in 4:6 & 12, then, is addressed in both cases to the sectarians.[176] The term בני אמת תבל should likewise not be taken as referring only to the sectarians (again, tending to associate spirituality solely with the Qumran community) but as referring to mankind in general.[177]

In 4:15 באלה refers not to the two spirits but to the great variety of spiritual qualities enumerated in 4:2-6 and 4:9-11, and תולדות should not be translated as "generations" but as "natures" (as also in 3:13 & 19).[178] Correspondingly, במפלגיהן in verse 15 should not be understood as meaning "in their (*i.e.* the two spirits') divisions" but "in their (*i.e.* the two spirits') *numerous* divisions" with "divisions" referring to the various good and bad qualities just enumerated in 4:2-6 & 9-11.[179] Two antithetical groups of people, then, are not mentioned here.[180] Also, the mention of a greater and lesser "inheritance" in verse 16 refers to the two"spirits" given to man in his creation.[181] Understood in the light of the phrase בד בבד in the same verse, the meaning is that these two dispositions or "spirits" may vary in amount from person to person, but in each individual they are always in perfect balance and are equally strong.[182] When one notes, then, that the basic contrast of verse 17 is between "truth" and "perversion," it becomes clear that the struggle in 4:15-17 is not

---

[176] *Ibid.*, p. 429.

[177] *Ibid.*, p. 429.

[178] *Ibid.*, p. 431.

[179] *Ibid.*, pp. 431-2.

[180] *Ibid.*, p. 432.

[181] *Ibid.*, p. 433.

[182] *Ibid.* If Wernberg-Møller is correct, this must mean the author of this verse assumed that the greatest enemies of the sect had the potential of becoming its greatest supporters without any fundamental change in their spirituality.

between two groups of people but between two perfectly balanced inclinations in the heart of each man.[183]

In 4:18 & 24 the subject of the verb "they walk" is not men (which would then give us the picture of two antithetic groups of people) but rather the two dispositions.[184]

In 4:19-22a there is no contrast between "truth" (as the sole possession of the community) and the "dominion of evil" seen as a sphere external to the community and in opposition to its "truth." Rather, the "truth" and the "dominion of evil" refer simply to the good and evil inclinations in each heart.[185]

In 4:22b-23a the sectarians are described as being elected by God. This, however, does not imply a consitutional difference of a spiritual nature between them and non-members due to the influence of "opposed metaphysical principles."[186]

In 4:23b the "spirits" refer to the two opposing, dispositions in man.[187]

For 4:24a, *cf.* 4:18 above.

In 4:24b-25 the statement concerning one's inheritance in truth or iniquity is not meant to explain why different individuals have different reactions to truth and iniquity (thus creating the basis for a constitutional difference between sectarians and non-sectarians) but is to be understood as referring to each individual; *i.e.*, the author is explaining why each individual (including the sectarian) hates not only iniquity but also the truth. The reason, again, is that God has placed both good and bad inclinations in a balanced measure in each heart.[188]

---

[183]*Ibid.*, p. 432. Wernberg-Møller does not comment on the 3rd m. pl. suffix on *mplgh* in verse 17. This suffix would seem to indicate that in this case the division refers to groups of men rather than to the "spirits" or their "qualities"; however, it may be a mistake of a copyist: *cf.* Osten-Sacken, *Gott und Beial*, p. 23 n. 4.

[184]*Ibid.*, pp. 432 & 433-4.

[185]*Ibid.*, pp. 423 & 434.

[186]*Ibid.*, p. 424.

[187]*Ibid.*, p. 422.

[188]*Ibid.*, p. 433.

In 4:26 the phrase "good and evil" refers to each individual rather than to the sectarian and non-sectarian, respectively.[189]

Before Wernberg-Møller ends his article, he makes the following observations on the chapters just preceding 1QS 3-4:

In 1:23f. (as in 3:21f.) he notes that the community members considered themselves to be "under the dominion of Belial" and yet called themselves "sons of righteousness."[190] This is because they recognized the difference between what they were and what they ought to be.[191] This, then, explains the true nature of the blessings and curses of 2:1-18. The intent of this section is not to indicate a basic spiritual difference between the sectarian and non-sectarian with one group worthy of a blessing and the other of a curse; its true intent, rather, was to speak to the sectarian in both blessings and curses since the "spirit" of darkness dwelt in him too and he needed to be put in fear of the consequences of letting this spirit dominate him.[192]

In 2:20 Wernberg-Møller notes that the sectarian is to be judged according to the "quantity" of the spirits in him, a concept which may anticipate the ideas of 4:16.[193]

In the light of the outline above, it can be seen that Wernberg-Møller's investigation of 1QS 3-4 resulted in two views or lines of interpretation original with him, *viz.*, 1) there is no trace in the Scrolls of cosmic dualism with its good and evil spiritual powers externally influencing man's conduct, and 2) nothing portrays the sectarian as essentially different spiritually from the non-sectarian.

---

[189]*Ibid.*, p. 434.

[190]*Ibid.*, p. 435. Note that the text here uses ב rather than ביד ("under the authority of") as in 1QS 3:20.

[191]*Ibid.*, p. 436.

[192]*Ibid.*, pp. 436-7. This section, then, presumably should not be used to show that the author or redactor (*cf. ibid.*, pp. 417-8) of 1QS had two fundamentally distinct and hostile communities in mind against which 3:13-4:26 should be interpreted.

[193]*Ibid.*, p. 437. Wernberg-Møller does not explain here how rank in the community is determined on the basis of the sectarian's *spirit* when all spirits have an equal balance of good and evil within them.

In section three of this chapter we will trace significant reactions to Wernberg-Møller's thesis.

At the same time that Wernberg-Møller's article appeared in *Revue de Qumrân*, an article by M. Treves appeared in the same journal which, along with Wernberg-Møller, questioned the view that 1QS 3-4 presents the two spirits as cosmic entities.[194] Man, rather, has freedom of choice, and the two spirits are simply tendencies in every heart, similar to the *yetzer* theology of later Judaism.[195] In reading May's assessment of Treves, one receives the impression that Treves along with Wernberg-Møller also denied the presence of any cosmic dualism in 1QS 3-4,[196] but this is not the case. Treves does not deny the cosmic status of the two angels in 1QS 3-4 or their connection to Zoroastrianism,[197] nor does he deny that men are are dominated by these angels depending on the impluse (spirit) to which they yield themselves (thus creating the basis for community dualism).[198] Treves, in fact, does not differ that much from previous scholars who questioned the angelic or cosmic

---

[194]Treves, "Two Spirits," pp. 449-452.

[195]*Ibid.*, pp. 451 & 449.

[196]May, "Cosmological Reference," p. 1: "P. Wernberg-Møller and M. Treves, in recent articles in *Revue de Qumran* have set themselves in solid opposition to Albright, Burrows. . . and others in finding in the Qumran doctrine of the two spirits in the Rule of the Community (1QS 3:13-4:26) no evidence of cosmic dualism or determinism and no Zoroastrian influence."

[197]Treves, "Two Spirits," p. 451 n. 10: "I do not deny Iranian and Greek influence on the doctrine of our covenanters. The conception of the two angels and the use of the words 'light' and 'darkness to symbolize righteousness and iniquity probably derive from the Zoroastrian religion."

Treves adds, however, that all these influences were adapted to Jewish monotheism.

[198]*Ibid.*, p. 450: "Each man with his free will may choose between these two impulses. If he yields to the evil impulse he falls under the domination of the Angel of Darkness and commits all kinds of sins. But if he follows the good impulse he is governed by the Prince of Lights and obeys God's righteous laws."

status of the two spirits[199] or the view of sectarian theology as deterministic and predestinarian.[200] However, his view that the two spirits should not be identified with the two angels because the Old Testament does not use *ruaḥ* to mean "angel" is somewhat unique since it does not account for the use of *ruaḥ* in this way in intertestamental literature,[201] and it assumes that 1QS should be read in isolation from other sectarian documents which use *ruaḥ* in reference to angelic beings.[202]

In summary, the position that the Scrolls contain no elements of cosmic dualism at all is essentially unique to Wernberg-Møller, although a number of scholars before him did question the strength and the Iranian origin of this dualism and also maintained that the two spirits (but not the two angels) were only dispositions in man with no independent, metaphysical existence. The denial that sectarians saw themselves as spiritually different from non-sectarians (community dualism) due to opposed metaphysical principles also seems to be unique to him in the form in which he presents it.[203] Finally, we should note that Wernberg-Møller's interpretation of 1QS would not eliminate the basic tension between the pneumatology of 1QS and that of 1QH (as understood by Sjöberg and

---

[199]*Cf.* n. 164 above.

[200]*Cf.* n. 167 above.

[201]*Cf.* Charlesworth, "Comparison," p. 82 n. 27: "It is quite surprising, however, to discover that Treves has examined the Qumranic treatise only by means of the interpretation of *ruaḥ* found in the Old Testament. . . . But one dare not overlook the additional meaning obtained by this noun during the intertestamental period."

[202]*Cf.* Treves, "Two Spirits," p. 452: Treves notes that 1QH and 1QM both call angels "spirits," but he does not consider these texts relevant because he believes that they are later in date than the *Rule of the Community* and were written by different authors.

[203]Scholars such as Treves, of course, would view the sectarian and non-sectarian alike as having both a good and an evil *yetzer*, but they would not deny the fundamentally greater spiritual potential of the sectarians for obeying God's law due to the spiritual influence and domination of the cosmic Prince of Lights over their community; *cf.* nn. 163 and 198.

others) since 1QH in Sjöberg's view describes man by nature as being in need of a *Neuschöpfung* in order to participate in the spirituality of the Qumran community, whereas 1QS 3-4 in Wernberg-Møller's view describes the sectarian as having the same spiritual constitution as the non-sectarian.

d. Conclusion to section 2, chapter 2.

In secion *2a* we noted that the views of E. Sjöberg in his 1955 article, "Neuschöpfung," were in tension with both K. G. Kuhn's view of sectarian pneumatology and that of the general consensus of scholarship. For Kuhn it became difficult to maintain that the sectarian's spirituality was simply a natural disposition inherited at birth, and it appears that by the early 1960's he moved away from this position in favor of an approach more like that of Sjöberg. The effect of Sjöberg's work on the general consensus of that time is harder to trace directly, but the following seems to be clear: scholarship after Sjöberg increasingly tended to recognize along with him the strong contrast in 1QH between man's weak and sinful spiritual condition by nature and the new life he receives through the power and grace of God's holy Spirit at his entrance into the sectarian community. As this view of pneumatology in 1QH became more widely known and accepted, it became increasingly evident that it was in tension with the pneumatology of 1QS 3-4 as this was usually understood in terms of Iranian, cosmic dualism, *viz.*, that men are divided into two mutually exclusive camps by a divine predestination in which they each "inherit" at birth an appropriate spiritual nature dominated either by an angelic spirit of truth or spirit of iniquity.

Eventually, two mutually exclusive trends of interpretation crystallized which were critical of the majority position that 1QS 3-4 should be interpreted in terms of Iranian, cosmic dualism as the dominant and underlying pneumatology of the Scrolls. One trend (outlined in section *2b*) agreed that sectarian pneumatology was influenced by Iranian, cosmic dualism but denied that the most representative passage of this dualism, 1QS 3:13-4:26, was at all characteristic of the dominant sectarian pneumatology of the Scrolls or even in harmony with it.

The other trend (outlined in section *2c*) agreed that sectarian pneumatology should be understood and interpreted as a whole but disagreed that Iranian cosmic dualism was an essential part of it, while a major study on this issue doubted the presence of any dualism at all in 1QS 3-4 or elsewhere in the Scrolls. By 1961, then, three conflicting approaches to sectarian pneumatology are evident: 1) The majority position, which viewed sectarian pneumatology as an essential unity dominated by the Iranian, cosmic dualism of its two-spirit theology, 2) a trend which questioned the unity of this pneumatology and the dominant position of the two-spirit teaching within it, and finally 3) a position which viewed sectarian pneumatology as a unity but denied that this involved the presence of a strong cosmic dualism, Iranian or otherwise.

3. The issue of *ruaḥ* from 1962 to the present.

a. Preliminary observations.

From the early 1960's, literary criticism of the sectarian literature of Qumran grew significantly in complexity largely through the efforts of the *Qumranforschungsgemeinschaft* at Heidelberg under the direction of K. G. Kuhn[204] as well as through the work of others.[205] This growth in literary-critical research would influence the discussion on the meaning of *ruaḥ*

---

[204]*Cf.* the remarks of Otto Betz in a review of J. Becker's *Das Heil Gottes* in the *Journal of Biblical Literature*, 84 (1965), p. 186, who notes that the Heidelberg school in subjecting the Scrolls to literary criticism has found that they were written by different authors at different times. *Cf.* also the complementary remarks of J. Murphy-O'Connor in his review of H. W. Kuhn's *Enderwartung* in *Revue Biblique*, 75 (1968), p. 439, who placed Heidelberg under K. G. Kuhn's leadership at that time at the forefront of the scientific study of the Scrolls.

[205]*E.g.*, Jérôme Murphy-O'Connor, "La genèse littéraire de la Règle de la Communauté," *Revue Biblique*, 76 (1969), pp. 528-549; Osten-Sacken, *Gott und Belial*; and more recently Philip R. Davies, *1QM, the War Scroll from Qumran. Its Structure and History* (Rome: Biblical Institute Press, 1977), and *idem*, *The Damascus Covenant* (Sheffield: JSOT Press, 1982).

in various ways[206] but not always in a clear direction.[207] At present there seems to be a general agreement among scholars that the Scrolls should not be treated uncritically as a doctrinally homogeneous group of writings,[208] but there is still a good deal of disagreement over the nature and history of their diverse teachings and relationships to one another.[209] In the following

---

[206]*E.g.*, if Osten-Sacken in *Gott und Belial* is correct in his reconstruction of the evolution of dualistic thought in Qumran, H. W. Kuhn's attempt to understand some uses of *ruaḥ* in 1QH (*e.g.*, 4:31; *cf.* H. W. Kuhn, *Enderwartung*, pp. 120-130) against the background of 1QS 3-4 would be incorrect since 1QH (especially the hymns of the Teacher of Righteousness) would have preceded the advent of the dualism of 1QS 3-4; *cf.* Osten-Sacken, *Gott und Belial*, pp. 131, 136-7 & 165ff.

[207]*Cf.* Lichtenberger, *Studien*, pp. 195-6: although Lichtenberger regards Iranian dualism (*e.g.*, as seen in 1QS 3:13-4:26) as influencing the sectarians right from the beginning of their history (against Osten-Sacken in *Gott und Belial*, pp. 165ff. and 239-40, who views Iranian dualism as a later stage in Qumranian thought, chronologically subsequent to 1QH), he still agrees with Osten-Sacken against H. W. Kuhn (*cf.* n. 206 above) that there is no evidence of Iranian, dualistic influence on 1QH. He regards this as an "auffällige Beobachtung."

[208]*Cf.* the Comments of J. Murphy-O'Connor in a review of Lichtenberger's *Studien* in *Revue Biblique*, 89 (1982), p. 154: "The early period of Qumran research was characterized by thematic studies which assumed the homogeneity of the documents. Thus material derived from one text could be used to fill out a picture derived from another. Any possibility of internal development or of different trends within the same community was studiously ignored. As the form-critical and source-critical analysis of the scrolls progressed, it became steadily more evident that all the sectarian documents were compilations which clearly betrayed the evolution of the community. The earlier thematic syntheses were thereby revealed as entirely artificial constructions that would have to be redone in order to acquire any validity."

[209]*E.g.*, see Huppenbauer's review of Osten-Sacken's *Gott und Belial* in *Revue de Qumrân*, 7 (1970), p. 296: Huppenbauer analyzes Osten-Sacken's reconstruction of the development of dualistic thinking at Qumran and concludes that the basic thesis of his work is incorrect, possibly due to "a linear conception of history which cannot be

paragraphs to the end of this chapter we will trace the general direction of the debate involving *ruaḥ* from 1962 to the present in terms of the three basic positions outlined immediately above at the conclusion of section two of this chapter. In chapters 3-7 we will attempt to isolate linguistic patterns of *ruaḥ* (primarily syntactical in nature) which may have a meaning independent of their specific contexts, the identification of which may aid in the understanding of ambiguous or disputed contexts (*e.g.*, 1QS 3:13-4:26; *cf.* chapter 8).

b. The position that sectarian pneumatology is an essential unity dominated by the Iranian, cosmic dualism of its two-spirit pneumatology.

As noted above, this position was the majority consensus through 1961,[210] and it seems clear that this essentially continued to be the case until the late 1960's before the work of H. W. Kuhn became widely known.[211] Virtually every scholar from 1962 through 1967 who expressed an opinion on the unity of sectarian pneumatology (with the exception of J. Becker[212] and, of

---

applied to pre-Christian Judaism, and probably caused by a failure to take Jewish apocalyptic literature sufficiently into account." *Cf.* also Osten-Sacken's criticisms in *Gott und Belial,* pp. 13-14 of Huppenbauer in *Der Mensch,* of J. Becker in *Heil Gottes, Heils- und Sündengegriffe in den Qumran-texten und im Neuen Testamentum,* Studien zur Umwelt des Neuen Testaments, 3 (Göttingen: Vandenboeck & Ruprecht, 1964), and of Otto Böcher in *Der johanneische Dualismus im Zusammenhang des nachbiblischen Judentums,* (Gütersloh: Gerd Mohn, 1965); note also Lichtenberger's rejection in *Studien,* p. 200 of Osten-Sacken's reconstruction in *Gott und Belial* of the historical development of dualistic thinking in Qumran. On the other hand, the basic methodology of Lichtenberger's work in *Studien* has been criticised as being too quick to isolate literary units from their broader contexts: *cf.* James C. VanderKam's review of Lichtenberger's *Studien* in the *Catholic Biblical Quarterly,* 43 (1981), p. 447.

[210]See nn. 19 and 104 above (especially the comments of Irwin).

[211]H W. Kuhn, *Enderwartung,* 1966.

[212]Becker, *Das Heil Gottes,* p. 60; Becker notes that the dualistic world view of 1QS 3:13-4:26 is absent in the hymns of the Teacher of

course H. W. Kuhn in *Enderwartung*) regarded it as an integrated whole under the domination of its two-spirit teaching[213] although there seems to less emphasis on Persia as its source.[214] All of these scholars agreed, however, that the pneumatology of 1QS 3:13-4:26 (as understood within some type of cosmic dualism) should be regarded as reflecting the standard teaching of the Scrolls in the light of which *ruaḥ* in the rest of sectarian literature should be understood.[215] This basic position involved two different approaches in relating the general pneumatology

---

Righteousness (*cf. ibid.*, pp. 53ff. for Becker's identification of these hymns, which comprise most of 1QH 2 through 8); the same lack of two-spirit pneumatology is also found in the rest of 1QH (*cf. ibid.*, p. 138) so that the "holy Spirit" of these hymns is best described not as the "spirit of truth" but as a "Kraft" sent from God (*ibid.*, p. 162).

[213](Cited by date), *e.g.*, Arnold A. Anderson, "The Use of 'Ruah' in 1QS, 1QH and 1QM," *Journal of Semitic Studies*, 7 (1962), pp. 298 & 301; M. Delcor, *Les Hymns de Qumran (Hodayot). Texte hebreu, introduction traduction, commentaire* (Paris: Letouzey et Ané, 1962), p. 52; Werner Foerster, "Der Heilige Geist in Spätjudentum," *New Testament Studies*, 8 (1962), p. 130; Annie Jaubert, *La notion d'alliance dans le Judaïsme aux abords de l'ere Chretienne*, Patristica Sorbonensia, 6 (Paris: Éditions du Seuil, 1963), 241-2; Helmer Ringgren, *The Faith of Qumran, Theology of the Dead Sea Scrolls*, trans. by E. T. Sander (Philadelphia: Fortress Press, 1963), p. 89; Böcher, *Dualismus*, p. 39; Schreiner, "Geistbegabung," pp. 173-4; A. R. C. Leaney, *The Rule of Qumran and its Meaning, Introduction, translation and commentary*, The New Testament Library (London: SCM Press, 1966), pp. 53-55; and David Hill, *Greek Words and Hebrew Meanings: Studies in the Semantics of Soteriological Terms*, Society for New Testament Studies Monograph Series, 5 (Cambridge, 1967), pp. 238-9.

[214]Among the scholars listed in n. 213 above, only Ringgren in *Faith*, pp. 78-80 argues for a strong Iranian influence on sectarian pneumatology.

[215]*Cf.* n. 213 above. Lichtenberger in *Studien*, p. 174 notes that scholars have often used 1QS 3-4 as a "*Richtschnur*" for sectarian anthropology. The same is true of sectarian pneumatology as Lichtenberger also notes in *ibid.*, p. 174 n. 1 (quoting Irwin in *Spirit-Dualism*, p. 1): "The Two-Spirit theology . . . is *not* as has been widely assumed the dominant pneumatology of the other writings."

of the Scrolls (as in 1QH) to the teaching of the two spirits of 1QS 3-4. The predominant approach viewed the two spirits as cosmic angels (as well as spiritual forces within men) and tended to regard God's holy Spirit as the good spirit of the two spirits and hence, as an angel.[216] The other approach also could understand the two spirits as being both psychological and cosmic in nature, but regarded God's Spirit (*i.e.* God's רוח קודש) in most instances as essentially no more than a spiritual disposition within man.[217] In both of these approaches, however, the goal was to understand sectarian pneumatology as an integrated whole.

Most of the scholars representing the predominant approach to sectarian pneumatology as outlined above tended to assume rather than present in an analytical and clear fashion

---

[216]*E.g.*, Anderson, "'Ruah'," pp. 298-9 & 301; Böcher, *Dualismus*, pp. 36-39 & 101; Foerster, "Geist," pp. 128-130: Foerster identifies the spirit of truth with the holy Spirit (*ibid.*, p. 130) and although he is uncertain as to the angelic status of the spirit of truth (*ibid.*, p. 129), he does not explicitly deny the angelic status of either spirit; *cf.* also Hill, *Greek Words*, pp. 236 & 238-9; Leaney, *Rule*, pp. 43-44, 53-55 & 159; and Ringgren, *Faith*, pp. 78, 82 & 89.

[217]*E.g.*, Schreiner, "Geistbegabung," p. 180. Schreiner, citing Otzen in "Sektenschriften," p. 135, recognizes with him both a macrocosmic as well as a microcosmic dimension to the teaching of the two spirits in 1QS 3-4 (*cf.* Schreiner, "Geistbegabung," p. 173), but the precise relationship between the two spirits and two angels in 1QS 3-4 is not entirely clear in either Otzen or Schreiner. Both may distinguish between the spirits and angels and regard the two spirits as no more than spiritual potentials within men (*i.e.*, the macrocosmic aspect of sectarian dualism would apply only to the two angels); but *cf.* Burrows in *More Light*, p. 281, who understands Otzen as regarding the two spirits themselves (and not just the two angels) as external mythological entities under the macrocosmic aspect of dualism. If Schreiner does regard the spirit of truth as a cosmic entity in its macrocosmic aspect, this would presumably mean that his equasion of the spirit of truth with the purely anthropological "holy spirit" of 1QH (*cf.* Schreiner, "Geistbegabung," p. 174) would apply only to the microcosmic aspect of the "spirit of truth."

the basis for their positions.[218] An exception to this was the work of W. Foerster.[219] Although the general theme of his article was to show how God's holy Spirit was active in a prophetic sense at Qumran,[220] a portion of it dealt with the relationship between the holy Spirit in 1QH and the spirit of

---

[218]A lack of clarity in describing the precise relationship between the "spirit of truth" and the "holy Spirit" (*e.g.*, in 1QH) can be seen in a number of authors at this time. Ringgren in *Faith*, for example, equates the "holy spirit" with the "spirit of truth" just after equating the "spirit of truth" with the mythological Prince of Lights (*cf. ibid.*, pp. 89 & 82), but he then goes on to describe the "holy spirit" as an impersonal quality or power (*viz.*,"a manifestation of God's grace," "a power granted by God," *ibid.*, p. 89). A similar situation can be seen in Hill, *Greek Words*: he equates the "spirit of truth" with both the "holy spirit" and the angelic Prince of Lights (*ibid.*, pp. 236 & 238) and then describes the "holy spirit" impersonally as "the influence on a man of the acknowledge holiness and will of God" (*ibid.*, pp. 239-240). However, if the "holy spirit" is the same as the "spirit of truth," which in turn is the same as the angelic Prince of Lights, Hill and Ringgren should make it clear that verses such as 1QH 7:6-7 are not simply referring to an impersonal "power" or divine "influence" of some kind but are actually describing a personal, angelic figure being "poured out" or "waved over" a pious sectarian. The same lack of precision in this respect can also be seen in Böcher, *Dualismus*, who defines "der heilige Geist" as impersonal (*ibid.*, p. 38), equates it with "der Geist der Wahrheit" (*ibid.*, p. 39) and then equates both "der Geist der Wahrheit" and "der Geist des Lichts" with the angelic "Fürst der Lichter." What is unclear, then, is how the impersonal "holy Spirit" can be identified with the "spirit of truth" while at the same time identifying the "spirit of truth" with the personal and mythological "Prince of Lights." A similar criticism was directed at J. Carmignac and G. Graystone by H. Braun in *Qumran*, vol. II, pp. 255, 258 & 263: according to Braun, the "spirit" at Qumran cannot be described as impersonal since "für Qumran sind die Geister durchaus auch hypostasierte Wesen," (*ibid.*, p. 258). If the "holy Spirit" at Qumran is to be described as impersonal, then, scholars need to show how this concept can be distinguished from the various personal, angelic figures surrounding it.

[219]Foerster, "Geist," pp. 117-134.

[220]*Ibid.*, pp. 122ff.

truth in 1QS 3-4.[221] He compared what was said about the work and effects of these spirits in their respective contexts and concluded that they were essentially the same and that Betz in *Offenbarung* had overstated the difference between them in his *Geist/Geisterlehre* distinction.[222] It should be noted, however, that neither Foerster nor anyone else supporting his position really dealt with the most striking differences seen by Betz in the sectarians' various understandings of *ruaḥ*.[223] It should also be noted that Betz did not maintain that the Qumran community itself was aware of the differences between the *Geist/Geisterlehre*.[224] These two traditions, even though they were essentially incompatable, tended to merge in the thinking of the sect. It is not a conclusive argument against Betz' position, then, if Foerster and others can demonstrate an overlapping in the use of "holy Spirit" and "spirit of truth" in the sectarian writings.[225]

---

[221]*Ibid.*, pp. 128-130.

[222]*Ibid.*, p. 130 n. 1.

[223]*E.g.*, the contrast between the "spirit of truth" as an inherited, spiritual status associated with angelic mediation and the "holy Spirit" (often found in 1QH) as received at one's entrance into the community directly from God; *cf.* n. 225 below.

[224]Betz, *Offenbarung*, p. 143.

[225]*Cf.* for example, Osten-Sacken, *Gott und Belial*, who agrees with Foerster's comparisons of *ruaḥ* in 1QS 3-4 and 1QH (*ibid.*, p. 136 n. 5) but notes at the same time that there is no direct connection between the pneumatologies of these two writings (*ibid.*, pp. 135 & 138). This is because the dualistic traditions of 1QH preceded those of 1QS 3-4 (*ibid.*, pp. 131 & 152ff.), and it was not until the later stage (as seen in 1QS 3:13-4:14) that Iranian influences made themselves felt in the teaching of the two spirits (*ibid.*, pp. 138ff.). The result is that "die Lehre von den beiden mit der Schöpfung gesetzten Geistern in S III, 17bf. nicht als einfache Ausformung des in den Hodajoth bezeugten *ruah*-Verständnisses zu verstehen" (*ibid.*, p. 138). The pneumatology of 1QH, in fact, with its view of *ruaḥ* as man's natural, perverted spirit in contrast to God's Spirit received at one's entrance into the community (*cf. ibid.*, p. 145) offers "keine Brücke. . . zu den nach S III, 17bff. bei der Schöpfung gesetzten beiden Geistern" (*ibid.*, p. 135).

The second approach to sectarian pneumatology mentioned above involves a view of God's רוח קודש as no more than a spiritual disposition within men. This spirit, then, can be regarded as a spiritual quality of those belonging to the "spirit of truth" (understood both cosmically and psychologically)[226] or, if the "spirit of truth" is understood as no more than a spiritual dispostion in man, the term "holy spirit" can be regarded as simply an alternative way of describing it.[227] Although the view of God's "holy spirit" as simply a disposition in man (in contrast to the Spirit of God as such, which defines the power of God and exists independently of man) has its origin in a 1953 monograph of J. Coppens,[228] the use of this position in relating the pneumatology of 1QS 3-4 to that of 1QH seems to have its beginning with Licht.[229] Generally speaking, scholarship has not followed Licht on this point,[230] but in 1965 his position re-

---

[226]*E.g.*, Licht, "Doctrine," p. 91-2; *idem, The Thanksgiving Scroll. A Scroll from the Wilderness of Judaea. Text, Introduction, Commentary and Glossary* (Jerusalem: Bialik Institute, 1957), p. 38; and *idem, The Rule Scroll. A Scroll from the Wilderness of Judaea. 1QS, 1QSa, 1QSb. Text, Intrroduction and Commentary* (Jerusalem: Bialik Institute, 1965), pp. 74-5; for Licht's view of the two spirits as having both psychological and cosmic dimensions, *cf. idem*, "Analysis," p. 93.

[227]*E.g.*, Schreiner, "Geistbegabung," p. 174; cf. n. 217 above.

[228]Coppens, "Documents," p. 36 n. 46.

[229]*Cf.* n. 226 above.

[230]Most scholars seem to understand God's רוח קודש in 1QH not only as involving man's spirituality but also as describing a spiritual force or entity of some kind beyond him. Besides Coppens and Schreiner, the only scholars I have found who regard God's רוח קודש in the present as generally involving no more than a good disposition within man are G. R. Driver and A. R. C. Leaney (*cf.* chapter 3, n. 10 below), although Coppens later adopted the majority position on this in response to Sjöberg's article "Neuschöpfung;" *cf.* Joseph Coppens, "le don de l'esprit d'après les textes de Qumrân et le Quatrième évangile," *L'Évangile de Jean. Études et Problèmes, Recherches bibliques*, 3(Louvain, 1958), p. 217-9. However, Coppens still minimizes the presence of God's Spirit, as such, at Qumran by recognizing its presence only as "les prémices"; *ibid.*, p. 216.

ceived some support in an article by Joseph Schreiner.[231] Schreiner's basic position was that *ruaḥ* in the sectarian writings should be understood in terms of its priestly (rather than prophetic) usage in the Old Testament, *i.e.*, as a description of man's worth or quality rather than as a charismatic gift endowing men with supernatural abilities or prophetic functions.[232] The "holy Spirit" (*e.g.*, in 1QH), then, would be the good "*Geistanteil*" given to men from birth and essentially the same as the "spirit of truth" described in 1QS 3-4.[233] At a man's entrance into the community, his inherent "holy spirit" is strengthened in its good resolve (against the "spirit of iniquity," which he and men generally also have from birth in varying degrees), but there is no essential transformation of man's nature at this or any other time on the basis of a new or supernatural presence of God's Spirit within the sectarian.[234]

In conclusion, from 1962 to the present the general trend among scholars who understand sectarian pneumatology as an essential unity under the domination of its two-spirit teaching in 1QS 3-4 has been to assume rather than to present analytically the basis for their position. Only W. Foerster and J. Schreiner offer significant exceptions to this general rule, but Schreiner stands virtually alone in his overall definition of God's רוח קודש in the Scrolls[235] and the results of Foerster's work do not seem to be ultimately incompatable with the view that the pneumatology of 1QS 3-4 is in conflict with the much of the pneumatology of 1QH.

---

[231]Schreiner, "Geistbegabung," p. 180.

[232]*Ibid.*, p. 170.

[233]*Ibid.*, pp. 174 & 180.

[234]*Ibid.*, p. 180: "Die Gemeinde von Qumran spricht nie von *ruah* in der Weise, daß sie Gott selbst 'Geist' nennen würde, etwa in Sinn von Is 31, 3."

[235]Coppens did not maintain his purely anthropological view of the "holy spirit" (*cf.* n. 230 above), and unlike Schreiner (*cf.* n. 227 above) Licht does not identify the "holy spirit" of 1QH with the "spirit of truth" (*cf.* n. 226 above); the same seems to be true for Driver and Leaney (*cf.* chapter 3, n. 10 below and chapter 8, n. 17 below).

c. The position which questions the unity of sectarian pneumatology and the dominant position of the two spirit teaching within it.

As noted above, most scholars who offered an opinion of the internal consistency of sectarian pneumatology before the work of H. W. Kuhn in *Enderwartung* tended to regard it as an integrated whole dominated by the two-spirit doctrine of 1QS 3-4. After Kuhn, however, only a few scholars continued to reflect this consensus.[236] Most scholars now recognize with him a diversity within sectarian pneumatology and are therefore less inclined than previously to interpret varied and diverse uses of *ruaḥ* in the Scrolls against the background of a standard, two-spirit dualism.[237]

---

[236]*E.g.*, E. E. Ellis, "'Spiritual' Gifts in the Pauline Community," *New Testament Studies*, 20 (1974), p. 135; George T. Montague, *The Holy Spirit: Growth of a Biblical Tradition* (New York: Paulist Press, 1976) pp. 116ff.; *cf.* also Delcor, "Doctrines," col. 973, who appears to equate "l'Esprit Saint" with "l'Esprit de Vérité" but at the same time recognizes that the spirit of truth is is given to man in his creation (*ibid.*, col. 960) and is a created, angelic being (*ibid.*, cols. 963-4), whereas the holy Spirit is given to man at his entrance into the community and (unlike an angel or a created being) is not clearly "distingué de Dieu" (*ibid.*, col. 973).

[237](Cited by date) *Cf.* F. F. Bruce, "Holy Spirit in the Qumran Texts," *The Annual of Leeds University Oriental Society*, 6 (1966-68), Dead Sea Scrolls Studies 1969 (Leiden, 1969), p. 50; Ehrhard Kamlah, "Geist," *Theologisches Begriffslexikon zum Neuen Testament*, 3, eds. L. Coenen, E. Beyreuther and H. Bietenhard (Wuppertal: Theologischer Verlag Rolf Brockhaus, 1967), p. 428; for Osten-Sacken, *Gott und Belial*, *cf.* the comments in this chapter below; Gerhard Maier, *Mensch und Freier Wille. Nach den jüdischen Religionsparteien zwischen Ben Sira und Paulus, Wissenschaftliche Untersuchungen zum Neuen Testament*, 12 (Tübingen: Mohr, 1971), pp. 188-9: Hauschild, *Geist*, p. 251 n. 51; Max-Alain Chevallier, *Souffle de Dieu, le Saint-Esprit dans le Nouveau Testament*, vol. I, le Point Théologique, 26 (Paris: Editions Beauchesne, 1978), p. 52ff.; Roland Bergmeier, *Glaube als Gabe nach Johannes. Religions- und theologiegeschichtliche Studien zum prädestinatianischen Dualismus in vierten Evangelium*, Beiträge zur Wissenschaft vom Alten und Neuen Testaments, 60 (Stuttgart:

A key work in helping to shape the present consensus, then, is H. W. Kuhn's *Enderwartung*. His primary goal was to investigate the nature of eschatological thought in the community hymns of the *Hodayoth*.[238] The results of his study were basically that some hymns view salvation in a traditional, future sense[239] while others seem to present salvation (*e.g.*, resurrection, communion with God and the angels, renewal) as an eschatological event already present.[240] The relevance of these results for *ruaḥ* has to do with the presence of God's Spirit as a possible element within this eschalogical event. Does 1QH view *ruaḥ* as a gift of God already present in Qumran's eschatological community? Kuhn found that there were a number of places in which *ruaḥ* could be understood in this way,[241] but in a number of other places he could also detect another, conflicting use of *ruaḥ*, *viz.*, the origin of man' spirituality is not seen as a supernatural gift of God's spirit experienced at one's entrance into the community, but rather the sectarian's spirituality is traced back to a positive, spiritual nature given to him at birth and ordained by God before his existence.[242] *ruaḥ* here, then, is man's predestined being, whether good (as in the members of the community) or evil (as in the community's enemies). This use of *ruaḥ* for Kuhn clearly does not have its origins in the Old Testament but is to be sought in Iran together with the origin of the two-spirit teaching of 1QS 3-4, with which it is "*religionsgeschichtlich*" related.[243]

The next major work of significance for *ruaḥ* in the Scrolls is P. von der Osten-Sacken's *Gott und Belial*. Osten-Sacken's goal

---

Kohlhammer, 1980), pp. 64 & 69-70; for Lichtenberger in *Studien*, *cf.* the comments in this chapter below; finally, *cf.* Dombkowski Hopkins, "Community," pp. 339-342 & 349.

[238]H. W. Kuhn, *Enderwartung*, p. 11.

[239]*Ibid.*, pp. 34ff.

[240]*Ibid.*, pp. 44-112.

[241]*Ibid.*, p. 130ff. However, Kuhn notes that God's Spirit is not explicitly desecribed as eschatological in 1QH; *cf. ibid.*, pp. 138-9.

[242]*Ibid.*, pp. 120-130; *cf.* n. 104 above.

[243]*Ibid.*, p. 122.

here was to trace the evolution of dualistic thought at Qumran, and his conclusions were basically that the earliest stage could be found in 1QM as a development of concepts already present in the Old Testament.[244] An Iranian influence did not affect Qumran until a time after the Teacher of Righteousness (who wrote 1QH 2:1-9, 31-39 ; 3:1-18; 4:5-29a; 5:5-19; 5:20-7:5; 7:6-25; and 8:4-40)[245] as can be seen in the later stage of 1QS 3:13-4:14.[246] Iranian influence, then, cannot be regarded as a formative element at the beginning of sectarian thought. Osten-Sacken therefore contests H. W. Kuhn's view discussed above that the use of *ruaḥ* in 1QH as man's predestined being is to be related "*religionsgeschlichtlich*" to the two-spirit teaching of 1QS 3-4. Iranian links to *ruaḥ* as man's predestined being are weak at best, whereas it is easy to explain this use as an effect of basic Old Testament concepts involving man's weakness and God's omnipotence.[247] Unlike Kuhn, then, Osten-Sacken is not interested in contrasting this use of *ruaḥ* with *ruaḥ* understood as God's gift to the sectarian at his entrance into the community. As we noted previously, however, Osten-Sacken still sees a clear contrast between the pneumatology of 1QS 3:13-4:14 (which he regards as affected by Iranian thought) and that of 1QH (which he believes draws its views ultimately from the Old Testament).[248]

After Osten-Sacken's *Gott und Belial,* the next (and last) major work having a bearing on the consistency of sectarian pneumatology was the 1980 publication of Lichtenberger's *Studien*. This dealt with the specific question of sectarian anthropology[249] but, as we have seen, it also pointed to the diverse

---

[244]Osten-Sacken, *Gott und Belial,* p. 239.

[245]*Ibid.,* p. 69 n. 2.

[246]*Ibid.,* pp. 138ff. & 165ff.

[247]*Ibid.,* pp. 136-7.

[248]*Cf.* n. 225 above.

[249]Lichtenberger, *Studien,* p. 11. A good summary of the basic diversity within sectarian anthropology as uncovered by Lichtenberger can be seen in J. Becker's review of Lichtenberger's *Studien* in *Theologische Literaturzeitung,* 107 (1982), p. 269: "als Hauptproblem sach-

and conflicting elements involved in sectarian pneumatology.[250] Since 1970, most scholars have touched on the issue of sectarian pneumatology only in passing, but they have also recognized that the Scrolls contain a clear diversity of thought on this matter.[251] And although there was some support which continued after the work of H. W. Kuhn in *Enderwartung* for the previous consensus of the late 1950's and early 1960's,[252] there has been no real attempt since Kuhn to support it in the light of current research.

In summary, the scholarly consensus on sectarian pneumatology during the first half of the 1960's tended to uphold the consensus of the late 1950's that this pneumatology was an essential unity dominated by its two-spirit teaching as understood in terms of a cosmic dualism influenced by Iran. After the work of H. W. Kuhn in *Enderwartung* became known, a definite shift in the consensus is noticeable toward the view of sectarian pneumatology as containing diverse and sometimes conflicting elements.

d. The position which views sectarian pneumatology as a unity but denies that this involves the presence of cosmic dualism, Iranian or otherwise.

As noted in section 2*c* of this chapter, this position received its most forceful expression in Wernberg-Møller's "Reconsideration" in a form which utilized earlier scholarship but which was also unique to him in two basic respects, *viz.*, that there is no cosmic dualism at all in sectarian thought and no

---

licher Art ergeben sich: (a) Die verschiedene Auffassung vom Menschen: Einmal ist er als unterstes Glied im Herrschaftsbereich dualistischer Mächte vorgestellt, wobei die jeweilige Zuordnung prädestinatianisch gestellt, das andere Mall kann er aufgrund der Wahlfreiheit dem Gesetz folgen oder sich ihm versagen. (b) Die verschiedene Bestimmung der Sünde: Sei es, daß sie auf die niedrige Kreatürlichkeit zurückgeführt wird, sei es, daß sie durch verführung der Geistermächte zustande kommt."

[250]*Cf.* n. 104 above.

[251]*Cf.* n. 237 above.

[252]*Cf.* n. 236 above.

evidence that the sectarians regarded themselves as being essentially different spiritually from non-sectarians due to opposed metaphysical principles.[253] In subsequent scholarship it appears that no one has supported Wermberg-Møller's position without qualification, although a certain amount of qualified (and, at times, ambiguous) support can be found in the work of a few scholars. J. Pryke, for example, seems to be supportive of Wernberg-Møller's position that the two spirits of 1QS 3-4 should be understood in terms of the two impulses (with the qualification that the former has to do with two groups whereas the later has to do with the individual),[254] and he may even regard the two angels as no more than personifications of the abstract concepts of Good and Evil,[255] but he nevertheless still describes the dualism of 1QS 3-4 as cosmic in nature with the consequent spiritual division of humanity into two clearly defined groups of good and evil.[256] D. Hill, on the other hand, seems to be supportive of Wernberg-Møller's position that 1QS 3-4 should not be understood against the background of a cosmic dualism (Iranian or otherwise)[257] and that the two spirits therefore should be understood in terms of the good and evil inclinations,[258] but this support is qualified by Hill's identification of these spirits as angels[259] and his apparent support of H. G. May's understanding of them as cosmic beings.[260] Finally, S. F. Noll has more recently defined the two spirits of

---

[253]*Cf.* nn. 162 and 163 above.

[254]John Pryke, "'Spirit' and 'Flesh' in the Qumran Documents and Some New Testament Texts," *Revue de Qumrân*, 5 (1965), 350-1.

[255]*Cf. ibid.*, p. 350. Pryke calls the two angels "personifications of Good and Evil," but his position is unclear: does he mean that the angels were *no more* than personifications of these concepts and, if so, is this the way the sectarian himself understood them?

[256]*Ibid.*, pp. 350-1: "A marked predestinarian outlook was coupled with an ethical cosmic dualism. . . . Mankind is divided into two classes: the good and the bad. . . ."

[257]Hill, *Greek Words*, p. 236.

[258]*Ibid.*, p. 238.

[259]*Ibid.*, pp. 235-6.

[260]*Ibid.*, p. 237 n 1.

1QS 3-4 as related most closely to the meaning "disposition" and only distantly to that of "angel,"[261] but he also notes that the presence of angels in 1QS 3-4 gives the dualism of this section a cosmic dimension.[262]

Most responses to Wernberg-Møller's position in "Reconsideration" have, in fact, been unsupportive[263] with the most detailed criticism coming from H. G. May[264] and J. H. Charlesworth.[265] May's basic criticisms were that Wernberg-Møller had ignored the creation context of 1QS 3-4 (which, in itself, should indicate the cosmic sweep of this section)[266] and that he had not taken into sufficient account its apocalyptic framework, which envisioned all of humanity as predestined to a good or evil realm under the cosmic domination of a good or vil angel.[267] These oversights are especially significant in the light of the fact that the roots of cosmic dualism can be found in the Old Testament itself,[268] and it is precisely against the Old Testament (as well as other Jewish literature) that Wernberg-Møller wished to understand sectarian thought.[269] The criticisms of Charlesworth are basically the same as those of May,

---

[261]Noll, "Angelology," p. 137.

[262]*Ibid.*, p. 141: "The presence of angels should itself be a sign of the cosmic dimension of the writer's thought."

[263](Cited by date) *e.g.*, Anderson, "'Ruah'," pp. 298-9; for May, "Cosmological Reference," see this chapter below; Ringgren, *Faith*, p. 78; Osten-Sacken, *Gott und Belial*, p. 141; G. Maier, *Mensch*, p. 236; for Charlesworth, "Comparison," see this chapter below; Gammie, "Dualism," p. 381; Benedikt Otzen, "Old Testament Wisdom Literature and Dualistic Thinking in Late Judaism," *Vetus Testamentum*, Supplements, 28 (1975), pp. 147-8 n. 4; Lichtenberger, *Studien*, pp. 127-8; and Dombkowski Hopkins, "Community," p. 342.

[264]May, "Cosmological Reference," 1963.

[265]Charlesworth, "Comparison," 1972.

[266]May, "Cosmological Reference," pp. 1ff.

[267]*Ibid.*, pp. 3ff.

[268]*Ibid.*, pp. 6-14. This line of argumentation is not new: *cf.* Molin, *Söhne*, p. 129 and especially Nötscher, *Terminologie*, pp. 86-93.

[269]Wernberg-Møller, "Reconsideration," p. 416.

but Charlesworth also cites the work of J. Strugnell,[270] J. Allegro,[271] Holm-Nielsen and Delcor.[272] In summary, then, Wernberg-Møller in "reconsideration" has not had much direct influence on the interpretation of sectarian pneumatology. His work, nevertheless, has stimulated an impressive debate which still continues today.

e. Conclusion to section 3, chapter 2.

Literary criticism of the Dead Sea Scrolls has grown increasingly complex since the early 1960's, and this has had an impact on how scholars have understood the meaning of *ruaḥ* in sectarian thought. Although the consensus of the late 1950's (*i.e.*, that the various uses of *ruaḥ* in the Scrolls should be viewed within the two-spirit teaching of 1QS 3-4 understood in terms of an Iranian cosmic dualism) continued well into the 1960's, this seems to have disappeared after H. W. Kuhn's *Enderwartung* became known, as most scholars began to recognize elements of diversity and even tension within sectarian pneumatology. At present, the majority of scholars recognize the existence of some form of cosmic dualism in 1QS 3-4 and tend not to make a simple equation between, *e.g.*, the pneumatology of 1QS 3-4 and 1QH.

---

[270]Charlesworth, "Comparison," p. 86: "J. Strugnell has shown that the angelology of [4QSl] is celestial. . . . The cosmic dimension of the document increases the probability that the dualism in 1QS 3:13ff. is cosmic since both seem to date from the same early stage in the development of Qumran theology."

[271]*Ibid.* Charlesworth cites the work of Allegro on 4Q186, which describes the effect of the stars on the spiritual nature man receives at birth.

[272]*Ibid.* Charlesworth notes that both Holm-Nielsen and Delcor in their respective commentaries of 1QH have shown that 1QH contains a cosmic dualism: *cf.* Delcor, *Hymns*, pp. 64 & 68 and Svend Holm-Nielsen, *Hodayot, Psalms from Qumran* (Aarhus: Universitetsforlaget I, 1960), pp. 40-52.

4. Conclusion to chapter 2.

The history of research into the meaning of *ruaḥ* in Qumran can be divided into three basic periods. The first period (1950 through 1955) was a time of basic shifts of opinion among major scholars together with initial attempts to understand sectarian pneumatology in terms of its relationship to Iranian and Christian thought. It soon became evident to the majority of investigators that *ruaḥ* in the Scrolls should not be interpreted as a Christian concept, and some would later strongly doubt the evidence for Iranian influence. Most scholars, however, would eventually agree that Iranian thought had influenced Qumran to some degree, but the precise extent and nature of this influence is still being debated. In any case, it does not seem that the question of Iranian influence has had a direct bearing on how scholars have distinguished between the most basic meanings of *ruaḥ* in the Scrolls (*e.g.*, as God's Spirit, man's spirit, angel, *etc.*),[273] although it is true that scholars who have seen a strong Iranian influence on Qumran have also tended to understand the two sprits of 1QS 3-4 as cosmic beings. The most important development of this period, however, was the work of E. Sjöberg in his 1955 article, "Neuschöpfung." In it, Sjöberg defined the sectarian understanding of *ruaḥ* in 1QH (as this relates to the source of their spirituality) as having to do with God's Spirit received at one's entrance into the community. This view of *ruaḥ* would later have significant implications for the understanding of sectarian pneumatology in general, as can be

---

[273]The most important factor on the definition of *ruaḥ* in the Scrolls has been whether or not to read the Scrolls in the light of 1QS 3-4. If a scholar does use 1QS 3-4 as the foundation stone of sectarian pneumatology, many instances of *ruaḥ* in the rest of the Scrolls will be understood as referring to a cosmic angel or to a predestined, spirituality given to the sectarian at birth; this will generally be the case even if the scholar does not depend on Iranian sources as the basis of his interpretations. *Cf.* for example, Anderson, "'Ruah'," pp. 298 & 301, who makes no appeal to Iranian sources but identifies רוח קודש in 1QS and 1QH as the "spirit of truth" (1QS 3:18) which, in turn, is defined as an angelic being.

seen in the second period of research into the meaning of *ruaḥ* outlined immediately below.

The second period of research (1956 through 1961) can be understood as reflecting a growing dissatisfaction with the scholarly consensus of that time which viewed sectarian pneumatology as an integrated whole under the domination of its two-spirit teaching in 1QS 3-4 as understood in terms of an Iranian, cosmic dualism. In this view, man's spirituality is regarded as something he "inherits" at birth by divine predestination, *i.e.*, men are created as either basically good or evil and through divine predestination are subject not directly to God but to the intermediate, spiritual domination of either a good or evil angel of cosmic proportions. With the growing popularity of Sjöberg's view of *ruaḥ* in 1QH, however, an increasing tension can be seen between this view (with its emphasis on receiving a "*Neuschöpfung*" through God's Spirit at work in the Qumran community) and that of the majority described above. It became increasingly clear that diverse and contradictory traditions might underlie sectarian pneumatology, and a number of scholars became convinced that the sectarian view of *ruaḥ* should not be understood as an integrated whole under the domination of an Iranian, two-spirit cosmic dualism. A second response to the majority consensus was to deny that sectarian thought had been influenced by cosmic dualism (Iranian or otherwise) in the first place. This view did not deny the unity of sectarian pneumatology but only its relationship to cosmic dualism as such, and it sought to understand the basis of sectarian spirituality in terms of the later rabbinic doctrine of the two impulses. It should be noted that this view of 1QS 3-4 is as difficult to reconcile to the interpretive trend of 1QH initiated by Sjöberg as was the consensus of the late 1950's and early 1960's. This is because its view of 1QS 3-4 as involving no more than two balanced impulses in the individual leaves no room for the insistence of 1QH (according to Sjöberg) that men are in need of a basic spiritual *Neuschöpfung* if they wish to obey the law of God properly.

The third period of research (from 1962 to the present) witnessed a significant growth in the complexity of the literary criticism of the Scrolls which, in general, has supported the position that a traditional and more biblically oriented pneumatology (*e.g.*, as seen in Sjöberg's interpretion of 1QH in "Neuschöpfung") experienced an influence of some sort from Iran (as seen especially in 1QS 3-4) and that this influence created a conflict in how the sectarians understood *ruaḥ* as the source of their spirituality, *i.e.*, as either an inherited, godly disposition or as a spiritual *Neuschöpfung* through the work of God's eschatological Spirit. This shift in the consensus from that of the late 1950's and early 1960's is perhaps related to the appearance of H. W. Kuhn's *Enderwartung* in 1966 in which *ruaḥ* as the predestined being of man (related "*religionsgeschichtlicht*" to the Iranian two-spirit dualism of 1QS 3-4) was understood as being in conceptual tension with the more traditional and biblical understanding of *ruaḥ* as God's eschatological Spirit received within the sectarian community. Although Kuhn's views have not gone entirely unchallenged, no one in support of the older consensus has yet addressed the questions he and other have raised against the view of *ruaḥ* as an integrated concept within sectarian thought.

It appears, then, that most scholars today recognize a cosmic dualism of some sort in the Scrolls (especially in 1QS 3-4) due to some degree to Iranian influence and that they also recognize the difficulty of harmonizing in every case the Scrolls' diverse and sometimes conflicting uses of *ruaḥ*.

CHAPTER 3

RUAḤ AS GOD'S SPIRIT

1. Basic syntactical characteristics of *ruaḥ* as God's Spirit.

Ruaḥ is found thirty-five times in the published, non-biblical Hebrew literature of the Scrolls as God's Spirit, including five cases in which it is reconstructed (1QH f 2:13 & 1Q34bis II 6/7) or partially reconstructed (1QH 14:13; 4Q171, 3-10 IV 25 and 11QMelch 3 II 18). It is always found in the singular, and except for 11QMelch 3 II 18 it never has the article.

The Scrolls do not give us much information about the gender of *ruaḥ* in relationship to God, but the available evidence indicates that it is feminine.[1] This would tend to support the contention of F. Nötscher and others that God's Spirit was not regarded by the sectarians as a personal being distinct from God (*e.g.*, as an angel) but as an impersonal power.[2] The general rarity of the definite article with *ruaḥ* as God's Spirit would also seem to point in this direction, but it should be noted that the article is very infrequent for all meanings of *ruaḥ* in Qumran's

---

[1]In 1QS 4:6 (*cf.* this chapter below) the author talks about the Spirit and those who walk "in it" (בה) and in 1QS 3:7 (*cf.* this chapter below) *ruaḥ* is modified by קדושה. Irwin, *Spirit-Dualism*, p. 203 n. 10, believes that קדושה should be pointed as קדושה ("holiness"), but this is unlikely since a clear use of this noun does not seem to be present elsewhere in the Scrolls. Note that the evidence of 4QSa (which reads רוח קודשו in place of רוח קדושה in 1QS 3:7) indicates the synonymity of both expressions (*cf.* this chapter below). *Ruaḥ* as God's Spirit never appears as masculine in the non-biblical Scrolls. Lys in *Ruaḥ*, p. 32 n. 2 notes that God's Spirit in the Old Testament (except for its oldest texts) is found primarily in the impersonal feminine gender.

[2]*Cf.* Nötscher, *Terminologie*, p. 42; *cf.* also Böcher, *Dualismus*, p. 38 and Becker, *Heil Gottes*, p. 162.

non-biblical, Hebrew literature even when it clearly refers to personal angelic or demonic beings.[3]

2. Specific syntactical patterns of *ruaḥ* as God's Spirit.

a. General overview.

The most frequent means of referring to God's Spirit in the published, non-biblical Hebrew literature of Qumran is with the singular of *ruaḥ* as a *nomen regens* in construct with the singular of קודש plus the pronominal suffix (כה/ך or ו) referring to God (seventeen times: 1QS 8:16; 1QH 7:6; 9:32; 12:12; 14:13; 16:2, 3, 7 & 12; 17:26; f 2:9 & 13 {recon.}; CD 2:12; 1Q34bis II 6/7; 1Q39,1:6; 4Q287, 4, 13; and 4Q504, 1-2 V 15); related to this category are the expressions רוח הקודש (two times: 4QDe {270} 2 II 13-14b and 4Q506, 131-132, 11) and רוח רחמיך (one time: 1QH 16:9). The next most frequent method of referring to God's Spirit is the use of the singular of *ruaḥ* without qualifying expressions, as in ברוח אשר נתתה בי;[4] this particular expression is found four times (1QH12:11; 13:19; 16:11; and f 3:14), and an additional three cases of an unqualified *ruaḥ* are סודי רוח (1QS 4:6), [. . .]רוח (1QH 16:6) and משיחי רוח (4QDe {270}2 II, 13-14 a).[5] In five cases the syntactically indefinite form רוח קודש is found (1QS 4:21a, *cf.* chapter eight; 9:3; 1QSb 2:24; 4Q171, 3-10 IV 25; and 4Q504, 4, 5); and finally there are three unrelated and unique cases which require special attention: רוח קודשה (1QS 3:7), רוח דעה (1QH 14:25), and משיח הרוח (11QMelch 3 II 18).

b. The singular of *ruaḥ* as a *nomen regens* in construct with a suffixed singular of קודש referring to God: רוח ק{ו}דש {ו or כה/ך}

---

[3]*Cf.* chapter 1 n. 15 above; the definite article occurs only two times (both as כול הרוחות) in the 58 possible occurrences of *ruaḥ* as an angel or demon (*cf.* 4Q185, 14 I 2, and 8Q5, 2, 6).

[4]The preposition in itself does not qualify *ruaḥ* but simply relates it to the other elements of the sentence.

[5]Note that the genitive *ruaḥ* qualifies the preceding *nomen regens* rather than the reverse; *cf.* E. Kautzsch, *Gesenius' Hebrew Grammar* (2nd. English edition; Oxford: Clarendon, 1910), §§89a, 128f & x.

(found seventeen times; see the list of references for these occurrences in section 2*a* above).

We should note, first of all, that only CD 5:11 and 7:4 contain forms of *ruaḥ* (sg.) in construct with the genitive קודש which a majority of scholars consider to be a reference to the human spirit.[6] These cases will be treated in chapter four, which deals with *ruaḥ* as man's spirit, but for now we may note that the plural of the genitive קודש in CD 5:11 and 7:4 (whatever its meaning) provides a clear syntactical device for differentiating between the *ruaḥ* of God and man. If these passages in CD do refer to the human spirit, this would not be evidence that *ruaḥ* followed by the *singular* genitive of קודש could be used ambiguously to refer to either God or man. It may, in fact, indicate the opposite. The unusual use of the plural genitive of קודש with *ruaḥ* to refer to man's spirit may indicate that

---

[6]See, *e.g.*, Otto Betz, "Die Geburt der Gemeinde durch den Lehrer," *New Testament Studies*, 3 (1957), p. 324; also *idem*, *Offenbarung*, pp. 126-7; F.-M. Braun, "arriere-fond," p. 35 n.3; Bruce, "Holy Spirit," p. 54; Burrows, *More Light*, p. 129; Coppens, "Documents," p. 36 n. 46; Graystone, "Scrolls," vol. 23, 33 n. 3; Hauschild, *Gottes Geist*, p. 248; Hill, *Greek Words*, p. 240; Irwin, *Spirit-Dualism*, pp. 54 & 194; Jaubert, *notion*, p. 243; George Johnston, "Spirit and Holy Spirit in the Qumran Literature," *New Testament Sidelights*, Essays in Honor of A. C. Purdy (Hartford, 1960), p. 33; Pryke, "'Spirit'," p. 345; Chaim Rabin, *The Zadokite Documents* (2nd. edition; Oxford: Clarendon, 1954), p. 19 n. 11/3 & p. 36 n. 4/1; Schreiner, "Geistbegabung," pp. 170-1; Eduard Schweizer, "Die sieben Geister in der Apokalypse," *Evangelische Theologie* 11, (1951/2), p. 506 n. 25; *idem*, "Gegenwart des Geistes," p. 494 n. 1; *idem*, "πνεῦμα," p. 392 n. 345; and Eric Sjöberg, "πνεῦμα, πνματικός," *Theological Dictionary of the New Testament*, 6 (1961), p. 378. A number of scholars also appear to regard CD 5:11 and 7:4 as referring to God's Spirit: *cf.* Jean-Paul Audet, "Affinites literaires et doctrinales du 'Manuel de Discipline'," *Revue Biblique*, 60 (1953), p. 65; Beaven, "Ruah," p. 76; Delcor, *Hymns*, pp. 46-7; *idem*, "Doctrines," cols. 972-3; Dupont-Sommer, *écrits*, p. 147; Huppenbauer, *Mensch*, p. 59 n. 221; Johann Maier, *Die Texte vom Toten Meer*, vol, II (München: Reinhardt Verlag, 1960), p. 206; Manns, *symbole*, p. 71 n. 15 & p. 90 n. 55; Nötscher, "Heiligkeit im Qumranschriften," *Revue de Qûmran*, 2 (1959/60), p. 338.

ruaḥ with a singular genitive of קודש could *not* be used by the sectarians for this purpose[7] even if the contextual or syntactical pointers (such as the pronominal suffix on קודש) pointed clearly to the spirit of man: *ruaḥ* with קודש in the singular would in itself be too strongly associated with the autonomous nature of God's Spirit to be associated with *ruaḥ* as something which could be subject to the decisions and control of men.

As indicated above, a majority of scholars regard our expression as referring to the Spirit of God.[8] I have found only

---

[7]This does not necessarily mean that the plural genitive of קודש is reserved for man; *cf.* 1QIsa 63:10-11 with the MT. It is possible that the plural in CD 5:11 and 7:4 is one of abstraction (*viz.*, "his/their sacred spirit") and that of 1QIsa 63:10-11 one of majesty (*viz.*, "His most Holy Spirit"); *cf.* Kautzsch, *Grammar*, §124 d, f, g, & h.

[8]The Qumran doctrine of God's Spirit has been understood in various ways by scholars; for example, among the majority who see a clear reference in our expression to the Spirit of God, there are different views of how God's Spirit relates to the two spirits of 1QS 3-4 (*cf.* chapter 2 above). With this in mind, then, the following scholars understand the seventeen occurrences of our expression as referring (in some sense) to God's Spirit as an entity external to man (although internally influencing man's spirit): Anderson, "'Ruah'," p. 302; Beaven , "Ruah," pp. 78, 92-3 & 99-100; Becker, *Heil Gottes*, p. 162; Betz, *Offenbarung*, pp. 119-120, 124, 126 & 130; *idem*, "'To Worship God in Spirit and in Truth': Reflections on John 4:20-26," *Standing Before God* (ed. by A. Finkel and L. Frizzell; New York: Ktav, 1981), p. 63; Böcher, *Dualismus*, p. 38; H. Braun, *Qumran*, vol. II p. 253; Bruce, "Holy Spirit,"pp. 51-2; J. Carmignac and P. Guilbert, *Les Textes de Qumran Traduits et Annotés*, vol. I (Paris: Editions Letouzey et Ané, 1961), p. 155 n. 9; J. Carmignac, É. Cothonet et H. Lignée, *Les Textes de Qumran Traduits et Annotés*, vol. II (Paris: Éditions Letouzey et Ané, 1963), pp. 154 & 155 n. 24; Chevallier, *Souffle de Dieu*, pp. 54-55; Coppens, "don," p. 219; M. de Jonge and A. S. van der Woude, "Melchizedek and the New Testament," *New Testament Studies*, 12 (July, 1966) p. 306; Delcor, "Doctrines," cols. 972-3; *idem*, *Hymns*, pp.45-47; Dietzel, "Beten," pp. 19 & 23-25; Ellis, "Gifts," p. 136; David Flusser, "The Dead Sea Sect and Pre-Pauline Christianity," *Scripta Hierosolymitana*, IV (1958), pp. 256 & 259; *idem*, "The Dualism of 'Flesh and Spirit' in the Dead Sea Scrolls and the New Testament," *Tarbis*, 27 (1958) p. 162; Foester, "Heilige

five scholars who believe that this expression may refer generally to no more than a human spirit or dispostion (whether inborn[9] or acquired in the community[10] in contrast to a force or entity sent from God), and only one of them has described his position at any length.[11] The majority opinion, however, seems to be correct for various reasons which will be outlined in the following paragraphs.

1) The suffix on קודש (sg.) in the Scrolls always refers to God. This is perhaps the most obvious syntactical feature of the seventeen occurrences of our expression and perhaps also the most important for determining its meaning. Although it is true that Jewish sources do at times describe man's spirit as the holy

---

Geist," pp. 129-130; Graystone, "Scrolls," vol. 23, pp. 33-4; Holm-Nielsen, *Hodayot,* pp. 288-9; Hans Hübner, "Anthropologischer Dualismus in den Hodayoth?" *New Testament Studies,* 18 (1972), p. 283; Huppenbauer, *Mensch,* p. 70; Irwin, "Spirit-Dualism," pp. 58, 69, 72 192-4 & 225 n. 68; Jaubert, *notion,* pp. 239 & 242-4; Johnston, "Spirit," pp. 34-5 & 38-40; H. W. Kuhn, *Enderwartung,* pp. 132 & 134-5; G. Maier, *Mensch,* pp. 188-9; J. Maier, *Texte,* vol. II, 206; May, "Cosmological Reference," p. 5 n. 17; Montague, *Holy Spirit,* p.121; Osten-Sacken, *Gott und Belial,* pp. 133 & 138; Ringgren, *Faith,* pp. 87-89; Schnackenburg, "'Anbetung'," pp. 91-2; Sjöberg, "Neuschöpfung," p. 135; and *idem,* "πνεῦμα," p. 358.

[9]*Cf.* Schreiner, "Geistbegabung."

[10]*Cf.* Licht, "Doctrine," p. 92: concerning the holy spirit he says that a man who has been given it "gains by it *further* qualities" [emphasis mine], and on the same page he notes that the acquisition of diverse noble qualities "if viewed as a gradual process, can be seen as a sort of climb on the ladder of moral perfection." *Cf.* also Coppens, "Document," p. 36 n. 46 (he later modified his position, *cf.* "don," p. 217); Godfrey R. Driver, *The Judean Scrolls,* (Oxford: Blackwell, 1965), p. 538; and Leaney, *Rule,* p. 35. I have also found two scholars who see a specific instance of our expression as referring to man's spirit but understand the others as referring to a power or Spirit from God: *cf.* Hauschild, *Gottes Geist,* pp. 248-9 (on 1QH 12:12) and Nötscher, "Geist," p. 307 (on CD 2:12).

[11]Schreiner, "Geistbegabung."

spirit of *God*,[12] it is difficult to know exactly how old this type of expression might be.[13] In other sources which are datable to the general period of the Scrolls, this kind of language never occurs as a description of man's spirit.[14] Occasionally the human spirit is called "holy,"[15] but whenever there is a syntactical indication of possession with this meaning, the reference is to man and not to God.[16] This is parallel to the situation in the Scrolls: the two contextually clearest examples of a reference to man's spirit as "holy" (pl.) with a syntactical indication of

---

[12]*E.g.*, the Heb. *Test. of Naphtali* 10:9 and Targum *JI* on Gen. 6:3. I do not know of any other occurrence of this kind of language in possible early Hebrew sources. *Cf.* Beaven, "Ruah."

[13]*Cf.* Charles' opposition to M. Gaster's view that the Heb. *Test. of Naphtali* is original in R. H. Charles, *The Greek Versions of the Testaments of the Twelve Patriarchs* (Hildesheim: Georg Olms Verlagsbuchhandlung, 1960 reprint), pp. li-liii; *cf.* also Kee's support of Charles on the late Hebrew style of the version in H. C. Kee, "Testament of the Twelve Patriarchs," *The Old Testament Pseudepigrapha*, vol. I (ed. by J. H. Charlesworth; Garden City: Doubleday & Company, Inc., 1983), 776. For a recent investigation on the relationship between the Greek and Hebrew *Tests. of Naphtali, cf.* Th. Korteweg, "The Meaning of Naphtali's visions," *Studies on the Testaments of the Twelve Patriarchs, Text and Interpretation* (ed. by M. de Jonge; Leiden: Brill, 1975), pp. 261-290, who believes that these versions are separate redactions of the original, *ibid.*, pp. 281-2. For the possible pre-Christian, oral origin of the Targum *JI*, see M. McNamara, *The New Testament and the Palestinian Targum to the Pentateuch* (Rome: Pontifical Biblical Institute, 1966); McNamara also notes, however, that passages in *JI* may have a late date, *ibid.*, pp. 35 & 65-6.

[14]Beaven in "Ruah," for example, finds no examples of this kind of language outside of the Heb. *Test. of Naphtali* 10:9.

[15]*Cf.* Jubilees 1:21 & 23 and LXX Daniel 5:12 & 6:3; D. S. Russell, *The Method and Message of Jewish Apocalyptic* (London: SCM Press, 1964) p. 403 lists the above occurrences of "spirit" under the heading "the fundamental aspect of human personality."

[16]*Cf.* for example, Theodotion's version of Susanna 45: "God aroused the holy spirit of a lad named Daniel."

possession have suffixes which refer to man rather than to God.[17]

2) The Hodayot in which 11 of the seventeen occurrences are found (with one reconstruction, 1QH f 2:13) tends to present man's spirit in strongly negative terms. This is part of a general theological view of man in 1QH which Licht calls "an almost pathological abhorrence of human nature."[18] There are contexts in which 1QH seems to present the natural, human spirit as a source of spirituality,[19] but its general tendency is to describe the sectarian's spirit as sinful by nature and in need of God's help. This need, furthermore, applies not only to the sectarian's past[20] but also to his present,[21] especially as his spirit/spirituality forms a contrast to the power and righteousness of God.[22] Against this background, then, it is difficult to

---

[17]CD. 5:11 and 7:4.

[18]Licht, "Doctrine," p. 10.

[19]*Cf.* especially 1QH 15:13 & 22.

[20]*Cf.* 1QH 3:21 and 11:12.

[21]Thus, in 1QH 1:22 the psalmist calls himself a "perverted spirit" while confessing that he has no defense before God (vv. 25-6) and that God alone is righteous (vv. 26-7; *cf.* also 4:29-30); in 1QH 13:13ff. he confesses that he is a spirit of flesh; and finally, in 1QH 17 he asks God for help in the future against sin and evil spirits (v. 23) since he has but a "spirit of flesh" (v. 25). *Cf.* also Holm-Nielsen, *Hodayot*, p. 288, who summarizes this fundamental emphasis in 1QH by noting that the psalmist "in no way distinguishes between himself and mortal man. . . . He is able, thus, to describe his ear which has heard the word of God as uncircumsised (18:20), and his heart as as heart of dust (18:24), that is to say human; his spirit is carnal (17:25) and perverted (3:31); the same is said of his heart (17:19)."

[22]*Cf.* Licht, "Doctrine," pp. 11-12: "Man is necessarily sinful, or morally imperfect, because perfection or righteousness can be attributed only to God. . . . The conviction of human sinfulness thus turns out be be the logical consequence of absolute divine righteousness. . . . [Sinfulness] is, the author of DST [*i.e.*, 1QH] feels, an inseparable part of human baseness and turpitude--the ultimate cause of his deep self-disgust and despair."

understand the psalmist as standing before God with the claim of having immovable strength (1QH 7:6-7), knowledge of God's wondrous counsel (12:12) and access to divine purity (16:12) because of the holiness of his own personal spirit (whether inborn or acquired in the community).[23] A more consistent approach here would be to understand the predominant teaching of 1QH as presenting man's spirit as essentially inadequate in spiritual matters and prone to failure even within the sectarian community.[24] The human spirit of the sectarian, then, would be totally dependent on the constant external intervention of God's holy Spirit for spiritual strength and insight. Thus, the psalmist knows that God has given him strength and knowledge by His holy Spirit in the past (1QH 7:6/7 & 12:11-13)) and implores God for His holy Spirit in the future to complete the good work already begun in him so that he might always have access to God's presence (16:11ff.).[25]

---

[23]1QH 4:31 & 36 are perhaps the clearest passages in 1QH (besides 15:13, 22) which speak of the sectarian's spirit as taking an active role in the spirituality of the community, with *ruaḥ* being used probably in the sense of the eschatological transformation of man's spirit (*i.e.*, religious disposition) as seen in Ezk. 36:26. But even here the psalmist credits his spirituality to God rather than to himself (vv. 27ff.), who grants this to him even though he will never be worthy of it (vv. 29ff.); thus, the psalmist's sinfulness by nature (*i.e.*, his natural spiritual condition apart from the eschatological intervention of God's transforming and life-giving Spirit) makes him constantly dependent on the mercy and power of God at work in the community.

[24]Thus, the psalmist remembers his past failures within the community in 1QH 4:33-35 (*cf.* n. 23 above); *cf.* also 1QH 17:20ff. in which the sectarian calls upon God to help him from falling in the future since he is a "spirit of flesh"; *cf.* also Wolverton, "Man," pp. 171-2.

[25]A problem in the study of the poetic language of 1QH is the time element of its verbal patterns, (*cf.* H. W. Kuhn, *Enderwartung*, pp. 20-1). A special study of this matter has been made by S. J. De Vries, "Consecutive Constructions in the 1Q Sectarian Scrolls," *Doron Hebraic Studies*, Essays in Honor of Professor Abraham L. Katsh (New York, 1965), pp. 75-87 and *idem*, "The Syntax of Tenses and Interpretation in the Hodayot," *Revue de Qumrân*, 5 (1965), pp. 375-414. As to the consecutive construction in the Cave 1 Scrolls (including 1QH), De

3) There are a number of diverse contexts in which our construction is presented in the Scrolls as a force from God external to man, whereas there is no context which requires it to be understood as no more than a human disposition.[26] Thus, God sheds (1QH 7:6/7; 17:26; and f 2:9)[27] His holy Spirit on the psalmist or pours (4Q504, 1-2 V 15) it on his people; through it he delights (1QH 9:32), instructs (1QH 14:13), makes atonement

---

Vries concludes in "Consecutive Construction," p. 80 that "the perfect consecutive never refers to the past in the scrolls under study. Conversely, the imperfect consecutive, which has a wide range of possible meanings in Biblical Hebrew is always past, with two exceptions, in the Scrolls. The exceptions are one example of a futuristric meaning following a prophetic perfect in a direct quotation of Numbers 24:17-19, and a present perfect signification with the stative verb *yd'*, whether this occurs in the perfect or in the imperfect consecutive." As to the other tense significations in 1QH, De Vries concludes in "Syntax of Tenses," p. 412 that "the participle is employed according to the biblical model. This is true of the infinitive as well, although this verbal form seems to be used chiefly in purpose clauses. The perfect always refers in the passages studied, to completed past events, unless it has the stative force. The imperfect is used to express continuing actions in the present or future, but often refers as well to past events, in which case it generally indicates the actions of the poet's enemies and has a durative or frequentive force, or constitutes a circumstantial statement."

[26]So also most scholars; *cf.* n. 8 above.

[27]There is disagreement among scholars about the meaning הניף as either "wave" or "shed." Its predominant meaning in the Old Testament is "wave," but the meaning "sprinkle/shed" is also attested (*e.g.*, Ps. 68:10; *cf.* also Ben Sira 43:17). The meaning "sprinkle/shed" is probably correct in our expression since this would be most conceptually analogous to the use of similar expressions with *ruaḥ* as God's Spirit in the Old Testament (*e.g.*, שפך in Ezk. 39:29 and Joel 3:1-2, יצק in Is. 44: 3, and ערה in Is. 32:15); *cf.* also 1 Enoch 62:2 and 91:1. This possibility is further supported by the pre-Essene fragment 4Q504, 1-2 V 15, which is almost an exact syntactical equivalent of 1QH 17:26 except that יצק is used instead of הניף. Note that the speakers in 4Q504, 1-2 view themselves as the eschatological generation of Is. 44:3; *cf.* Maurice Baillet, *Discoveries in the Judaean Desert*, VII: *Qumran Grotte 4* (Oxford: Clarendon Press, 1982), p. 147 line 15 and also n. 38 below.

for (f 2:13) and cleanses (16:12) the psalmist; and through those anointed by it (*e.g.*, 4Q287, 4, 13 & CD 2:12)[28] and through its "words" (1Q34bis II 6/7),[29] God provides instruction and covenantal rule for his people. This activity often occurs in a context in which the sectarian's sin and helplessness are emphasized.[30] The impression these texts convey, then, is not that the sectarian has an inborn "holy spirit" or even that God creates a new spirit or disposition in him through which he is then able to save himself (although the sectarian believes that God has given him a new disposition, *e.g.*, as in Ezk. 36:26). It is God, rather, who acts, and He acts through a *ruaḥ* consistently identified as His Spirit on behalf of the sectarian who is repeatedly described as sinful and helpless within himself. Those passages, then, in which the *sectarian* seems to be acting though the power of *ruaḥ*, *e.g.*, in listening to God (1QH12:12) or in strengthening himself by it (16:7), should be read in the light of his frequent confessions of personal weakness, *e.g.*, 1QH 12:32-35. Although the psalmist seems to act rather than God, this does not mean that he is acting in the

---

[28]*Cf.* de Jonge and van der Woude, "Melchizedek," p. 306 n. 2, who note that most scholars believe that משיחו should be corrected to משיחי. *Cf.* also J. T. Milik's comments in "Milkî-resa' dans le anciens écrits juifs et chrétiens," *Journal of Jewish Studies*, XXIII (1972), p. 134.

[29]Note Milik's translation of this expression in D. Barthélemy, J. T. Milik, *et. al.* in *Discoveries in the Judaean Desert*, I: *Qumran Cave I* (Oxford: Clarendon, 1955), 154 as "les Paroles de ton (Esprit) Saint" and his comment in *ibid.*, note 6/7 that this relates to the doctrine of inspiration.

[30]Thus, the psalmist even as a faithful sectarian is near despair in 1QH 9:1-7, but in v. 12 God "establishes"and "founds" the psalmist's spirit and turns his despair into delight (v. 31). In 1QH 16:11 the psalmist acknowledges that apart from God no one can be righteous, and so he pleads with God to complete His work of purifying him (v. 12). Finally, after giving thanks to God for revealing His light to him (1QH 18:1ff.), the psalmist asks God to continue to help him hold to the covenant (18:12), and he confesses that as "dust" (i. e., in his natural, spiritual condition) he is not worthy (18:12ff. & 25ff.) or capable (18:19ff.) of knowing the truth or teaching it to others.

power of his own spirituality. A similar situation can be observed in 1QS 8:16. Syntactically this passage forms a close parallel to those in question (1QH 12:12 and 16:7), but because of its content (*viz.*, the prophets [plural] reveal God's law by His [not their] holy Spirit), it is universally accepted by scholars as referring to the Sprit of God even though it is the prophets rather than the Spirit of God which syntactically does the revealing.[31] The prophets act, but not in the power of an inborn or acquired spirituality under their personal control; the same is true of the sectarian's attempt to lead a God-pleasing life against enemies both within and without.[32] This does not mean, however, that 1QH never traces positive spiritual functions to the new, transformed *ruaḥ* eschatologically given to the sectarian (*e.g.*, 1QH 4:31 & 36) or even to the "natural" *ruaḥ* given to the sectarian in birth (*e.g.*, 1QH 15:13 & 22). We will discuss these passages in chapter 4 below.

4) Finally, we should note that a number of passages cited in paragraph 3 directly above have associations with biblical concepts and vocabulary which further indicate an influence of God's Spirit external to man, *viz.*, God's activity of "shedding" (1QH 7:6/7; 17:26: and f 2:9) or "pouring out" (4Q504, 1-2 V 15)

---

[31]I am not aware of any scholar who sees something other than God's Spirit in 1QS 8:16. Even Schreiner in "Geistbegabung," p. 179, for example, understands this verse as referring to God's Spirit in contrast to the "holy spirit" of man.

[32]*Cf.* Foerster, "Geist," p. 117, who comments on this function of the holy Spirit at this time as follows: "Fragen wir nach dem Heiligen Geist im Späjudentum, so fragen wir nach Gottes Geist in seiner soteriologischen Wirksamkeit. Es ist die einhellige Ansicht des Spätjudentums, daß dieser Heilige Geist in den Männern des Alten Testamentes gewirkt hat und zwar nicht nur in der Niederschrift der biblischen Bücher, sondern auch in ihrem ganzen Tun und Leben, doch wird später die Inspiration mehr auf die Abfassung der heiligen Schriften begrenzt." This pneumatology, then, was already available to the sectarians as they thought of God's holy Spirit as eschatologically present in their group.

His Spirit[33] and of "cleansing" His people as He gives them His Spirit (*cf.* 1QS3:7; 4:21a; & especially 1QH 16:12 with Ezk. 36:27-33); note also the possible link between Is. 61:1 and CD 2:12; 4Q287, 4, 13; 4QDe {270} 2 II 13-14a and 11QMelch 3 II 18 on those "anointed" with the Spirit.[34] The ideas of "cleansing" and especially of "shedding/pouring out" are found in eschatological contexts of the Old Testament;[35] and given the scholarly consensus that the Qumran sectarians viewed themselves in some sense as an eschatological community,[36] they probably

---

[33]*Cf.* n. 27 above for the Old Testament parallels; *cf.* also 1 Enoch 62:2 & 91:1.

[34]For the use of משיח at Qumran and its connection to Is. 61:1, *cf.* M. de Jonge, "The Use of the Word 'Anointed' in the Time of Jesus," *Novum Testamentum*, VIII (1966), pp. 132-148. De Jonge notes that this term can be used for the future high priest as well as for the future Davidic Messiah (*ibid.*, p. 139) and that in addition to referring to the Old Testament prophets (*cf.* 1QM 11:7-8) it can also refer to the prophet who is to come (*ibid.*, pp. 141-2). In relationship to *ruaḥ*, however, משיח denotes a future figure in only one sectarian text (11QMelch 3 II 18), which seems to have been influenced by Is. 61:1 and appears to be describing a prophet who will attend the coming of "Melchizedek" (*ibid.*, p. 142); all the other occurrences of משיח with *ruaḥ* have to do with the Old Testament prophets (CD 2:12; 4QDe {270} 2 II 13-14a; and 4Q287, 4, 13; *cf.* also J. T. Milik, "Milkî-resa," p. 134). This close relationship in the Scrolls between God's holy Spirit and the prophetic use of משיח reflects the general tendency of this time to associate prophecy with the Spirit of God; *cf.* the comments of Joachim Jeremias, *New Testament Theology* (trans. by J. Bowden; New York: Charles Scribner's Sons, 1971), p. 79, who notes that at this time "the synagogue regarded the possession of the holy spirit, *i.e.*, the spirit of God, as *the* mark of prophecy" [emphasis his]. The holy Spirit was not restricted to this function at this time, however; *cf.* n. 32 above.

[35]The eschatological "cleansing" of Ezekiel 36 together with the granting of God's Spirit seems to have had a major impact on sectarian thought and expression; *cf.* below in this chapter. Also, whenever *ruaḥ* is associated with a concept of shedding or pouring out in the Old Testament, the context is always eschatological in nature: *cf.* Is. 32:15; 44:3; Ezk. 39:29; and Joel 3:1-2.

also understood God's Spirit in this context as an eschatological gift of God's power, reaching far beyond their own, natural capabilities.

c. Expressions related to רוח הק{ו}דש: רוח ק{ו}דש{ו or כה/ך} (4QDe {270} 2 II 13-14b and 4Q506, 131-132, 11) and רוח רחמיך (1QH 16:9).

The syntactical characteristic which relates these expressions to the expression analyzed immediately above (section *2b*) is that they have definite genitives in construct with the singular of *ruaḥ*.

The expression רוח הקודש is unusual in the Scrolls. The two passages listed above are the only places in which *ruaḥ* followed by the genitive קודש is defined by the article rather than a suffix. Its occurrence in 4QDe {270} 2 II 13-14b is perhaps the most instructive. It is in apposition to משיחי רוח (which will be treated below in section *2d*), and together with this expression it forms a composite expression analogous to משיחי רוח קודשו in 4Q287, 4, 13 and משיחי רוח קדשו[37] in CD 2:12. It seems clear, then, that רוח הקודש should be understood here as God's own Spirit at work in those "anointed" by it, *i.e.*, the Old Testament prophets (*cf.* Ps. 105:15 and 1 Chron. 16:22). 4Q506, 131-132, 11 also seems to refer to God's Spirit, *e.g.*, in the sense of 4Q504, 1-2 V 15, which both belong to the same work (The Words of the Heavenly Lights); *cf.* n. 38 below. It is doubtful that the speakers here are claiming (in God's presence) to have a disposition of personal holiness since immediately after claiming that they have this kind of a *ruaḥ*, they ask for God's forgiveness not only for the sins of the past but also for those of the present

[36]*Cf.* for example, Vermes, *Perspective*, pp. 182ff. and 197. *Cf.* also S. F. Noll, "Communion of Angels and Men in Realized Eschatology in the Dead Sea Scrolls," *Proceedings of the Eighth World Congress of Jewish Studies*, Division A., 1981 (1982), pp. 91-97, who questions H. W. Kuhn's strongly eschatological interpretation of sectarian theology in *Enderwartung*, but he still notes that the sectarians saw themselves "in the beginning of the 'end of days';" Noll, "Communion," p. 96.

[37]Instead of משיחו; *cf.* n. 28 above.

(as is also the attitude of much of 1QH; *cf.* section *2b2* above). Of special interest here is that these pre-sectarian Hasidim thought of their group as a whole (and not just a few prophets) as having received divine knowledge and the holy Spirit.[38]

The second expression noted above, רוח רחמיך, could perhaps be understood in 1QH 16:9 as a human disposition given to man by God,[39] but the context seems to be more oriented to the external activity of God than to the personal spirituality of the psalmist. Thus, the "favor" (חסד) preceding and paralleling our expression and the "radiance(?) of Your glory" (...ור כבודך) following it both belong to God and do not necessarily imply that the psalmist as the beneficiary of these divine favors has himself become a source of them, as the last half of v. 9 appears to say.[40] God's "Spirit of mercy," then, should probably be understood as describing an external, spiritual power from God which creates within the psalmist a sense of God's love and acceptance of him. It is possible that this expression is synonymous with God's "Spirit of holiness" (as analyzed in section *2b* above), but the limited context of רוח רחמיך makes this difficult to determine. This is the only place in the Scrolls in which רוח in construct with רחמיך occurs. If God's "Spirit of mercy" and "Spirit of holiness" are not completely synonymous, however, the difference may lie in their function: God's Spirit of holiness may be more associated with the communication of divine knowledge (*e.g.*, 1QH 12:12), empowerment (1QH 16:7) and cleansing activity (1QH 16:12) and His Spirit of mercy with a communication of favor to His people (לעשות חסד).

---

[38]*Cf.* Baillet, *Discoveries*, VII, 137, who regards 4Q504 (4Q505 and 4Q506 are copies) as a pre-Essene, Hasidic writing; the viewpoints here are important for understanding sectarian beliefs since the sectarians (whatever their precise identification may be) were the spiritual heirs of the Hasidim and probably thought of themselves in the much the same way.

[39]*Cf.* Licht, *Thanksgiving Scroll*, p. 38.

[40]"To You, You, belongs righteousness, for it is You who have done all these things!"

d. The singular of *ruaḥ* used without qualifying expressions: (found 7 times; see the list of references for these occurrences in section *2a* above).

Two basic observations which show that *ruaḥ* without qualifying expressions can be used to mean the "Spirit of God" are its use in contexts parallel to the pattern analyzed in section *2b* above (identified as God's Spirit), and its association with biblical vocabulary often used with *ruaḥ* as God's Spirit.

1) Parallel contexts. *Ruaḥ* without qualifying expressions in contexts parallel to the patterns analyzed in section *2b* can be found in 1QH 12:11-12 and 4QDe {270} 2 II 13-14 a. In 1QH 12:11-12, the clause containing ברוח is poetically parallel to the following clause containing ברוח קודשכה.[41] In both clauses the psalmist claims spiritual knowledge,[42] and in both the ב preceding their respective expressions of *ruaḥ* can have an instrumental sense indicating the means by which the psalmist has this knowledge. It seems clear, then, that in the first clause as well as in the second, the psalmist is confessing that it is by means of God's Spirit rather than his own that he knows God and His wonderful counsel. The same idea is made explicit at the end of this hymn in vv. 31ff. It is possible, however, that these two clauses are only partially parallel and that ברוח in the first clause refers simply to a spiritual disposition given by God to the psalmist by which he is able to know him. As we have seen, however, the predominant teaching of 1QH portrays the spirit of the sectarian as being in *need* of spiritual qualities such as strength and insight rather than as being the source of them.[43] Finally, we note that 4Q506, 131-132, 10-11

---

[41]For the parallelism here, *cf.* Holm-Nielsen, *Hodayot,* p, 204 n. 38; *cf.* also Menahem Mansoor, *The Thanksgiving Hymns,* Studies on the Texts of Judah, 3 (Leiden: Brill, 1961), 174 and Geza Vermes, *The Dead Sea Scrolls in English* (Baltimore: Penguin Books, 1968), p. 189. Note that the ב before *ruaḥ* does not qualify it but simply relates its to the rest of the members of the sentence.

[42]*Cf.* 1QH 13:18-19 and f 3:14 for additional examples of *ruaḥ* (used without qualifications) as the source of divine knowledge.

[43]*Cf.* nn. 21-24 above.

explicitly attributes spiritual knowledge to the gift of God's holy Spirit, whereas there is in the Scrolls no clear reference in which the sectarian regards his own spirit (whether inborn or acquired in the community) as the source of his divine knowledge.[44]

The second case in which *ruaḥ* can be found in a usage parallel to that of section *2b* above is in 4QDe {270} 2 II 13-14a, משיחי רוח. This verse has already been treated above in section *2c* in connection with רוח הקודש, in which it was noted that this expression is in apposition to משיחי רוח and with it forms a compound expression equivalent to משיחי רוח קודשו found in CD 2:12 and 4Q287, 4, 3. However, if the compound expression in 4QDe {270} 2 II 13-14 as a whole refers to the Spirit of God, what does משיחי רוח mean by itself and why does it require the further definition of רוח הקודש? The best solution appears to be as follows: whenever an unqualified form of *ruaḥ* refers to God's Spirit (as indicated by the context), it is describing this Spirit in its most abstract sense as "divine power."[45] The further definition of it here as רוח הקודש or in 1QH 12: 11-12 as רוח קודשכה specifies the precise nature of this power, *i.e.*, it is God's specific Spirit of holiness (as indicated by the article or pronominal suffix) in contrast, for example, to God's Spirit of mercy (*cf.* 1QH 16:9 and the analysis of this expression in section *2c* above).

---

[44]Note that even 1QH 4:31-32 does not present the sectarian's (new) spirit or disposition as the source of his spiritual knowledge or behavior (*cf.* n. 23 above): it is not the sectarian's spirit that establishes his way, but it is God Himself who does this through the new disposition which he creates for His people so that they may have an understanding of His merciful work on their behalf. But without God's constant support through His Spirit (*cf.* 1QH 7:6ff.& 16:7), the beleaguered sectarian with only the power of his own spirit (however transformed it may be) would soon lose his ability to remain faithful to God and fall into transgression (1QH 4:33-35). The sectarian's new "spirit," of course, is not totally inactive: it responds to God's mercy toward it by "holding on" (החזיקה) to what it has been given (1QH 4:36).

[45]*Cf.* Lys' comments in *Ruaḥ*, p. 130 on a similar use of *ruaḥ* in Ezekiel: "ainse, pour Ezéchiel *ruah* est assez impersonelle: sans article, du genre féminin, elle exprime action puissante plutôt qu' entité."

2) The absolute use of *ruaḥ* in its association with biblical vocabulary. The combination of משיח in construct with *ruaḥ* has already been treated in n. 34 above. In 4QDe {270} 2 II 13-14 this combination in itself (even without the appositive (רוח הקודש) shows that the sectarians could refer to God's Spirit with an unqualified *ruaḥ*: משיח here refers to the Old Testament prophets, and the connection between prophecy and God's Spirit at this time was strong in Jewish thought.[46]

The next most frequent occurrence of the absolute form of *ruaḥ* is in the phrase ברוח אשר נתתה בי , an expression which is limited to the later hymns of 1QH and one of its fragments.[47] It seems to be based primarily upon *ruaḥ* as it is found in Ezk. 36 and 37. Here we read that God will put His "breath" or "spirit"[48] in His people at some future time. What is important for this study is that only in these passages in the Hebrew literature known to have been used in Qumran do we have such a close analogy syntactically and conceptually to the sectarian expression cited above.[49] Ezk. 37:6 promises that God will place (נתן) *ruaḥ* (used without qualifiers) in (ב) His people, and in verse 14 this *ruaḥ* is defined (again with the verb נתן + ב) as *God's ruaḥ*.[50] All of this is immediately preceded by a promise of God's Spirit in 36:27 (using much the same language as in 37:6 & 14), which will transform the *heart* of the people so that they will live in purity. God will also *cleanse* them (36:29a and esp. 33a with טהר), resulting in many blessings, and this in turn will lead the people to *loath* themselves for their sins (36:31). All of this will be done by God in spite of the fact that His people are *unworthy* of it (36:32). The goal and outcome of this

---

[46]*Cf*. n. 34 above.

[47]1QH 12:11; 13:19; 16:11; and f 3:14.

[48]Ezk. 36:27; 37:6 & 14.

[49]2 Kings 19:7 is syntactically similar to our expression but not in terms of its content since it is not in an eschatological context. *Ruaḥ* in this passage probably means an interior disposition of fear or error; *cf*. P. van Imschoot, *Theology of the Old Testament*, I (trans. by K. Sullivan and F. Buck; New York: Desclee, 1965), 184 n. 28.

[50]*Cf*. Lys, *Ruaḥ*, p. 132.

whole eschatological process is clear: "Then they will *know* that I am the LORD" (36:32). The recurrence of these themes and even much of the vocabulary in connection with the sectarian expression in question is striking. Thus, in 1QH 16 the psalmist notes that he desires to serve God with a whole *heart* (*cf.* 16:7 with Ezk. 36:26); he sees that this is the work of God, who alone is righteous and yet still favors man, who in himself is *unworthy* (*cf.* 16:9 & 11 with Ezk. 36:32). The psalmist, therefore, implores God by the Spirit which He has placed in him to *cleanse* him (טהר) and to carry out his favor toward him (*cf.* 16: 11-12 with Ezk. 36:33ff.). In other contexts the psalmist affirms that he *knows* God and His work by the Spirit which God has put in him (*cf.* 1QH 12:11 and 13:18-19 with Ezk. 36:38). Closely associated with this knowledge are statements in which the psalmist expresses an almost pathological *loathing* for his sinful condition (*cf.* 1QH 12:24-28 and 13:15-16 with Ezk. 36:31). If these observations are valid, the "pathological abhorrence of human nature" noticed by Licht in 1QH (*cf.* n. 18 above) may be more the result of rhetorical or theological reflection based on Ezk. 36:31 than on actual feelings of this nature within the sectarians' psychological make-up. This becomes even more probable if the sectarians saw themselves as the eschatological heirs of Ezekiel's promise of the Spirit in Ezk. 36:27.

It seems, then, that the psalmist(s) patterned his expression of *ruaḥ* syntactically after Ezk. 37:6, but the meaning he gave to it is most closely related to Ezk. 36:27 & 37:14; it is possible that he simply equated its three uses in 36:27 and 37:6 & 14.[51] Why the psalmist did not use a suffix on *ruaḥ* (as in in Ezk. 36:27) is difficult to determine with certainty, but in doing so he was apparently following the idiom of the sect: *ruaḥ* (as "spirit") with a suffix referring to God is not found in the non-biblical, Hebrew Scrolls (but *cf.* 4Q185, 1-2 I 10 with *ruaḥ* as

[51]*Cf.* K. Elliger and W. Rudolph, eds., *Biblia Hebraica Stuttgartensia* (Stuttgart: Deutsche Bibelstiftung, 1977) on Ezk. 37:6 *in loco*, in which it is noted that the LXX reads "my spirit" in this place instead of simply "spirit."

"wind"). It is also interesting to note that the unqualified use of *ruaḥ* in referring to God's Spirit is twice as frequent in Ezekiel as in all the other Old Testament sources combined;[52] if the sectarians did view themselves as the recipients of Ezekiel's eschatological promise of the Spirit, this may help to explain their tendency to imitate his preference for this unqualified usage.

Finally, a preference for the unqualified use of *ruaḥ* in referring to God's Spirit may explain the difficult and unique form סודי רוח in 1QS 4:6. A number of scholars have seen here a reference to the good spirit of the two spirits (*cf.* 1QS 3:18-19)[53] and some have even thought that אמת has fallen out after *ruaḥ* (although they offer no textual evidence to support this).[54] This thinking is based in part on the idea that the pneumatology of the two spirits of 1QS 3:18ff. is basic to the thinking of the sect against which other expressions of *ruaḥ* should be understood. *Ruaḥ* in 1QS 4:6, however, is probably part of the traditional pneumatology of the sect (which knows nothing of the two spirits of 1QS 3:18ff.)[55] and should be interpreted in the light of its unqualified use as seen especially in 1QH. סודי רוח, then, should probably be translated as "Spirit-led counsels," *i.e.*, standards for holy living inspired by the eschatological Spirit of God already at work in the sectarian community, although it is clear that the author(s) of 1QS 3:13-4:26 wanted

---

[52]In Ezekiel: 2:2; 3:12, 14, & 24; 8:3; 11:1 & 24; and 43:5; outside of Ezekiel: Num. 27:18; Is. 32:15; (57:16?); and 1 Chron. 12:19. 2 Kings 19:7 (with its parallel passage in Is. 37:7) probably refers to an interior disposition (*cf.* n. 49 above).

[53]*E.g.*, Dupont-Sommer, "instruction," p. 25; Flusser, "Sect," p. 249; Foester, "Geist," p. 129; Irwin, "Spirit-Conflict," p. 191 (possibly); J. Hemple, "Christentum vor Christus? Die Handschriftenfunde vom Toten Meer und das Neue Testament," *Deutsches Pfarrerblatt*, 51 (1951), p. 484; Lichtenberger, *Studien*, p. 133 n. 43; and Ringgren, *Faith*, p. 70.

[54]*E.g.*, Dupont-Sommer, "instruction," p. 25 and Lichtenberger, *Studien*, p. 133 n. 43.

[55]*Cf.* the discussion of this passage in the conclusion of chapter 8 below.

to reinterpret this traditional understanding in the light of the new, two-spirit pneumatology of the Treatise (*cf.* the conclusion to chapter 8 below).

1QH 16:6 seems to be too fragmentary for meaningful analysis; its use of בקש with *ruaḥ* as its object is unique. It is categorized here with "God's Spirit" since it seems less likely that the psalmist would be "seeking" an angel or the spirit of man.

e. The syntactically indefinite form רוח קודש: (found 5 times; 1QS 4:21a, *cf.* chapter 8 below; 9:3; 1QSb 2:24; 4Q171, 3-10 IV 25; and 4Q504, 4, 5).

Most of the occurrences of this expression are somewhat more difficult to define contextually than those treated up to this point. Exceptions to this are 1QS 4:21a (*cf.* chapter 8 below) and 4Q504, 4, 5, in which the eschatological context shows *ruaḥ* to be a reference to God's Spirit.[56] Additional evidence for *ruaḥ* in 4Q504, 4, 5 as God's Spirit is its parallel fragment, 4Q506, 131-132, 11, which reads רוח הקודש in place of רוח קודש (*cf.* the analysis of *ruaḥ* in 4Q506, 131-132, 11 as the "Spirit of God" in section 2*c* above), but the other three occurrences of this expression are contextually more ambiguous and can be understood as either man's spirit[57] or the Spirit of God.[58] Nevertheless,

---

[56]*Cf.* n. 27 above. The author of 4Q504-506 ("Words of the Heavenly Lights") views his Hasidean community as the eschatological people, heirs of the promise of Is. 44:3. For the strange form חנואתנו, *cf.* Baillet, *Discoveries VII*, p. 155 n. 5, who believes that it is from the root חנן with the א serving as a *mater lexionis*.

[57]*E.g.*, for 1QS 9:3 and 1QSb 2:24 as man's spirit, *cf.* Burrows, *More Light*, p. 295 and Licht, *Thanksgiving Scroll*, p. 38; for 1QS 9:3 as man's spirit, *cf.* Coppens, "Documents," p. 36 n. 46; Driver, *Scrolls*, pp. 258-9; Hill, *Greek Words*, p. 241; J. Maier, *Texte*, vol. II, p. 206; Nötscher, "Geist," p. 307; and Schreiner, "Geistbegabung," pp. 174 & 180.

[58]Very few scholars have commented on the meaning of רוח קודש in 4Q171 IV 25 or 4Q504, 4, 5; for the latter, *cf.* T. H. Gaster, *The Dead Sea Scriptures* (3rd. ed.; Garden City: Anchor Press, 1975), p. 331, who translates this occurrence as "the Holy Spirit." However, the majority of scholars who have commented on *ruaḥ* in either (a) 1QS 9:3 or (b)1QSb 2:24 (or both) have understood it as God's Spirit: *cf.* Beaven,

רוח קודש in these contexts also is perhaps best understood as God's Spirit since this would be compatable with its meaning in the two clearer contexts of 1QS 4:21a and 4Q504, 4, 5 and there is no evidence in the contexts of 1QS 9:3, 1QSb 2:24 and 4Q171, 3-10 IV 2 to suggest that it means anything else. Thus, it is easy to understand 1QS 9:3 not only as the community's claim of being a "spiritually holy foundation" but also as a claim of being a spiritual foundation conducive to the presence of God's holy Spirit,[59] now eschatologically at work among God's people. Likewise, the blessing directed to the High Priest in 1QSb 2:24 can be understood not only as a request that God would grace him with a holy dispositon but also with the holy, spiritual power which makes such a disposition possible.[60] The same kind of spiritual power conducive to special leadership in the sect is probably also the meaning of [רו]ח קודש in 4Q171, 3-10 IV 5 since it is found in a context which alludes to the Teacher of Righteousness, who was probably considered to have been especially inspired by God's holy Spirit in his teaching and leadership capacity.[61]

f. Three unrelated and unique cases referring to God's Spirit: רוח דעה, 1QH 14:25; משיח הרוח, 11QMelch 3 II 18; and רוח קדושה, 1QS 3:7.

"Ruah," p. 102 (a only); Betz, *Offenbarung*, p. 120 (a only); Böcher, *Dualismus*, p. 38 (a only); Bruce, "Holy Spirit," p. 55 (a only); Carmignac and Guilbert, *Textes*, p. 155 n. 9 (a only); Carmignac, Cothenet and Lignée, *Textes*, p. 37 n. 20 (a & b); Delcor, "Doctrines," col. 972 (a & b); Irwin, "Spirit-Dualism," pp. 73 & 192 (b only); Johnston, "Spirit," p. 38 (a only); J. Maier, *Texte*, vol. II, 206 (b only); Manns, *symbole*, p. 80 (a only); Montague, *Holy Spirit*, p. 121 (a only); Nötscher, "Heiligkeit im Qumranschriften," *Revue de Qumrân*, 2 (1959/60), 339 (b only); and Ringgren, *Faith*, p. 89 (a only).

[59]So most scholars; *cf.* n. 58 above.

[60]*Ibid.*

[61]*Cf.* Foerster, "Geist," pp. 123-5; *cf.* also Schreiner, "Geistbegabung," p. 179, who recognizes this in his discussion of 1QH 7:6/7; so also most scholars: see n. 8 above.

The meaning of the expression רוח דעה is difficult to determine. It is possible that it is equivalent to רוח דעת in 1QS 4:4, 1QSb 5:25 and 6Q18, 5, 3, which probably refers to the spirit of man (*cf.* the analysis of this expression in chapter 4 above). But דעה, although it has the same basic meaning as דעת, still has a different form, and together with its associated syntax (*viz.*, ב + חנן), its form may have functioned as a semantic marker indicating its meaning as "God's Spirit." The broken context of 1QH 14:25 makes it difficult to say much more than this. Our position, then, that רוח דעה refers to the Spirit of God is based primarily on the similarity of its syntax with *ruaḥ* in 1QH 16:9 and 1QSb 2:24 (*i.e.*, as an object of the preposition ב following the verb חנן), both of which were interpreted in section *2e* above as referring to the Spirit of God.

The expression משיח הרוח in 11 QMelch 3 II 18 is the only time in the Scrolls in which *ruaḥ* as God's Spirit has the article. But even in this case the article on *ruaḥ* probably has no more significance for its meaning than the article on the genitive following *ruaḥ* in the expression רוח הקודש in 4Q506, 131-132, 11 and 4QDe {270} 2 II 13-14b (*cf.* section *2c* and *2d{1}* above). In the case of all three examples the article defines the whole construct phrase rather than just a part of it. The meaning of the article on *ruaḥ* in the context of 11QMelch 3 II 18, then, is not that the משיח will have *the* Spirit (*e.g.*, as if this were a personal being in contrast to an impersonal, divine power)[62] but rather that the "herald" (המבשר) of Isaiah (in 52:7) is that particular person anointed by the Spirit as promised by the prophet Daniel (in 9:27). We should note, finally, that the meaning of *ruaḥ* in this expression as "God's Spirit" is strongly indicated by its *nomen regens*, משיח.[63]

The final expression to be considered under the category of "God's Spirit" is רוח קדושה in 1QS 3:7. It appears to belong to this category for the following reasons: 1) the use of the root קדש to describe the spirit of man (or even the sectarian's spirit) is unusual, and when קדש is used for this purpose (e.g, in CD 5:11

---

[62]*Cf.* Lys' view of the article on *ruaḥ* in chapter 1, pp. 2-3 above.
[63]*Cf.* n. 34 above.

and 7:4), its syntactical markers, unlike our expression, clearly refer to man; 2) a copy of 1QS from Cave 4 (*viz.*, 4QSa) reads רוח קודשו rather than רוח קדושה;[64] this may indicate that these expressions were synonymous for the sectarians (*cf.* section *2b* above for the meaning of רוח קודשו as God's Spirit); and finally, 3) the work of רוח קדושה in 1QS 3:7 is to purify (טהר) God's people, and whenever טהר is used to describe the moral purification of man, God rather than man is the principle agent of this in the Scrolls.[65]

3. Conclusion.

For an analysis of this chapter and a comparison of its results with the results of chapters 4 - 6 (*ruaḥ* as man's spirit {ch. 4}, angel/demon {ch. 5}, and wind & breath {ch. 6}), see chapter 7 below.

---

[64]*Cf.* J. T. Milik's review of P. Wernberg-Møller, *The Manual of Discipline* in *Revue Biblique,* 67 (1960), p. 413, note on col. III, line 7.

[65]*Cf.* Manns in *symbole,* p. 83, who points out this pattern but only as it applies specifically to the Spirit of God in the context of 1QH 3:7 as the agent of purification. However, an inner *moral* cleansing, *e.g.*, from "iniquity" (עוון), seems in every case to be a result of God's activity throughout the Scrolls. 1QS 3:8-9 (*cf.* טהר in v. 8) should offer no difficulty if the ב is understood as indicating manner or circumstance rather than means (*cf.* Lohse, *Texte,* p. 11, who translates בענות נפשו as "wenn er sine Seele demütigt. . . ."), and other passages such as 1QM 7:2, CD 10:12, 4Q512 XII 1-15, 4Q514 1 I 1-10 and Temple Scroll 45:5, 47:14 & 49:14 which describe *man* as accomplishing a purification of one kind or another are concerned essentially with *ritual* purification. Note, finally, that טהר in 11QPsa Zion XXII, 11, 7 with "Zion" as its subject does not refer to the cleansing of individual people but of the city as a whole and that, in any case, this psalm together with the rest of the psalms in 11QPsa was probably not composed by the sectarians; *cf.* J. A. Sanders, *Discoveries in the Judaean Desert of Jordan,* IV: *The Psalm Scroll of Qumran Cave 11,* (Oxford: Clarendon Press, 1965), pp. 75-6.

CHAPTER 4

RUAḤ AS MAN'S SPIRIT

1. The basic semantic range of *ruaḥ* as man's spirit.

With the exception of 1QS 3:13-4:26, 1QH 15 and 4Q186, the basic semantic range for *ruaḥ* as man's spirit in the non-biblical, Hebrew Scrolls seems for the most part to reflect biblical categories[1] but with a more negative emphasis[2] and with a tendency to describe man as not only having a spirit but also as *being* one.[3] This tendency to stay within biblical categories means that there is no clear use of *ruaḥ* in any of the nonbiblical, Hebrew Scrolls to mean a disembodied specter or an aspect of human personality which survives death.[4] There also seems to be

---

[1]*Cf.* F. Brown, S. R. Driver and C. A. Briggs, *A Hebrew and English Lexicon* (Oxford: Clarendon Press, 1979), p. 925, who list six basic categories for the human spirit; *cf.* sections 3 - 8: 1) disposition, 2) spirit of life, 3) seat of emotion, 4) seat of the mind, 5) designation of the will, and 6) designation of the moral character. For corresponding examples in the Scrolls, *cf.* 1) Proverbs 15:13 with 1QM 11:10; 2) Zech. 12:1 with 1QH 1:15; 3) Job 7:11 with 1QS 10:18-19; 4) Isaiah 29:24 with 1QS 11:1a; 5) Ps 51: 12 with 1QH 9:2; and 6) Ps. 51:19 with 1QS 11:1c.

[2]This is largely because of the sectarians' view of human nature as found especially in 1QH; *cf.* chapter 3, section *2b2* above.

[3]*Cf.* 1QH 1:22; 2:15; 3:21; 7:11; 9:16; 13:13; 4Q510, 1, 6; and 4Q511, 10, 2.

[4]*Cf.* R. B. Laurin, "The Question of Immortality in the Qumran Hodayot," *Journal of Semitic Studies*, 3 (1958), 344-355 for a discussion of this issue. For a viewpoint which supports the hope of immortality in the Scrolls, *cf.* J. van der Ploeg, "The Belief in Immortality in the Writings of Qumran," *Bibliotheca Orientalis*, 18 (1961), pp. 118-124. Van der Ploeg is probably correct in his view that the sectarians had a hope of immortality, but as he himself notes, it is not at all clear from the Scrolls "how individual immortality is to be realized," *ibid.*, p 123. I

no clear use of *ruaḥ* (with the exception of 1QS 3:13-4:26, 1QH 15 and 4Q186) as a good or evil predestined "being" or "self" given to man at birth which unchangeably determines his spirituality, *i.e.*, his ability (or lack of it) to keep God's law properly. The predominantly negative view of the natural, spiritual condition of both sectarian and non-sectarian (as reflected especially in 1QH) has apparently discouraged much of this type of thinking.[5] The sectarian, of course, is often described as having a spiritually positive *ruaḥ* in the Scrolls but, as we have seen (chapter 3), many of these uses of *ruaḥ* should be understood as referring to God's Spirit, whereas other uses to be investigated below in this chapter probably refer to the spiritual dispositions, qualities and gifts which come to the sectarian as a member of Qumran's eschatological community (*cf.* Ezk. 36:26). Outside of 1QH 4:31 & 36 and 17:17, however, the Scrolls seem to have very little to say about this view of *ruaḥ*, probably because of the tendency of the writers (especially in 1QH) to place the sectarian in a position of humility before the majesty and righteousness of God.[6] Such a conception of *ruaḥ* may, on the other hand, be implicit in many of the references to man's spirit in 1QS which involve practical considerations of membership and rank in the community. The Qumran leaders could not see the invisible presence of God's eschatological Spirit in their members or in a prospective candidate, but they could see and evaluate the *effects* of this Spirit in the new "spirit" or disposition given to God's elect in the last days (*cf.* Ezk. 36:26) in greater or lesser degrees.

It is possible, of course, to interpret the anthropological use of *ruaḥ* in 1QS and the rest of the Scrolls against the back-

---

am aware of only one scholar who sees a *clear* use of *ruaḥ* to mean an entity which survives death (*viz.*, J. Carmignac, *La Règle de la Guerre* (Paris, 1958), p. 18 on 1QM 12:9 and 13:10), but no one seems to have followed him on this in so far as his suggestions involve the word *ruaḥ*. For an assessment of Carmignac's position, *cf.* J. van der Ploeg's review of Carmignac's *La Règle de la Guerre* in *Revue de Qumrân*, 2 (1958), 300.

[5]*Cf.* chapter 3, section *2b2* above.

[6]*Cf.* chapter 3, n. 23 above.

ground of 1QS 3:13-4:26, 1QH 15 and 4Q186 in which case a number of occurrences of *ruaḥ* beyond the confines of these three passages will be seen as reflecting the post-biblical ideas of the two-spirit theology of 1Q3 3:13-4:26 with its concept of man's spirit as a predestined, good or evil "self" given to him at birth.[7] There are good reasons, however, not to assume such a

---

[7]H. W. Kuhn, *Enderwartung*, pp. 120-136, believes that *ruaḥ* as man's predestined being given to him at birth is present also in 1QS 2:20; 5:21; 6:17; 9:14, 15, & 18 (all in *ibid.*, p. 122 n. 3); 1QH 1:9 (*ibid.*, pp. 125-6); 4:31 (*ibid.*, p. 126); 14:11 (*ibid.*, p. 132); 15:13-14 (*ibid.*, pp. 124-6); 15:22 (*ibid.*, pp. 123-5); and 16:10 (*ibid.*, p. 134). We should note that Kuhn along with most scholars regards the two spirits of 1QS 3:18ff. as cosmic angels (*cf. ibid.*, pp. 121-2) and that he relates these two spirits to *ruaḥ* as man's predestined being "*religionsgeschlichtlich*," *i.e.*, on the basis of their common historical origin in Iranian thought and their shared views on predestination (*ibid.*, p. 122). Osten-Sacken, on the other hand, denies this relationship (he also views the two-spirits as cosmic angels; *cf.* Osten-Sacken, *Gott und Belial*, p. 141) and seeks to find the conceptual origins of *ruaḥ* as man's predestined being in the Old Testament alone (*cf. ibid.*, pp. 136-7) while at the same time disagreeing with Kuhn on the extent of this concept of *ruaḥ* in the Scrolls. In 1QH, at least, he would limit its presence to 15:13 & 22 (*cf. ibid.*, p. 137 n. 11; *cf.* also Osten-Sacken's view of 4:31 in *ibid.*, p. 133). It appears that both scholars have valid points. Osten-Sacken seems to be correct in reading most of the occurrences of *ruaḥ* in the Scrolls against an Old Testament background as opposed to the background of 1QS 3-4, and he also seems to be correct in recognizing *ruaḥ* as the predestined being of man in 1QH only in 15:13 & 22. Kuhn, however, seems to be correct in seeing a strong connection between 1QS 3-4 and 1QH 15. This connection, in fact, is stronger than Kuhn supposes since not only does *ruaḥ* mean the predestined being of man in 1QH 15;13 & 22, but it also has the same meaning in 1QS 3:18ff. The two spirits, in fact, are not personal, cosmic entities at all but rather two predestined, religious dispositions of good and evil given to man at birth to varying degrees (*cf.* chapter 8 below). The only essential difference between 1QH 15:13 & 22 and 1QS 3:18ff. is that the latter has abstracted (perhaps under indirect Persian influence) the various types of religious dispositions found in men into two basic "spirits" which men then inherit in various degrees. The basic idea which 1QS 3-4, 1QH 15 and 4Q186 share, however (*i.e.*, that men are given at birth

back-ground uncritically,[8] and this is especially true in those instances in which such an understanding of *ruaḥ* is not indicated by the context itself and may even produce tensions with conceptual elements already present. Thus, 4Q186[9] can be under-

---

a basically good or evil religious disposition which unchangeably determines their future conduct), seems to be essentially foreign to Old Testament thought; in this case Kuhn is probably more correct than Osten-Sacken in tracing its origins to foreign (Persian) sources.

[8]Most of Kuhn's evidence for *ruaḥ* as man's predestined being in *Enderwartung* is based on an analysis of vocabulary patterns rather than context. Thus, expressions such as לכול מיני רוחותם and לפי רוחו found in 1QS 3:14 and 4:26 within the two-spirit Treatise indicate that similar expressions outside of it (*e.g.*, in 1QS 2:20, 9:14, *etc.*) should have the same meaning, *viz.*, man's predestined being (*cf. ibid.*, p. 122 n. 3). Likewise, פעולה (found in 1QS 3:16; 4:15 & 25) indicates by its presence in 1QH 1:9 and 14:12 that *ruaḥ* in these passages should be understood against the background of 1QS 3-4; other key vocabulary items used for this purpose are כון and יצר (*cf. ibid.*, p. 126). There are two problems with this approach, however. One is that Kuhn assumes too easily that the relatively few vocabulary items which 1QS 3:13-4:26 and various passages share (in the case of 1QH 4:31, only one item: יצר) should be read in the light of 1QS 3:13-4:26 as if this were a dominant conceptual touchstone for the sect; but even within 1QS itself, it is not clear that 1QS 3:13-4:26 had a basic linguistic or conceptual influence within it. Murphy-O'Connor in "Règle," pp. 537ff., for example,would place 1QS 1-4 as the last major element in the redaction of 1QS; and if the thesis of Osten-Sacken in *Gott und Belial* is correct, the two spirit dualism of 1QS would be late in the literary history of the sect and could not be used uncritially as a conceptual background against which to understand other sectarian compositions. A second problem is that Kuhn at times does not give full weight to the specific context which he is interpreting. Thus, for example, the psalmist in 1QH 4:31 appears to be contradicting himself in Kuhn's exegesis when he first identifies himself in vv. 29-30 with the rest of humanity as profoundly sinful by nature and then describes himself in vv. 31-32 as being *born* with a spirit capable of attaining perfection. Kuhn himself notes a similar tension in his interpretation of 1QH 14:11f. and 16:8-12 (*ibid.*, p. 132).

[9]*Cf.* John M. Allegro, "An Astrological Cryptic Document from Qumran," *Journal of Semitic Studies*, 9 (1964), pp. 291-4.

stood as an interpretation of 1QS 3-4 of how various mixtures of light and darkness are apportioned to men at birth, but this view of man is in tension with the rest of 1QS which envisions a yearly evaluation of the *changing* spiritual status of the sectarian.[10] The same is true for 1QS 3-4 and 1QH 15: if a man is born with a specific quality of "spirit" from which his works *necessarily* flow,[11] a yearly evaluation of either his spirit or works would seem to be unnecessary.

2. Basic syntactical characteristics of *ruaḥ* as man's spirit.

Ruaḥ is found 97 times in the published, non-biblical literature of the Scrolls as the spirit of man, including 4 cases in which it is implied (1QS 4:15 & 16; 4:25 & 26) and 6 cases in which it is reconstructed (1QH 5:28 and 1QSb 5:25a) or partially reconstructed (1QH f 12:6; 31:1 and 4Q266, 1 XVII 12). It is found as a singular 86 times, 6 times of which it serves as a collective (*e.g.*, רוחם "their spirits"); 7 times it is found as רוחות but never in a masculine plural form, *i.e.*, any form involving רוחים.[12]

Perhaps the most important characteristic of *ruaḥ* as man's spirit, however, is its consistently feminine gender. The evidence for this is quite strong. Thus, for example, *ruaḥ* in 1QS 2:14 is the subject of the feminine verb נספחה and is modified by the feminine adjective צמאה; in 1QS 7:18 & 23, 1QH 4:36, 9:16 and 13:15 it is the subject of the feminine verbs תזוע, שבה, החזיקה, תגבר and משלה (respectively); in 1QS 8:3 & 12, 11:1c and 1QH 1:22 it is modified by the feminine participial adjectives נשברה, נסוגה and נבעתה; in 1QH 15:22 the feminine suffix on פעולתה refers to it, and in 4Q186 1 II 7 and 4Q186 1 III 5 it is modified by the feminine numbers שש, שלש and אחת. The evidence that *ruaḥ* as man's spirit can be construed as masculine, on the other hand, is

---

[10]*Cf.* for example, 1QS 5:23-24.

[11]*Cf.* this description of 1QS 3-4 in H. W. Kuhn, *Enderwartung*, pp. 121-2.

[12]For a detailed listing of these 93 forms (excluding the 4 implied forms), *cf.* section *3a* of this chapter below.

not strong. There are only three cases in which this is possible (1QH 8:29; 15:13 and 16:10) and in only one of them (1QH 8:29) is this probable. In 1QH 15:13 it is possible that the masculine suffix on בראתו refers to *ruaḥ*, but it is more probable that it refers to the *nomen regens* יצר, especially in view of the feminine suffixal reference to *ruaḥ* on פעולתה only a few verses later (v. 22). In 1QH 16:10 it is possible that צדיק should be taken as an adjective modifying *ruaḥ*,[13] but it is equally possible that צדיק should be understood as a genitive in construct with *ruaḥ* as "the spirit of the righteous."[14] And even in 1QH 8:29, in which *ruaḥ* seems to be the subject of the masculine verb יחפש, there are alternative possibilities. Mansoor suggests, for example, that this verb can be understood either in terms of במתים חפשי in Ps. 88:6 and translated as "set adrift" or related to the Aramaic root חפש with the meaning "to deliver."[15] In both cases God would be the subject of the verb with *ruaḥ* as the object and its gender would not be an issue. If this verb is understood in terms of Ps. 77:7, however, the poet's *ruaḥ* is probably its subject

---

[13]*E.g.*, Mansoor, *Hymns*, p. 186.

[14]So apparently most scholars: *cf.* Hans Bardtke, *Die Handschriftenfunde am Toten Meer* (2nd. ed.; Berlin: Evangelische Haupt-Bibelgesellschaft, 1961), p. 256; Carmignac and Guilbert, *Textes*, p. 164; Dupont-Sommer, *écrits*, p. 261; Holm-Nielsen, *Hodayot*, p. 236; Lohse, *Texte*, p. 169; J. Maier, *Texte*, vol. I, p. 113; and Vermes, *Scrolls in English*, p. 196. From the syntactical indications it would seem best to regard צדיק as a genitive substantive in construct with *ruaḥ* by analogy, *e.g.*, with רוח כושלים in 1QH 8:36. The genitive relationship with *ruaḥ* is the most common pattern in the Scrolls for describing man's spirit (39 times, *cf.* section *3a* below), whereas an adjectival modifier is less common (8 times, *cf.* section *3d* below) and unlike צדיק, it is always participial in form. There are only three other cases of a non-participial, adjectival modifier following *ruaḥ* in the published, non-bibical Hebrew Scrolls, but they do not refer to man's spirit and they all involve special circumstances: see רוח קודושה (1QS 3:7) in chapter 3 above (changed to רוח קודשו in 4QSa), and רוח רעה (4Q511, 15, 7 and 4Q511, 81, 3) in chapter 5 below (apparently in imitation of Jgs. 9:23 and 1 Sam. 16:14).

[15]*Cf.* Mansoor, *Hymns*, p. 156 n. 14.

(whatever it may mean),[16] but this may still not be conclusive evidence of actual sectarian expression. It is possible that the sectarian psalmist was simply imitating the biblical author of Ps. 77:7 syntactically as he sought to imitate him conceptually in his feelings of despair over God's lack of help and concern for him.[17] This possibility is strengthened in the light of the fact that the phrase יחפש/ש רוחי occurs only in Ps. 77:7 in the Old Testament and only in 1QH 8:29 in the Scrolls published so far.[18]

3. Specific syntactical patterns of *ruaḥ* as man's spirit.

a. General overview.

The most frequent and descriptive means of referring to man's spirit in the Scrolls is with *ruaḥ* (usually in the singular) in construct with one or more genitives; occasionally, the first genitive serves as the *nomen regens* of the second and in two cases *ruaḥ* is both a genitive and a *nomen regens* (39 times): רוח

[16]*Cf.* Gert Jeremias, *Der Lehrer der Gerechtigkeit*, Studien zur Umwelt des Neuen Testaments, 2 (Göttingen: Vandenhoeck & Rupricht, 1963), p. 251 n. 1, who suggests that this verb should be translated "*ängstlich sein/sich ängstigen*" on the basis of its relationship to the word חפז. Other suggestions are "sink low/conceal oneself" (Holm-Nielsen, *Hodayot*, p. 157 n. 61), "imprisoned/shut up" (Vermes, *Scrolls in English*, pp. 178 & 185), "*sucht*" [with *ruaḥ* as the object] (J. Maier, *Texte*, vol. I, p. 96), and "*était en quête*" [with *ruaḥ* as the subject] (Dupont-Sommer, *écrits*, p. 244).

[17]The connection between 1QH 8:28/29 (with עם מתים) and Ps 88:6 (with במתים) is clear, but the connection between 1QH 8:29 and Ps. 77:7 seems to be especially strong. Thus, in Ps. 77:4 the psalmist complains that his spirit is faint (תתעטף רוחי) and in v. 5 that God has deprived him of sleep (אחזת שמרות עיני); likewise, the sectarian in 1QH 8:29 complains that his soul is faint (תתעטף נפשי) and in v. 30 that he has no rest (לאין מנוח). Note also that the content of 1QH 8:26-35 and 8:35-40 can be understood as extended reflections by the sectarian on נפעמתי and לא אדבר, respectively, of Ps. 77:5.

[18]In 1QH 8:29 the author was probably weaving together the language of Ps. 77:7 and 88:6; *cf.* Mansoor, *Hymns*, p. 28, who notes that "in numerous places the text sounds virtually like a mosaic of Biblical phrases and quotations."

אדם (1QH 1:15), רוח אמונה ודעת (11QPsa Plea 19:14), רוח אמת (1QS 4:21b and 4Q177, 12-13 I 5), רוח אנוש (1QH 1:32), רוח בינה (4Q510, 1, 6 and 4Q511, 10, 2), רוח בשר (1QH 13:13 and 17:25), רוח דעת (1QS 4:4; 1QSb 5:25b; and 6Q18, 5, 3), רוח הוות (1QH 7:11), רוח הסתר (1QS 9:22), רוח זידות (1Q29, 14:1), רוח זנות (1QS 4:10, רוח יושר וענוה (1QH 3:8), רוח כול חי (4Q504, 6, 22), רוח כושלים (1QH 8:36), רוח נדה (1QS 4:22), רוח עולה (1QS 4:9, and 4:20 with the *nomen regens* כול), רוח עורף ק[שה] (1QH f 12:4), רוח ענוה (1QS 4:3), [רוח ע]צה (1QSb 5:25a), רוח עצת אמת (1QS 3:6), רוח צדיק (1QH 16:10), רוח קנאה (1QH 2:15), רוח רשע {קנאת} (1QS 5:26),[19] רוח רשעה (1QS 10:18/19); included here are also 5 cases of a genitive with a suffix: רוח בינתי (4Q511, 18, II 6), רוח עבדך (1QH 10:22 {reconstructed}, and 16:14), רוח קדשיהם (CD 5:11) and רוח קדשיו (CD 7:4); two cases of a genitive with the article: ר[ו]ח החיים (4Q266 Da 1 XVII 12) and רוח התועה (1QH 1:22); one case of *ruaḥ* in the plural in construct with indefinite genitives: רוחות אור וחשך (1QS 3:25); and another case with genitives having the article: רוחות האמת והעול (1QS 3:18-19).

The next most frequent means of referring to man's spirit is with a suffix on *ruaḥ* referring to man (24 times): רוחו (1QS 2:14; 4:26b; 6:17; 7:18 & 23; 9:15 & 18; 1QH f 31:1; CD 3:3; 20:24; and 4Q184, 4, 4) and רוחי (1QH 4:36; 8:29; 9:12a & 12b); there are various forms of the 3rd. m. pl. suffix: רוחם (1QS 5:24; 1QH f 6:4; 11:4; and CD 3:7), רוחום (1QS 5:21 and 9:14)[20] and רוחמה (5Q13, 2,

---

[19]There is a possibility that רשע here should be understood as an adjective (רָשָׁע) rather than a noun (רֶשַׁע), thus indicating the gender of *ruaḥ* as masculine. The use of רשע (*cf.* also רשעה in 1QS 10:18-19) as a noun in 1QS 5:26 is the most probable, however, since every case in which a form of רשע in association with a form of *ruaḥ* can be evaluated, it always turns out to be a noun; *cf.* 1QH f 5:4 רוחות רשעה, 1QM 15:14 כול רוחי רש[עה], and 4Q511, 1, 6 רוחי רשע.

[20] = רוחם; *cf.*, Lohse, *Texte*, p. 18 note e, and p. 34 note e. For the interchange of םָ and ום with other words, *cf.* 1QS 1:21 (גבורתום) and 1QH 11:27 (עולום).

9);[21] finally, there are two cases of *ruaḥ* in the plural with the 3rd. m. pl. suffix: רוחותם (1QS 2:20 and 3:14).

The next most frequent use of *ruaḥ* is in the singular without qualifying expressions (19 times): it is found by itself[22] (1QH 5:28 {reconstructed}; 5:36; 9:16a; 15:22; 4Q186 1 II 7; 4Q186 1 III 5; and 4Q186 2 I 6), as the object of a preposition (ב in 1QH 4:31 and מ in 9:16b) and as a genitive (נכאי רוח in 1QH 18:15 and 1QM 11:10; עניי רוח in 1QH 14:3 and 1QM 14:7; רמי רוח in 1QS 11:1b; תועי רוח in 1QS 11:1a and 4Q183 1 II 6; and תמימי רוח in 1QM 7:5); finally, there are two cases of *ruaḥ* in the plural (רוחות) following the propositions לפי in 1QH 14:11 and מ in 1QH 17:17.

Next in frequency is the use of *ruaḥ* in the singular followed by one one or more participial adjectives (8 times): רוח נבונה ואורה (11QPsa DavComp 27: II 4), רוח נסוגה (1QS 8:12 as the genitive of יראת), רוח נעוה (1QH 3:21; 11:12; 13:15; and f 12:6) and רוח נשברה (1QS 8:3 and 11:1c).[23]

---

[21] = רוחם as an alternative paradigm; *cf.* M. H. Goshen-Gottstein, "Linguistic Structure and Tradition in the Qumran Documents," *Scripta Hierosolymitana,* IV (1958), pp. 118-119.

[22] Occasionally a *waw* precedes *ruaḥ,* but this does not affect is meaning.

[23] For an alternative view of the syntax of רוח נבונה ואורה and רוח נעוה, *cf.* Baillet, *Discoveries,* VII, pp. 222 and 231-2, respectively. Concerning רוח נבונה ואורה, Baillet differs with Sanders' view in J. A. Sanders, *Discoveries in the Judaean Desert of Jordan,* IV: *The Psalms Scroll of Qumran Cave 11* (Oxford: Clarendon Press, 1965), p. 92 that אורה and נבונה should be read as participles and prefers, instead, to understand them as nouns. It seems that either view is possible, but if Baillet is correct, this would not essentially effect the analysis of this expression in section *3e* of this chapter below. As for נעוה, Baillet suggests that the usual understanding of it as a participle is brought into question by the form נעוותי in 4Q511, 118 II 9, which he understands as a nominal plural of נעוה (thus showing נעוה to be a noun). However, it seems possible that נעוותי is simply a fem. pl. Niphal participle functioning as an abstract substantive much in the same way as, *e.g.,* נפלאותיו in Ps. 96:3 (*cf.* Kautzsch, *Grammar,* §§116g and 122q). Note also the parallel construction between נעוה and the particple נבערה in 1QH 1:22.

Finally, there are a few uses of *ruaḥ* which require special attention: הרוח (4Q266 Da 1 XVII 6; this form together with רוח החיים in verse 12 of the same fragment will be treated in section *3f* of this chapter below); יצר כול רוח (1QH 15:13; this will be treated with רוח in v. 22 of the same column in section *3d2* of this chapter below); and שתי רוחות (1QS 3:18; this will be analyzed as part of the two-spirit Treatise in chapter 8 below).

b. The meaning of *ruaḥ* as a *nomen regens* in construct with the genitive: (39 times; *cf.* section *3a* of this chapter above for references; the nine occurrences of this pattern in the two-spirit Treatise will be handled in chapter 8 below, *viz.*, 1QS 3:18/19; 3:25; 4:3, 4, 9, 10, 20, 21b & 22. Note also that 4Q266 Da 1 XVII 12 will be treated in section *3f* of this chapter below).

Perhaps the best way to handle this pattern of *ruaḥ* is to divide it into the three following categories: those occurrences which are regarded by almost all scholars as referring to man's spirit, those over which scholars have divided opinions, and those which have remained largely untreated.

1) Occurrences of *ruaḥ* regarded by a strong consensus of scholars as referring to man's spirit: 1QS 5:25/26; 9:22; 1QH 1:15, 22, & 32; 2:15; 8:36; 10:22 {reconstructed}; 13:13; 16:10 & 14; and 17:25.[24] This consensus seems to be essentially correct. Thus, the psalmist describes himself as not only having a "spirit" but also as *being* a spirit, *e.g.*, of flesh (רוח בשר, 1QH 13:13), of zeal (רוח קנאה, 1QH 2:15), or of error (רוח התועה, 1QH 1:22), *i.e.*, as being a fleshly, zealous or error prone *person*.[25] In two cases *ruaḥ* is qualified with the genitives אדם and אנוש, once in a clear allusion to the natural, human spirit as described in Zech. 12:1 (note that 1QH 1:15 and Zech. 12:1 share the terms רוח אדם and יצר)

[24]I have found no clear disagreement among scholars on the meaning of *ruaḥ* in these texts as referring in some sense to the spirit of man; a possible exception, however, is the opinion of Ringgren in *Faith*, p. 88 in which he defines *ruaḥ* in 1QH 16:10 somewhat ambiguously as either "the spirit of truth" or "God's turn of mind."

[25]*Cf.* Anderson, "'Ruah'," pp. 294ff.

and another time in the chatacteristic position of man's natural spirit as being in fundamental need of God's help (*viz.*, 1QH 1:32; the רוח אנוש receives strength from God in adversity).[26] In 1QH 8:36 the *ruaḥ* of the כושלים needs not only God's help but also the help of the sectarian leader, who acts in God's power when this is available to him (*cf.* vv. 21ff.). In 1QH 16:14 also, the psalmist seems to be referring to God's help in the form of a divine association of some kind which he either has or will receive: God(?) is to become "part" (התערב) of the spirit of the עבד;[27] a similar expression in 1QH 17:25 (רוח בש]ר ל[עבדך) reinforces our impression of the spirit of the servant as continually standing in need of God's help, *i.e.*, it remains only "flesh." On the other hand, if the reconstruction [רוח עבדך] יצרתה is correct in 1QH 10:22,[28] it is not entirely clear from the context whether this refers to the servant's natural, "fleshly" spirit given to him at birth (as in 1QH 17:25) or to the new, more capable spirit (*i.e.*, religious disposition) created by God only for the sectarian (as in 1QH 4:31 & 36; *cf.* section *3d* below), although it is clear that this would still be the sectarian's spirit in contrast to the Spirit of God or an angel.[29] However, *ruaḥ* as a simple good or evil disposition can be seen in 1QS 5:25/26 and 9:22 in which it is presented as the responsibility of the sectarian in a context of various qualities which he is to purge or cultivate within himself; thus, in 1QS 5:25/26 the sectarian is not to speak to his brother in anger, stubbornness or in קנאת רוח רשע, and in 1QS 9:22 the משכיל is to hate the "men of the pit" with a רוח הסתר, *i.e.*, in an attitude of secrecy, while resisting any desire for their wealth. Finally, the object of the verb רשמתה in

[26]*Cf.* nn. 18, 21 & 22 in chapter 3 above.

[27]*Cf.* Mansoor, *Hymns*, p. 186 n. 16, who compares התערב here to the technical meaning of ערב in the Talmud in which it has to do with a voluntary association of mutual help and co-operation.

[28]*Cf.* Lohse, *Texte*, p. 150; for an alternative reconstruction (רוחי), *cf.* Mansoor, *Hymns*, p. 165 n. 6.

[29]Note that *ruaḥ*, however it may be reconstructed, is parallel to the 1st. per. sg. suffix (refering to the psalmist) on the following verb הכין.

1QH 16:10 (*viz.*, רוח צדיק)[30] is probably nothing more than a reference to any righteous member of the sect, whatever the precise meaning of רשמתה may be.[31] *Ruaḥ*, then, does not refer here to a part of the sectarian in contrast, for example, to his "flesh," but as in 1QH 9: 12 in which God "establishes" (v. 12a) or "founds" (v. 12b) the "spirit" of the sectarian, *ruaḥ* could be dropped completely (with only a reference to the sectarian and other qualifiers remaining) and there would be little or no change in meaning.[32]

2) Occurrences of *ruaḥ* over whose meaning scholars have divided opinions: 1QS 3:6 & 8; 10:18; 1QSb 5:25a & 25b; 1QH 7:11; f 12:4; CD 5:11; 7:4; and 11QPsa Plea 19:14.

1QS 3:6 & 8: רוח עצת אמת & רוח יושר וענוה, respectively. Scholars seem to be evenly divided on whether to understand *ruaḥ* in 1QS 3:6 & 8 as a disposition in man or as the Spirit of God,[33] but

---

[30]*Viz.*, "(the) spirit of (the) righteous."

[31]*Cf.* Carmignac and Guilbert, *Textes*, p. 165 n. 21 and Mansoor, *Hymns*, p. 186 n. 4.

[32]*Cf.* Irwin, "Spirit-Dualism," p. 188: "A personal pronoun or a reflexive may be substituted with little change in signification." *Cf.* also 1QH 13:13 and 17:25.

[33]Most scholars who comment on both 1QS 3:6 & 8 understand *ruaḥ* in both verses in the same sense, but *cf.* Anderson, "'Ruah'," p. 296, who understands *ruaḥ* in v. 8 as a disposition in the sectarian but thinks that *ruaḥ* in v. 6 might refer to the Spirit of God (*ibid.*, p. 301); *cf.* also Nötscher, "Heiligkeit," p. 341, who understands v. 6 as a reference to the holy Spirit from God and v. 8 as referring to the spiritual cooperation of the sect members. Scholars who think that vv. 6 & 8 refer to man's spirit or disposition are as follows: Burrows, *More Light*, p. 195; Coppens, "don," p. 210 (comments on v. 8 only); Carmignac and Guilbert, *Textes*, p. 30 n. 72; Hill, *Greek Words*, p. 234 (comments on v. 8 only); Irwin, "Spirit-Dualism," p. 18; Kamlah, "Geist," p. 482; Leaney, *Rule*, pp. 34-35 (comments on v. 8 only); Licht, *Rule*, p. 75; J. Maier, *Texte*, vol. II, p. 206 (comments on v. 6 only); Manns, *symbole*, pp. 82-3; Nötscher, "Geist," pp. 307 & 309; and Pryke, "'Spirit'," p. 345. Scholars who think that vv. 6 & 8 refer to the Spirit of God (sometimes equated with the spirit of truth in 1QS 3:18/19; *cf.* nn. 108, 213 & 318 in chapter 2 above) are as follows: Charlesworth, "Comparison," p. 100 (comments

however *ruaḥ* is understood in these passages, it seems clear (as we will try to show below) that they should be understood together. A slight problem of translation exists in 1QS 3:6 in which אל can be understood either as אֵל or אַל,[34] but a decision in favor of אֵל would not in itself identify *ruaḥ* here as God's Spirit since אֵל would directly qualify not *ruaḥ* but rather אמת or עצת אמת.[35] There is, however, a basic reason why *ruaḥ* in 1QS 3:6 & 8 is describing a human disposition (*i.e.*, in the sense of the new spirit of Ezk. 36:26 which only the sectarian has) rather than the Spirit of God. This has to do with an observation of F. Manns that atonement (כפר) in this context (*cf.* vv. 9-12) is an act of *man's* spirit rather than of God's Spirit.[36] In Both 3:6 and 8, man's iniquities (עוונותיו v. 6) or sin (חטתו v. 8) undergo atonement (pual imperfect of כפר in both verses) through (instrumental ב in both verses) either a spirit of true counsel (v. 6) or a spirit of uprightness and humility (v. 8). These verses,

---

on v. 6 only); Chevallier, *Souffle*, pp. 54-5 (sees a mixture of divine and human elements); Delcor, "Doctrines," col. 973; Flusser, "Dualism," pp. 159-60; Graystone, "Scrolls," 23, p. 27 n. 4 (comments on v. 6 only); Hauschild, *Gottes Geist*, p. 249; Jaubert, *notion*, pp. 239 & 241; Johnston, "Spirit," pp. 38 & 40 (comments on v. 6 only); Lichtenberger, *Studien*, p. 120 (comments on v.6 only); Montague, *Holy Spirit*, p. 120 (sees a mixture of divine and human elements); Osten-Sacken, *Gott und Belial*, pp. 133-4 (comments on v. 8 only); and Sjöberg, "Neuschöpfung," p. 135.

[34]For אֵל, *cf.* Lohse, *Texte*, p. 10 and P. Wernberg-Møller, *The Manual of Discipline, Translated and Annotated with an Introduction*, Studies on the Texts of the Desert of Judah, I (Grand Rapids: Eerdmans, 1957), 24. For אַל *cf.* Leaney, *Rule*, p. 137 and Vermes, *Scrolls in English*, p. 75.

[35]Most scholars who understand אל as אֵל translate the construct phrase רוח עצת אמת־אֵל as "the spirit of God's true counsel" or something similar, which could refer to a proper religious disposition within the sectarian. Note that Wernberg-Møller in *Manual*, pp. 24 & 61 n. 18 understands עצת as "council."

[36]Manns, *symbole*, p. 83. God, however, can also atone for sin in the Scrolls (*cf.* כפר in 1QS 2:8 & 11:14 and 9:3 in relationship to God's Spirit); for additional references to men making atonement, *cf.* 1QS 5:6; 8:6 & 10; and 9:4.

then, belong together as conceptual and syntactical parallels and form a contrast to v. 7 (with רוח קדושה) which deals not with atonement for iniquity but with an attainment of purity which is able to avoid sin (יטהר מכול עוונותו) and can be granted only by God or His Spirit.[37] Note, finally, that the forms of *ruaḥ* in both v. 6 and v. 8 are unique in the Scrolls published so far (*cf.*, however, 1QS 3:6 with 1QS 4:3 רוח ענוה).

1QS 10:18; רוח רשעה. Although most scholars consider *ruaḥ* in this verse to be a reference to man's spirit either as something he has[38] or something he is,[39] at least two scholars understand its use differently. G. Baumbach understands it as referring to an evil spirit[40] and J. Licht thinks that it is עולה כמו רוח (*cf.* 1QS 4:9), which in turn refers to the evil spirit of the two (cosmic) spirits of 1QS 3:18ff.[41] The majority opinion, however, seems to be correct in this instance. It is true that רשע and רשעה are found as genitives in construct with *ruaḥ* as "demons,"[42] but *ruaḥ* in these cases is always plural and it is very rare in any case for the sectarians to use the singular of *ruaḥ* in reference to

---

[37]For moral purity in man as an act of God rather than of man in the Scrolls, *cf.* n. 65, chapter 3 above. The meaning of 1QS 3:8b & 9a, then, would be that a lack of proper humility toward the sectarian interpretation of the law prevents true, moral purification from taking place.

[38]*E.g.*, G. Maier, *Mensch*, pp. 186-7; J. Maier, *Texte*, vol. I, p. 42 and vol. II, p. 206; and Noll, "Angelology," p. 136. In this case, the ב is translated as indicating circumstance or manner.

[39]*E.g.*, Anderson, "'Ruah'," p. 295; William H. Brownlee, "The Dead Sea Manual of Discipline translation and Notes," *Bulletin of the American Schools of Oriental Research, Supplementary Studies*, 10-12 (New Haven, 1951), p. 42; and Irwin, "Spirit-Dualism," pp. 188 & 191. In this case, the ב is taken with the verb קנא as indicating the direct object.

[40]Günther Baumbach, *Qumran und das Johannes-Evangelium*, Aufsätze und Vorträge zur Theologie und Religionswissenschaft, 6 (Berlin: Evangelische Verlagsanstalt, 1958), p. 14.

[41]Licht, *Rule*, p. 219.

[42]*E.g.*, 1QM 15:14; 1QH f 5:4; and 4Q511, 1, 6.

an angel or evil spirit.[43] And if it were true that רוח רשעה should be understood as the evil spirit of 1QS 3:18ff., this would still not identify it as an angelic being since both the good and evil spirits of 1QS 3:18ff. are essentially dispositions within men with no personal, angelic status (*cf.* chapter 8 below). Given the observations, then, 1) that the closest syntactical and conceptual analogy to ברוח רשעה is רוח רשע בקנאת in 1QS 5:26 (which has to do with a human attitude or disposition)[44] and 2) that *ruaḥ* in 10:18 appears to be conceptually parallel to נפשי in the following verse,[45] it is clear that no more than the psalmist's disposition is involved here. He simply wishes to avoid being zealous "in" or "with" an evil spiritual disposition.

1QSb 5:25a and 25b; [רוח עצ]ה and רוח דעת, respectively. We should note first of all that 1QSb 5:25a is a reconstruction based on Is. 11:2 to which 1QSb 5:25 alludes. A majority of scholars consider v. 25a along with the expression רוח דעת in v. 25b to be references to God's Spirit,[46] but it is probably best to regard

---

[43]*Cf.* Noll, "Angelology," p. 136: "Angelic spirits almost invariably occur in the plural (exceptions: כול רוח in 1QH vii 29; x 8, if it is referring to angels at all, is syntactically pl.; 4QBer^{a} 10 II 7 - רו]ח האב[דון refers to Belial; 4QSirSabb (unpublished) - רוח קודש עולמים is without context; on 11QPs^{a} Plea xix 5 see below), and they never occur in pairs." Another use of the singular of *ruaḥ* as a "demon" is in col. 20 of the Aramaic 1QapGen, but this work (like 11QPs^{a} Plea, *cf.* Sanders, *Discoveries*, IV, pp. 75-6) is probably not sectarian in origin and should be used with caution in reconstructing the content and expressions of sectarian pneumatology (*cf.* Joseph A. Fitzmyer, *The Genesis Apocryphon of Qumran Cave I* (2nd. ed.; Rome: Pontifical Biblical Institute, 1971), pp. 11-13 and also Walter Kirchschläger, "Exorzismus in Qumran?" *Kairos*, 18 (1976), pp. 135-153). We should also note that the expression רוח רעה in 4Q511, 15, 7 and 4Q511, 81, 3 may refer to a demon (*cf.* chapter 5 below).

[44]*Cf.* the analysis of this expression in paragraph *1)* directly above.

[45]*Cf.* Wernberg-Møller, *Manual*, p. 147 n. 58.

[46]*Cf.* Dupont-Sommer, *écrits*, p. 126 (comments on v.25b only); Foerster, "Geist," p. 119; Jaubert, *notion*, p. 144 (comments on v. 25b only); Manns, *symbole*, pp. 77-8 (comments on v. 25a only); Nötscher,

these as referring to various spiritual dispositions possessed by the נשיא here as the *effects* of God's Spirit[47] available to the sectarian community as a whole rather than as referring to a special presence of God's Spirit itself (*e.g.*, for special leadership or prophetic activity). Two considerations point in this direction. The first is that there are no clear links between expressions of *ruaḥ* in the non-biblical Scrolls which refer to God's Spirit and *ruaḥ* in 25a and 25b, whereas the expressions רוח עצת אמת in 1QS 3:6 and רוח דעת in 1QS 4:4 & 6Q18, 5,3 are similar to *ruaḥ* in 1QSb 5:25a & 25b (respectively) and both are best understood as referring to man's spirit.[48] A second, more basic consideration, however, is that the Scrolls never clearly describe the future, kingly Messiah (נשיא העדה)[49] in relationship to God's Spirit.[50] This may be because the Spirit of God was re-

---

Terminologie, p. 42 (comments on v. 25a only); and Schreiner, "Geistbegabung," p. 179 (comments on v. 25b only). On the other hand, J. Maier in *Texte*, vol. II, p. 206 lists *ruaḥ* in both passages under "Geist (des Menschen), Gesinnung"; Milik in Berthélemy and Milik, *Discoveries*, I, p. 155 translates both as "esprit," and Irwin in "Spirit-Dualism," pp. 74-5 & 192 thinks that both could refer either to a disposition in man or to God's Spirit.

[47]This is how P. van Imschoot in *Theology of the Old Testament*, I (trans. by K. Sullivan and F. Buck; New York: Desclee, 1965), pp. 182-3 n. 23 understands the original meaning of the "spirit of wisdom" in Is. 11:2 (and presumably the following two uses of *ruaḥ*); but *cf.* Lys, *Ruaḥ*, p. 81, who understands all four uses of *ruaḥ* in Is. 11:2 as referring essentially to God's Spirit.

[48]For *ruaḥ* in 1QS 3:6 as a reference to man's spirit, *cf.* above in this paragraph; for *ruaḥ* in 1QS 4:4 as man's spirit, *cf.* chapter 8 below; for *ruaḥ* in 6Q18, 5, 3 as man's spirit, *cf.* paragraph 3) of this section below.

[49]*Cf.* Milik's comments on this expression in Barthélemy and Milik, *Discoveries*, I, pp. 128-130.

[50]*Cf.* W. D. Davies, "Paul," p. 176: "If we reject the strictly messianic reference in 1QS iv 20, and in CD ii, 9ff., then in no case in the Scrolls is the spirit specifically connected with the Messiah(s), although in 1QS iv, 20f., it is connected with the end." Note also the remarks of Chevallier in his 1978 work, *Souffle*, p. 62: "Ces deux chapitres [*i.e.*, Levi 18 and Judah 24 in the *Test. of the XII Patriarchs*]

garded as a normal possession of all the members of the sectarian community and was therefore taken for granted as working within the coming Prince, but more probably this silence is intentional. A special mention of the presence of God's Spirit within such an important leader of the Sect might have indicated that his authority even in religious matters (*e.g.*, as a prophet)[51] would transcend the authority of the normal, priestly leadership of the sect, and it is clear that Qumran's priestly leadership wanted to avoid this kind of situation.[52]

1QH 7:11; רוח הוות. Scholars are divided over the meaning of *ruaḥ* in this verse as either an evil angel/demon[53] or an evil person.[54] However, *ruaḥ* here is probably a reference to man as a "spirit" for the following reasons: 1) it is rare for the Scrolls to refer to an angel or demon with the singular of *ruaḥ*;[55] 2) *ruaḥ* is otherwise never associated with the word הוות or any form of it, whereas הוות is used to describe man in 1QH 5:25 with the syntactically analogous expression בני הוות; 3) the expression אין פה לרוח הוות is followed by the parallel expression לא מענה לשון לכל בני אשמה, which refers to men and seems to define more

sont en effet les seuls textes des pseudépigraphes qui attribuent la *ruaḥ* divine au Messie. . . , et ils donnent des précisions. . . qui contrastent avec l'obscurité des fragments repéres à ce sujet dans les écrits de Qumran." Chevallier also notes here that it is uncertain whether or not the *Test. of the XII Patriarchs* represents late Judaism; for a view of this work as having a Christian origin, *cf.* M. de Jonge, *The Testaments of the Twelve Patriarchs: A Study of their Text, Composition and Origin* (Leiden, 1953).

[51]*Cf.* n. 32 in chapter 3 above.

[52]*Cf.* Vermes, *Perspective*, pp. 184-5.

[53]*Cf.* Huppenbauer, *Mensch*, p. 74; Irwin, "Spirit-Conflict," pp. 52 & 192; Johnston, "Spirit," and J. Maier, *Texte*, vol. II, p. 206.

[54]*Cf.* Anderson, "'Ruah'," p. 295; Hauschild, *Gottes Geist*, p. 254; Holm-Nielsen, *Hodayot*, p. 132 n. 13; Nötscher, "Geist," p. 305; Osten-Sacken, *Gott und Belial*, p. 138; and Pryke, "'Spirit'," p. 345.

[55]*Cf.* n. 43 above.

closely its preceding stich;[56] and finally, 4) it is not unusual in 1QH for men to be described as *ruaḥ*.[57]

1QH f 12:4; רוח עורף ק[שה]. I have found only two scholars who have commented on this verse. One regards *ruaḥ* here as a simple religious disposition[58] and the other as an impersonal power of evil standing behind man's sin and godlessness.[59] The expression רוח עורף קשה occurs only here (in a very fragmentary context), but it probably refers simply to a human disposition with no metaphysical or cosmic significance since syntactically and conceptually it fits in best with the most dominant and characteristic syntactical pattern in the Scrolls for describing man's spirit (*cf.* section *3a* above). In this pattern the singular of *ruaḥ* is in construct with a genitive which, in turn, is often descriptive of a good or evil moral quality, *e.g.*, אמונה, זנות, *etc.* Although this pattern is very commonly used for describing the character of man's spirit, is it never clearly used in the sectarian literature to describe an angel or demon.[60]

CD 5:11 & 7:4; רוח קדשיהם and רוח קדשיו, respectively. Most scholars believe that *ruaḥ* in these passages refers to man's spirit, although a strong minority believes that it refers in some sense to the Spirit of God.[61] The majority seems to be correct. As in chapter 3 (section *2b1*), which dealt with the importance of the suffix in defining רוח קודש as God's holy Spirit, a

---

[56]*Cf.* Holm-Nielsen, *Hodayot*, p. 132 n. 13.

[57]*E.g.*, 1QH 1:22; 2:15; 3:21; 9:16; and 13:13.

[58]Nötscher, "Geist," p. 309.

[59]H. W. Huppenbauer, "Belial in den Qumrantexten," *Theologische Zeitschrift*, 15 (1959), p. 84.

[60]Note that 11QPsa Plea 19 with רוח טמאה in v. 15 (which probably refers to a demon; *cf.* chapter 5 above) is probably not a sectarian composition; *cf.* Sanders, *Discoveries*, IV, 75-6. Note also that the genitive in the expression רו]ח האב[דון in 4Q286Bera 10 II 7-8 is not so much a moral description as a description of function. In any case, this expression is highly unusual since this is the only place in the Scrolls in which Belial (or the corresponding good angel, *viz.*, Michael, the Prince of Lights) is ever called a *ruaḥ*. Also, it is only rarely that any demon or angel is called a *ruaḥ* in the singular (*cf.* n. 43 above).

[61]*Cf.* the list of these scholars in n. 6 in chapter 3 above.

primary evidence for *ruaḥ* as man's spirit in CD 5:11 (and by analogy CD 7:4)[62] is the fact that the suffix on the genitive קדש in both cases refers to man. We noted in the analysis of chapter 3, section *2b1* that it is doubtful if the sectarians or anyone else at that time ever referred to man's spirit as the Spirit (or spirit) of *God*,[63] and this seems to be essentially true for man's spirit: there does not appear to be a clear place in sectarian literature in which *ruaḥ* as the Spirit of God is ever referred to as the spirit of *man* (*e.g.*, with a suffix or some other syntactical marker).[64] There is a biblical sense, of course, in which God imparts His "spirit" (*i.e.*, the capacity of *life* having its source only in Him) to men and they live, or He withdraws His spirit and they die,[65] and this kind of thinking may in part lie behind the language of CD 5:11 and 7:4. But even more basic to the thought of the sectarians, as we have seen in chapter 3, is their radical distinction (especially in 1QH) between God's Spirit and man's spirit.[66] In the context of this theology, then, if it has had any influence on CD at all, it is difficult to believe that CD regards man as having a dominance over God's Spirit even to the point of *defiling* it. *Ruaḥ* in CD 5:11 and 7:4 probably refers to the natural spirit of man which he has from birth (perhaps also renewed in the sense of Ezk. 36:26) as opposed to the transcendent and autonomous Spirit of God. This is confirmed by the following two observations: it is not unusual for

---

[62]Without the parallel passage CD 5:11, it might be possible to understand the suffix on קדש in 7:4 as referring to God; but *cf.* the syntactical and conceptual analogies between CD 7:4, 12:11, and Lev. 20:25 which strongly indicate that the suffix on the expression in CD 7:4 refers to man.

[63]*I.e.*, either directly or indirectly with a suffix or some other marker; *cf.* nn. 12-14 in chapter 3 above.

[64]*Cf.* however, 2 Kings 2:15 (and 1 Cor. 5:4 in the New Testament). This kind of language seems to be absent for the most part also in the intertestamental sources known to be used by the sectarians.

[65]*Cf.* Gen. 6:3 and Job 27:3. In these cases, however, *ruaḥ* expresses man's complete dependence on God's spirit rather than his possession or control over it; *cf.* Lys, *Ruaḥ*, pp. 321-315.

[66]*Cf.* nn. 18, 21 and 22 in chapter 3 above.

man's spirit at this time to be called "holy,"[67] and as E. Schweizer noted as early as 1952, the phrasiology of CD 7:4 is analogous to the levitical expression ולא תשקצו את נפשתיכם in Lev. 20:25 (*cf.* also CD 12:11 in which נפש is retained) and probably has a similar meaning.[68] The context of CD 5:11, on the other hand, makes use not of שקץ but of the conceptually analogous verb טמא and it is concerned less with ceremonial defilement than doctrinal and moral sins, but the rare form of its genitive (*i.e.*, the plural of קודש with a suffix referring to men) which it shares with 7:4 and the shared theme of men engaging in defiling, unclean activity indicates a similarity of meaning for *ruaḥ* in both passages.

11QPsa Plea 19:14; רוח אמונה ודעת. I have found only two scholars who take clear positions on the meaning of *ruaḥ* in this verse: Noll regards it as a reference to human psychological qualities[69] and Manns sees it as a reference to the Spirit of God.[70] Noll seems to be correct in this instance since the context of this pre-Essene psalm[71] is not that of a special, eschatological presence of God's Spirit in the end-time community, but rather has to do with the biblical psalmist's[72] forgiveness and cleansing from sin (vv. 13-14) and his desire to live henceforth in true knowledge and faithfulness to God (vv. 14-15).

---

[67]*Cf.* n. 15 in chapter 3 above.

[68]Eduard Schweizer, "Die sieben Geister in der Apokalypse," *Evangelische Theologie*, 11 (1951/1952), p. 506 n. 25. *Cf.* also the same connection in Chaim Rabin, *The Zadokite Documents* (2nd. ed.; Oxford: Clarendon Press, 1958), p. 26 n. 1 on line 4.

[69]Noll, "Angelology," p. 72.

[70]Manns, *symbole*, p. 71.

[71]*Cf.* Sanders, *Discoveries*, IV, pp. 75-6.

[72]*Cf.* n. 71 above. This is probably how the sectarians would have understood the authorship of this psalm, *i.e.*, the author by definition would not be part of their eschatological community. Note that if the author was thought to be David himself, he would not be praying for the prophetic Spirit of God as such, which he had from his youth (*cf.* 1 Sam. 16:13) but for a righteous disposition (*cf.* Ps. 51), which is the basic theme of this hymn.

3) Occurrences of *ruaḥ* which have remained largely untreated: 1Q29, 14, 1; 4Q177, 12-13, I, 5; 4Q504, 6, 22; 4Q510, 1, 6; 4Q511, 10, 2; 4Q511, 18 II 6; and 6Q18, 5, 3.

1Q29, 14, 1: רוח זידות. This expression is unique in the Scrolls and without a context, but its pattern of *ruaḥ* in the singular (which is uncharacteristic as a reference to an angel or demon)[73] followed by the genitive זידות (which cannot apply to God)[74] indicates that this phrase is descriptive of man's spirit or disposition.[75]

4Q177, 12-13, I, 5; רוח אמת. This expression is very interesting since this is one of the few places outside the two-spirit Treatise (*cf.* 1QS 3:18/19 and 4:21b) that any form of *ruaḥ* ever occurs with any form of אמת in the non-biblical, Hebrew Scrolls published so far.[76] Of even more interest is a phrase in the immediate context of our expression (v. 7) which seems to have been taken directly from 1QS 3:24: מלאך אמתו יעזור לכול בני אור. Although it is difficult to determine the meaning of רוח אמת in the fragmentary context of v. 5, the connection of verse 7 with 1QS 3:24 is a strong indication that רוח אמת should be understood in the light of רוחות האמת והעול in 1QS 3:18/19 as a disposition given to the sectarian at birth (*cf.* the analysis of *ruaḥ* in 1QS 3:18/19 in chapter 8 below as essentially a human disposition).

---

[73]*Cf.* nn. 43 and 60 above.

[74]This is probably a negative term; note Milik's translation in Barthélemy and Milik, *Discoveries*, I, p. 132 as "ambition."

[75]The singular of *ruaḥ* followed by a genitive indicating a good or evil moral quality is a common syntactical pattern for describing man's spirit in the Scrolls; *cf.* section *3a* above.

[76]1QM 13, which has a strong literary relationship with 1QS 3-4 (*cf.* Irwin, "Spirit-Dualism," p. 210), contains the expression רוחי אמת in v. 10; the only other occurrence of אמת with *ruaḥ* I have found is in 1QH 2:4 in which אמת was replaced with צדק by the scribe. Also, with the exception רוחות עולה in 1QH f 5:6, I have found no form of *ruaḥ* with any form of עול/עולה, אור (noun) or חשך outside of the two-spirit Treatise; *cf.* 1QS 3:18 & 25. If the consensus of the late 1950's and early 1960's were correct, which viewed the two-spirit Treatise as having a dominant position in sectarian pneumatology (*cf.* chapter 2 above), this almost total lack of contact with the two-spirit vocabulary of 1QS 3-4 would be astonishing.

Finally, we should note that an expresssion identical to our expression (*viz.*, רוח אמת) is found in 1QS 4:21b in which it appears at first sight to have the meaning "God's eschatological Spirit." However, as we will attempt to show in chapter 8 below, the author of this section of the two-spirit Treatise (4:15-26) is attempting to reinterpret the traditional pneumatology of the sect (as seen especially in 1QH) in terms of his two-spirit (*i.e.*, disposition) view, and he chose to use רוח אמת (= the good disposition of 3:18/19) in the context of 4:21 precisely because it reflected and supported this view.

4Q504, 6, 22; רוח כול חי. This expression is unique in the Scrolls. Its closest equivalent in the literature known and used by the sect seems to be נפש כל חי (*cf.* Job 12:10 and 11QPsa Plea 19: 3-4). These contexts would seem to indicate that *ruaḥ* in our expression refers to the breath of life in anything (man or animal) that has life, but perhaps it has to do chiefly with human life much like the expression כול חי in 1QS 4:26, 9:12 and 10:17.

4Q510, 1, 6 and 5Q511, 10, 2: רוח בינה. These two fragments are essentially parallel to each other (with 4Q511, 10 perhaps being an expanded recension) and so contain the same unique expression in essentially the same context.[77] In these fragments, as Baillet notes, the psalmist seeks "à la fois pour louer Dieu et pour chasser les mauvais esprits,"[78] *i.e.*, he praises God to throw fear into the demons (4Q510, 1, 4-5) who would otherwise פוגעים פתע פתאום לתעות רוח בינה ("strike unexpectedly for the leading astray of a spirit of knowledge," v. 6). It seems clear, that רוח בינה here refers to the sectarian himself or his fellow religionists for the following reasons: 1) the basic theme of this context is the psalmist's attempt to protect himself and other members of the sect from demonic attack (*cf.* 1QS 3:24); 2) it is not unusual in the Scrolls for the sectarian to describe himself or another person as a *ruaḥ* of one kind or another;[79] and finally,

---

[77]Baillet, *Discoveries*, VII, p. 226.

[78]*Ibid.*, p. 215.

[79]*E.g.*, 1QH 1:22; 2:15; 3:21; 9:16; and 13:13; *cf.* also 1QS 8:12. Note that most of the clear uses of *ruaḥ* in this manner are found in 1QH and compare this with Baillet's remarks in *ibid.*, p. 220 on the relation-

3) whenever the verb תעה has a logical subject (as intransitive) or an object (as transitive) in the Scrolls, such a subject or object is always a human being and often the sectarian himself[80] rather than, *e.g.*, an angel or a demon.

4Q511, 18 II 6; רוח בינתי. This expression is unique despite its similarity to רוח בינה treated immediately above, since this spirit is something which the psalmist *has* rather than something he is. This is also the only place except for CD 5:11 and 7:4 in the published, non-biblical Hebrew Scrolls in which *ruaḥ* as man's spirit is in construct with a genitive substantive with the suffix referring back to man as its possessor.[81] There is a certain formal similarity, then, between *ruaḥ* here and in CD 5:11 and 7:4, and as in these CD passages, *ruaḥ* in our passages belongs to man rather than to God. This is indicated by the basic theme of 4Q511, 18 II which has to do not with the Spirit of God as such but with the personal spirituality of a sectarian evidently trying to defend himself against opponents who are pointing out his shortcomings (vv. 9-10). The psalmist's mention of his "spirit of understanding" in v. 6, then, probably means no more than the expression דעת בינה in v. 8; it is simply his claim to have a disposition of understanding and acceptance of his community's doctrine and practice.

6Q18, 5, 3; רוח דעת. This expression occurs elsewhere only in 1QS 4:14 and 1QSb 5:25b, and in connection with *ruaḥ* the verb חזק occurs only in 1QH 16:7. The full expression of 6Q18, 5, 3 is [. . .]חזקו ברוח דעת in which, according to Baillet, חזקו can be read either as a piel or a hithpael.[82] If a hithpael form of חזק is understood here, this would give our expression a formal likeness

---

ship between 4Q510/511 and 1QH: "Les rappochements avec les Hodayôt sont si nombreux qu'il peut y avior une communauté d'auteur avec au moins certain passages."

[80]*E.g.*, 1QS 5:4 & 11; 11:1; and 1QH 4:25.

[81]*Cf.* the patterns for man's spirit in section *3c* in this chapter above. Note that the suffix on רוח עבדך (1QH 16:14) refers formally to God.

[82]*Cf.* M. Baillet, J. T. Milik and R. de Vaux, *Discoveries in the Judean Desert of Jordan, Textes*, III (Oxford: Clarendon Press, 1962), p. 134 n. 3.

to 1QH 16:7 in which *ruaḥ* was understood as referring to God's Spirit,[83] and perhaps with other evidence (*e.g.*, 1QH 14:25),[84] רוח דעת here could also be understood as God's Spirit. The hithpael reading is not certain, however, and even if it were, this form with ב is ambiguous in meaning. Baillet suggests, for example, that its meaning in 6Q18, 5, 3 should be understood in a reflexive sense by analogy with 1QSa 2:7 ("se tenir ferm"),[85] whereas G. Jeremias understands it in 1QH 4:39 & 18:9 as having an active meaning[86] and Mansoor in 1QH 16:7 as a passive.[87] The key to the meaning of our expression should probably be sought in the expression רוח דעת itself (given the fragmentary condition of this passage), which in its other occurrences means man's spirit[88] and probably also has the same meaning here.

c. The meaning of *ruaḥ* with a suffix: (24 times, *cf.* section *3a* above for references; 1QS 3:14 & 4:26b will be handled in chapter 8 below, and 1QH 4:36 will be handled below in section *3d* of this chapter in connection with 4:31).

If the consensus of scholarship on the interpretation of the above passages is correct, a significant pattern for determining the meaning of *ruaḥ* in the non-biblical, Hebrew Scrolls could be its use in the singular with an attached suffix (22 times; in 2 cases above *ruaḥ* is in the plural, *cf.* 1QS 2:20 & 3:14). Every time, in fact, that this pattern of *ruaḥ* is found in the non-biblical, Hebrew Scrolls (with only on exception: 4Q185, 1-2, I, 10), scholars almost unanimously regard it as referring in some sense to the spirit of man in contrast, *e.g.*, to God's Spirit or an angel.[89] This consensus seems to be correct for the following rea-

---

[83]*Cf.* section *2b3* in chapter 3 above.

[84]*Cf.* section *2f* in chapter 3 above.

[85]Baillet, Milik and de Vaux, *Discoveries*, III, p. 134 n. 3.

[86]G. Jeremias, *Lehrer*, p. 210 n. 11.

[87]Mansoor, *Hymns*, p. 185.

[88]*Cf.* paragraph 2 in this section above for 1QSb 5:25b and chapter 8 below for 1QS 4:4.

[89]I have found only three scholars who have commented on the verses associated with this pattern and who disagree somewhat with

sons: 1) there is no clear case in the non-biblical, Hebrew Scrolls in which *ruaḥ* as God's Spirit ever has an attached suffix;[90] 2) the singular of *ruaḥ* only rarely means "angel/demon"[91] and this never involves a suffix; 3) the most basic reason, however, supporting the above consensus is that the contexts themselves in the passages cited above indicate that *ruaḥ* refers to man's spirit (sometimes in the sense of Ezk. 36: 26) and nothing more. This is especially clear in contexts in which *ruaḥ* can be replaced by a personal pronoun referring to man without causing a basic change in meaning. Thus, in 1QS 2:14 the *ruaḥ* suffers destruction due to man's disobedience, or it "wavers" (זוע 1QS 7:18), "turns aside" from the truth (שוב 1QS 7:23) or is "imprisoned"(?) with the dead (חפש 1QH 8:29); in other passages God "establishes" (העמיד 1QH 9:12a) or "founds" (יסד 1QH 9;12b) the sectarian's *ruaḥ* in the face of opposition, and it apparently can experience salvation (*cf.* 1QH f 6:4, כן רוחם להושיע). In CD 3:3 and in the reconstruction of 3:7, the meaning of *ruaḥ* as man's natural, sinful dispositon is clear when Abraham is praised for not following the desire of his *ruaḥ* while the wilderness generation is criticized for following theirs.[92] One of the most important contexts of *ruaḥ* with the suffix, however, is in the regular promotion or demotion of the sectarian within

---

the consensus on their meaning: Dupont-Sommer in *Nouveaux aperçus sur les Manuscrits de la Mer Morte,* L'Orient ancient îllustré, 5 (Paris, 1953), p. 168 translates רוחו in 1QS 4:26b as "Son esprit" (but *cf.* Dupont-Sommer in his later work, *écrits,* p. 98 in which this is rendered "son esprit"); Ringgren in *Faith,* p. 72 (translated edition) renders the same verse somewhat ambiguously as "His (its) spirit"; finally, R. Murphy in *The Dead Sea Scrolls and the Bible* (Westminster: Newman Press, 1956), p. 69 describes *ruaḥ* in 1QS 5:21, 23/24 & 6:17 as standing "both for the opposing 'angels' as well as for the influence which they initiate and exert in the heart of man."

[90]For this pattern as the "wind" or "breath" of God, *cf.* the single case in 4Q185, 1-2, I, 10. This situation in the Scrolls is surprising since this pattern in reference to God is not unusual in the Old Testament; *e.g.,* Num. 11:29; Is. 44:3; and Ezk. 37:14

[91]*Cf.* n. 43 above.

[92]*Cf.* Ezk. 13:3.

his community on the basis of his "spirit" and works; *cf.* 1QS 5:21 & 23-24; 6:17; 9:14, 15 & 18; and also the plural in 2:20. A clear contextual indication of the meaning of *ruaḥ* in these passages (all of which share the same context, *viz.*, status in the community) is the close structural parallel between v. 14 and v. 17 of 1QS 6 in which *ruaḥ* in v. 17 replaces שכל in v. 14 with apparently little change in meaning.[93] The sectarian's spirit, as his insight, describes his personal and constantly evolving religious character, which serves as the basis for his changing rank in the community.

Finally, mention should be made of the expression לפי רוחו in CD 20:24 (found also in 1QS 2:20; 4:26b: and 9:14 with some variation). It is clear that *ruaḥ* here means a simple, spiritual disposition in man (perhaps in the sense of Ezk. 36:26) and nothing more since CD as a whole involves no two-spirit dualism (although a dualistic tradition of two opposed angelic forces is present to some extent).[94] The same meaning is probably also present in 1QS 2:20 and 9:14, although the two-spirit context of 1QS 4:26b shows that here man's spirit has to do with the predestined, good or evil "self" or "being" given to man at birth which totally determines the quality of his religious life.[95]

There are four additional occurrences of *ruaḥ* (all singular) with a suffix, but these are too isolated and fragmentary for much analysis. It seems clear from the context available, however, that these occurrences for the most part belong to the category of man's spirit. Thus, רוחמה in 5Q13, 2, 9 appears to refer to the spirit of the Levites, רוחם and רוחו in 1QH f 11:4 and 4Q184, 4, 4 (respectively), are in a context in which בני איש and אדם appear to be the topic of discussion, and סוד רוחו in 1QH f 31:1 is in association with בשר. The characteristic, however, which most strongly indicates that *ruaḥ* (sg.) in all these passages is man's

---

[93]*Cf.* Brownlee, *Manual*, p. 25 n. 35 and Licht, *Rule*, p. 150.

[94]*Cf.* Osten-Sacken, *Gott und Belial*, p. 194. As Osten-Sacken notes, however, Belial has no eschatological, cosmic dimensions in CD.

[95]*Cf.* H. W. Kuhn, *Enderwartung*, pp. 120-2.

spirit is its suffix. As noted above, there is only one clear case in the non-biblical Scrolls so far in which the singular of *ruaḥ* with a suffix does not refer to man (*viz.*, 4Q185, 1-2, I, 10), and there the context indicates without ambiguity that *ruaḥ* means "wind" or "breath" of God (*cf.* chapter 6 below).

d. The meaning of *ruaḥ* used without qualifying expressions: (19 times; *cf.* section *3a* above for references; note that 1QH 4:36 from section *3c* above will be handledhere together with 1QH 4:31 and that יצר כול רוח in 1QH 15:13 will be handled here together with 1QH 15:22).

Perhaps the best way to handle this pattern of *ruaḥ* is to divide it into two basic categories: those occurrences which are regarded by almost all scholars as referring to man's spirit and those over which there is some disagreement.

1) Occurrences of *ruaḥ* regarded by almost all scholars as referring to man's spirit; *category A*: 1QS 11:1a & 1b; 1QH 14:3; 18:15; 1QM 7:5; 11:10; 14:7; and 4Q183, 1 II 6; *category B*: 1QH 5:28 (reconstruction); 5:36; 4Q186, 1 II 7; 4Q186, 1 III 5; and 4Q186, 2, I, 6.[96]

The special syntactical characteristic of the unqualified use of *ruaḥ* in category A above is its use as a singular genitive of a *nomen regens* which, in turn, indicates a spiritual disposition or quality of character.[97] The pattern of a *nomen regens* followed by an unqualified, singular genitive of *ruaḥ* is found for meanings other than "man's spirit,"[98] but the *nomen regens* in these cases never indicates a spiritual disposition or quality.

---

[96]I have found only one scholar who has regarded any of these occurrences as referring to something other than man's spirit or disposition: *cf.* H. E. del Medico, *L'énigme des manuscrits de la Mer Morte* (Paris: Librairie Plon, 1957), p. 397, who translates נכאי רוח as "un souffle destructeur."

[97]Note that the genitive qualifies its *nomen regens* rather than the reverse; *cf.* Kautzsch, *Grammar*, §§ 89a and 128f & x.

[98]*E.g.*, סודי רוח 1QS 4:6, ארוכי רוח 1QM 6:12 (referring to a horse as "longwinded"; *cf.* chapter 6 below), עבותי רוח 1QH f 9:6, כנפי רוח f 19:3, and משיחי רוח 4QDe {270} 2 II 13-14a.

Whenever a *nomen regens* does indicate such a disposition or quality, if the consensus above is correct, an unqualified use of *ruaḥ* as its genitive always refers to man in the non-biblical, Hebrew Scrolls published so far. It should also be noted that such a *nomen regens* with *ruaḥ* as its genitive is found only with the unqualified, singular of *ruaḥ*.

It appears, in fact, that the consensus on category A above is correct. Thus, in 1QS 11:1 the משכיל teaches knowledge to his errant followers (לתועי רוח)[99] so that they may have the presence of mind to avoid angry religious debates with their proud enemies (רמי רוח), who are further identified in the following stich as אנשי מטה; it is not as clear, on the other hand, that תועי רוח in 4Q183, 1, II, 6 refers to erring sectarians due to its fragmentary context, but it is still clear that it has to do with human beings of some kind since the theme of this fragment is the struggle between two groups of men, *viz.*, sectarians and the non-Essene priests who defile the sanctuary with their impurity (v. 1). In 1QH 14:3, however, there seems to be a clear reference to the sectarians in the expression ענוי רוח, who are said to be "purified" (מזוקקים); this is an idea based on Mal. 3:3, which deals with God's purification of the Levitical priests who serve Him (a theme which recurs also in 1QH 5:16 and 4Q511, 35, 2),[100] and the same expression is parallel with כול תמימי דרך in 1QM 14:7 as descriptions of the Qumran faithful.[101] Note also the related expression תמימי רוח ובשר in 1QM 7:5, which in context distinguishes between those sectarians who are eligible to fight in the eschatological war and those who are not. The key difference between this expression in 1QM 7:5 and the one in 14:7 (כול תמימי דרך) is that 7:5 specifies a physical (בשר) as well as a spiritual (רוח) standard necessary for participation in the coming war, whereas 14:7 simply refers to the proper religious conduct expected from all sectarians. 1QM 7:5, then, has nothing to do with a hellenistic distinction between body and

---

[99]*Cf.* Is. 29:24; note that according to 1QS 9:16ff. the master is not to teach non-sectarians.

[100]*Cf.* Baillet, *Discoveries*, VII, p. 238 n. 2.

[101]*Cf.* Mansoor, *Hymns*, p. 104 n. 1.

soul. Finally, the expression נכאי רוח occurs in 1QM 11:10 and 1QH 18:15 (partially reconstructed)[102] as a description of the despondent sectarian. In 1QM 11:10 God is to set these seemingly ineffective people on fire, who will then consume ungodliness like straw until it exists no more, and in 1QH 18:15 it is these people who receive the good news of God's mercy from a sectarian leader especially gifted by God to proclaim this message to them (*cf.* vv. 10ff.).

Category B above has to do with the unqualified use of *ruaḥ* unattached to other parts of speech (except for *waw* in 4Q186, 1 III 5 and 2, I, 6). All the passages listed above in this category also refer clearly to man's spirit. Thus, in 1QH 5:36 (and in the parallel reconstruction in 5:28) the opposition which the psalmist faces from his enemies has a direct effect within his own person (בחוכמי עבדך v. 35), causing (his) spirit to stumble (להכשיל רוח, vv. 28 & 36) and (his) strength to be destroyed (להתם כוח vv. 28/29, and לכלות כוח v. 36). It seems clear that the unqualified use of *ruaḥ* in v. 36 (and probably v. 28) means approximately the same thing as the unqualified כוח following it in parallel construction, *i.e.*, both terms have to do with the sectarian's personal disposition and character. Finally, the three occurrences of *ruaḥ* in 4Q186 (*viz.*, 1 II 7; 1 III 5; and 2, I, 6) have to do with man's spirit, probably in the sense of 1QS 3-4 and 1QH 15 as the predestined being of man, but with the added precision that men's spirits are made up of mixtures of "light" and "darkness" determined by the formation of the stars at one's birth. Unlike 1QS 3-4, however, *ruaḥ* here is not set in relationship to two cosmic, angelic creatures dominating humanity.[103] In this respect *ruaḥ* in 4Q186 and 1QH 15 are similar. Neither has an interest in personal, cosmic intermediaries, which indicates that the two spirits of 1QS 3-4 (themselves essentially human dispositions; *cf.* chapter eight below) have no *necessary* conceptual relationship to the two angels of 1QS 3:20-25.

---

[102]*Cf. ibid.*, p. 192 n. 1.

[103]*Cf.* Dupont-Sommer, "documents," p. 251, who understands *ruaḥ* in these passages as simply "l'esprit de chaque individu."

2) Occurrences of *ruaḥ* used without qualification over which there is some disagreement among scholars: 1QH 4:31 & 36 (analyzed together); 9:16a & 16b; 14:11; 15:13 & 22 (analyzed together); and 17:17. Note that 1QH 4:36 and 15:13 do not belong in this syntactical category but are analyzed here for contextual reasons.

1QH 4:31, ברוח; and 4:36, רוחי. The meaning of *ruaḥ* in 1QH 4:31 has been at the center of the debate over sectarian pneumatology almost from the beginning of Qumranian studies to the present,[104] and during this time it has been understood in a number of different ways. Many scholars have regarded it as referring in some sense to the spirit of man[105], but it has also been

---

[104]The basic history of this verse is as follows: 1) K. G. Kuhn initially regarded it in 1950 as referring to a spiritual *Neuschöpfung* experienced at one's entrance into the sect, *cf.* K. G. Kuhn, "Texte," p. 201 and n. 7; 2) Sjöberg would contest this shortly afterwards and regard *ruaḥ* here as referring to the spirit of man given at birth, *cf.* Sjöberg, "Wiedergeburt," pp. 79ff.; 3) Kuhn appears subsequently in 1952 to agree with Sjöberg (although without citing this passage), *cf.* K. G. Kuhn, "Πειρασμός," pp. 214-5; 4) Sjöberg then decides in 1955 that Kuhn was originally correct and cites this verse (among others) as evidence of a spiritual "Neuschöpfung" at Qumran, *cf.* Sjöberg, "Neuschöpfung," p. 135 and n. 6; 5) Kuhn appears again in 1961 to agree with Sjöberg (but without citing this passage), *cf.* K. G. Kuhn, "Epheserbrief," p. 344; 6) in 1966, H. W. Kuhn, a student of K. G. Kuhn, defined *ruaḥ* here as the "predestined being" of man given to him at birth, *cf.* H. W. Kuhn, *Enderwartung*, p. 126 and n. 5; 6) not everyone, however, even in Heidelberg, was convinced of this, and in 1980 Lichtenberger (another student of K. G. Kuhn) defined *ruaḥ* in 1QH 4:31 as God's own Spirit, *cf.* Lichtenberger, *Studien*, pp. 67. It seems, in fact, that K. G. Kuhn's original position in 1950 was correct but with the added observation that the spiritual "Neuschöpfung" in 1QH 4:31 has its origin in the eschatological presence of God's Spirit at work in the sectarian community; *cf.* in this chapter below.

[105]*Cf.* Egon Brandenburger, *Fleisch und Geist, Paulus und die dualistische Weisheit*, Wissenschaftliche Monographien zum Alten und Neuen Testament, 29 (Neukirchen: Neukirchener Verlag, 1968), pp. 92-3; Hauschild, *Gottes Geist*, pp. 248-9; Irwin, "Spirit-Dualism," pp. 58, 192 & 224 n.60; Jaubert, *notion*, p. 243; G. Jeremias, *Lehrer*, p.209 n.4;

seen as God's Spirit (as distinct from the "spirit of truth" in 1QS 3-4)[106] or as the ambiguous Spirit of God/spirit of truth,[107] sometimes with more emphasis on one than another, but with no essential distinction made between them.[108] It appears, however, that those scholars who identify *ruaḥ* here with man's spirit are correct, especially those who see this spirit as a religious disposition characteristic of the sectarian.[109] A number of considerations point in this direction, the most immediate of which is the verb יצר in association with an unqualified, singular form of *ruaḥ* as its logical object. This syntactical pattern refers to man's spirit in contrast to God's Spirit or an angel for the following reasons: 1) there appears to be no place in the literature written or used by the sect in which God's Spirit is clearly ever the object of a creating activity;[110] 2) *ruaḥ* as

---

Johnston, "Spirit," p. 28; Kamlah, "Geist," p. 482; H. W. Kuhn, *Enderwartung*, p. 126; Licht, *Thanksgiving Scroll*, p. 38; Eugene H. Merrill, *Qumran and Predestination, A Theological Study of the Thanksgiving Hymns*, Studies on the Texts of the Desert of Judah, VIII (Leiden, Brill, 1975), p. 18; Molin, *Söhne*, p. 38; Nötscher, "Heiligkeit," pp. 337-8; Pryke, "'Spirit'," p. 345; Schreinder, "Geistbegabung," p. 165 n. 19; and Sjöberg, "Wiedergeburt," pp. 78-9 (but *cf.* n. 106 below).

[106]*Cf.* Chevallier, *Souffle*, p. 56; Dietzel, "Beten," p. 23; Hübner, "Dualismus," p. 284 n. 2; Lichtenberger, *Studien*, p. 67; J. Maier, *Texte*, vol. II, p. 206; Osten-Sacken, *Gott und Belial*, p. 133; Sjöberg, "Neuschöpfung," p. 135 and n. 6; and *idem*, "πνεῦμα," p. 385.

[107]*Cf.* Anderson, "'Ruah'," p. 293; H. Braun, *Qumran*, vol. II, p. 253; Carmignac and Guilbert, *Textes*, p. 211 n. 60; Delcor, "Doctrines," col. 973; *idem*, Hymns, p. 46; Dupont-Sommer, "instruction," p. 21; Flusser, "Sect," pp. 257 & 259; *idem*, "Dualism," p. 162 Foerster, "Geist," pp. 128-9; Holm-Nielsen, *Hodayot*, p. 20 n. 10 and p. 85 n. 77; Mansoor, *Hymns*, p. 76; Nötscher, "Geist," p. 306; Ringgren, *Faith*, p. 89; Schweizer, "πνεῦμα," p. 390 and n. 329; and Seitz, "Two Spirits," pp. 94-5.

[108]*Cf.* nn. 213, 215, 216 and 218 in chapter 2 above.

[109]*Cf.* Irwin, "Spirit-Dualism," pp. 58, 192 & 224 n. 60 and Merrill, *Qumran*, pp. 40-1 for a similar opinion.

[110]Both Chevallier in *Souffle*, p. 56 and Sjöberg in "Neuschöpfung," p. 135 & n. 6 understand *ruaḥ* in 1QH 4:31 as "God's Spirit," but they are unable to cite analogies in relevant literature in which God's Spirit is the object of a creating activity. Chevallier in

"angel," on the other hand, can be the object of יצר in the Scrolls,[111] but there is no evidence in the Scrolls for an unqualified use of *ruaḥ* in the singular as an angel or demon;[112] and finally, 3) *ruaḥ* in its immediate context in 1QH 4:31 can be best understood in terms of Ezk. 36:26 (*i.e.*, as a new disposition given by God to His eschatological people) in contrast to an understanding based on 1QS 3:13-4:26[113] in which the good spirituality of the sectarian is given to him from birth since the psalmist identifies himself with the rest of humanity as sinful by nature (*cf.* 1QH 4:29ff.). This stands in contrast, *e.g.*, to the context of 1QH 15 :13 & 22, which has to do with a good or evil predestined disposition received at birth and is probably best understood in the light of 1QS 3-4 (*cf.* the discussion of these passages below in this section). In the context of 1QH 15, the

---

Souffle, p. 63 suggest somewhat tentatively that Jubilees 1:21 & 23 (which speak of God creating a "holy spirit" in His people) may refer to God's Spirit, but the context of these passages seems to make this unlikely; *cf.* Sjöberg in "πνεῦμα," p. 378 & n.236,who regards this context as referring to man's spirit and also the same opinion in Russell, *Method*, p. 403.

[111]*E.g.*, 1QH 1:8-9

[112]There are rare uses, however, of a qualified *ruaḥ* in the singular as an angel or demon; *cf.* n. 43 above; note also that *ruaḥ* in רוח כול (*e.g.*, 1QH 1:10 & 10:8) is qualified in this case by its *nomen regens*, כול; *cf.* Kautzsch, *Grammar*, § 146c. For *ruaḥ* in 1QH 4:31 as the "spirit of truth" of 1QS 3:18-19 viewed as a cosmic angel, *cf.* Dupont-Sommer, "instruction," p. 21 and Holm-Nielsen, *Hodayot*, p. 20 n. 10 and p. 85 n. 77;

[113]*Cf.* Carmignac and Guilbert, *Textes*, p. 211 n. 60 and Seitz, "Two Spirits," pp. 94-5. A complicating factor in any discussion of the two spirits is their status as either simple dispositions in man or as angelic creatures which work within man but also transcend him. However, this question has no direct bearing on the issue at hand since with either view of the two spirits God stills creates men from the beginning as either essentially good or evil; thus, a scholar who views the two spirits as angels in 1QS 3-4 and then interprets 1QH 4:31in the light of 1QS 3-4 is not *necessarily* prevented from regarding *ruaḥ* in 1QH 4:31 as a predestined disposition rather than an angel; *cf.* for example, H. W. Kuhn, *Enderwartung*, p. 126.

sectarian cannot really put himself on a level by nature with the rest of sinful humanity since he believes that he and his fellow sectarians were created spiritually good from birth (*cf.* 1QH 15:14ff. and 1QS 3:17-19). He can, of course, note that man's righteousness has its source solely in God's ordination and creative power completely apart from all the efforts of mere "flesh" (1QH 15:12-13) and that men can do nothing to alter this situation in the least (*cf.* 1QH 15: 12-13 and 1QS 3:16), yet he still cannot identify himself by nature with humanity's *sinfulness* before God but only with its *dependence* upon Him. It is clear, then, that 1QH 4:31 does not share the same conceptual environment with 1QH 15 or 1QS 3-4 in spite of the fact that 1QH 4:38 and 15:13 & 17 share some common vocabulary: "You Yourself have created (ברא) the righteous (צדיק) and the wicked (רשע)." The basic conceptual framework of this shared vocabulary is different in the two contexts: in 1QH 15, God's creation of the righteous takes place individually in the womb, whereas in 1QH 4:38 this "creation" probably has to do with the birth of the eschatological community at the end of days.[114]

A major problem, however, with a view of *ruaḥ* in 1QH 4:31 as man's spirit is that it appears to be a *source* of spirituality for the psalmist, and normally in 1QH the sectarian's spirit is presented as being in *need* of spiritual help.[115] However, if the sectarians were as greatly influenced by Ezk. 36 & 37 as we believe,[116] it is reasonable that they viewed themselves not only as having received God's eschatolgical Spirit as promised in Ezk.. 36:27 & 37:14 but also as possessing the new heart and *ruaḥ* (*i.e.*, disposition) promised in these same verses (Ezk.

---

[114]Note that Jubilees 1:20-25 talks about God creating a righteous people in the latter days-- a promise that our author probably saw as fulfilled in his own community. He may have also had Isa. 45:7 in mind; *cf.* Wernberg-Møller, "Reconsideration," p. 415 n. 5: "The sentence [*i.e.*, 1QH 4:38] simply implies that God created everybody." *Cf.* also 4Q495 2 1 with 1QM 13:9.

[115]*Cf.* nn. 18-24 in chapter 3 above.

[116]*Cf.* section *2d2* in chapter 3 above.

36:26). Nevertheless, because of the requirement in Ezk. 36:31 that they assume a posture of unworthiness in spiritual matters, it was difficult for them to speak about their new spiritual worth and spiritual capabilities especially when addressing themselves to God Himself in their hymns. Nevertheless, this kind of language was not completely forbidden, and in 1QH 4:31 it emerges. The reference to the psalmist's spirit in 1QH 4:36 (רוחי), then, means essentially the same thing as *ruaḥ* in v. 31. In both verses the *ruaḥ* is seen as a *secondary* source of the psalmist's ability to lead a sanctified life with God's Spirit, of course, being the primary source. Thus, in 1QH 4:31 the general statement is made that God himself must create the kind of disposition in man which enables him to lead a godly life, and in v. 36 the psalmist says that it was this God-given disposition within him which overcame his weak and sinful nature (vv. 33ff.) and held firm (רוחי החזיקה) its stand in the face of persecution.

1QH 9:16a & 16b; רוח מרוח. Most scholars think that the two occurrences of *ruaḥ* in this verse refer in some sense to man's spirit,[117] although a few believe that they refer to angelic creatures[118] or even to the wind.[119] It appears however, that the majority is correct in this case for the following reasons: 1) there are no clear examples in the Hebrew, non-biblical Scrolls so far in which *ruaḥ* as "angel/demon" occurs in an unqualified, singular form[120] or as a feminine,[121] and 2) the immediate con-

---

[117]*Cf.* Betz, *Offenbarung*, p. 129; Carmignac and Guilbert, *Textes*, p. 245 n. 87; Hauschild, *Gottes Geist*, p. 248; Holm-Nielsen, *Hodayot*, p. 162 n. 118; Irwin, "Spirit-Dualism," p. 192; Leaney, *Rule*, p. 159; G. Maier, *Mensch*, p. 183; Noll, "Angelology," p. 136; Nötscher, "Geist," p. 308; Pryke, "'Spirit'," p. 345; and Schreiner, "Geistbegabung," p. 171.

[118]*Cf.* Huppenbauer, *Mensch*, p. 105 and n. 456 and Johnston, "Spirit," p. 37.

[119]*Cf.* J. Maier, *Texte*, vol. I, 98.

[120]*Cf.* n. 112 above.

[121]A possible exception to this is רוח רעה in 4Q511, 15, 7 and 4Q511, 81, 3, but this appears to be a direct borrowing from the Old Testament; *cf.* chapter 5 below. *Cf.* also the analysis of הרוח in section *3f* below.

text of our passage (vv. 15b-17) is concerned predominantly with the idea that men may differ in stature toward one another but all men in relationship to God amount to absolutely nothing at all. Thus, *ruaḥ* in our expression is immediately preceded by three parallel expressions all referring to man, and the third expression (בשר מיצר [חמר] יכבד) uses the words "flesh" and "creature of [clay]" as metaphorical descriptions of man and so prepares the reader for the author's further metaphorical reference to man as "*ruaḥ*."[122]

1QH 14:11; רוחות. The few scholars who have commented on this verse have understood רוחות here as a reference to the two spirits of 1QS 3-4 (understood as cosmic angels),[123] or as man's predestined being (related conceptually to the two spirits of 1QS 3-4 viewed as angels),[124] or as a simple reference to angels with no special relationship to 1QS 3-4.[125] Most scholars simply do not comment on this verse when they have the opportunity.[126] In light of the fragmentary condition of the text here,[127] this may be a wise policy, but there does seem to be enough evidence in the text as it stands (without excessive reliance on reconstruction) to indicate that רוחות refers to no more than good and evil religious dispositions which distinguish the pious from the wicked. We are referring to the use of the prepositional expression לפי before רוחות. In all the cases in which לפי is used before a form of *ruaḥ* in our material, *ruaḥ* always

---

[122]This use of *ruaḥ* to describe man is not unusual in 1QH; *cf.* n. 57 above.

[123]*Cf.* J. Maier, *Texte,* vol. II, p. 107 n. on 11/12 and p. 206; Merrill, *Qumran,* p. 28; and Ringgren, *Faith,* p. 76.

[124]H. W. Kuhn, *Enderwartung,* pp. 125 & 132.

[125]Irwin, "Spirit-Dualism," pp. 52 & 193.

[126]The five scholars above (nn. 123-125) and Domkowski Hopkins (*cf.* n. 127 below) are the only scholars I know who have offered specific opinions on רוחות in 1QH 14:11.

[127]*Cf.* Dombkowski Hopkins, "Community," p. 340, who notes that 1QH 14:11-12 "by no means offers clear evidence for the two spirits doctrine since the text is damaged and much reconstruction is necessary,"

means man's spirit in one sense or another,[128] and there would seem to be nothing to preclude the same meaning for *ruaḥ* in 1QH 14:11. It is true that scholars have suggested that רוחות should be understood as being in construct with עולם,[129] העולם,[130] or גורלם,[131] and if any of these suggestions is correct, this would indicate that רוחות here probably has to do with angelic beings of some kind rather than with man's spirit.[132] These suggested reconstructions, however, all face various textual and syntactical problems. עולם, for example, is not long enough to fill the gap in the text after רוחות,[133] and the form העולם, which seems to be long enough, is never found anywhere in the Scrolls, at least in association with any form of *ruaḥ*.[134] גורלם, finally, is perhaps a possible reading epigraphically, but the feminine plural form רוחות is never found with any form of גורל; and although גורל is frequently found as a genitive of רוחֵי,[135] it never has a suffix referring to man but is always found with a 3rd. m. sg. suffix referring to Belial. Perhaps the best reading for the words immediately following רוחות would be יבדילם (with the suffix referring to men),[136] which seems to be epigraphically possible and is

---

[128]*Cf.* 1QS 2:20; 4:26b; 9:14; & CD 20:24; *cf.* also the analysis of these verses in section *3c* of this chapter above.

[129]*E.g.*, Mansoor, *Hymns*, p. 181 n 4.

[130]*E.g.*, H. W. Kuhn, *Enderwartung*, p. 126 n. 1.

[131]*Cf.* Vermes, *Scrolls in English*, p. 192, who translates "the spirits of their lot."

[132]When a form of עולם or גורל is a genitive in construct with a form of *ruaḥ*, such an expression always means an angel or demon; *cf.* chapter 5 below.

[133]So Holm-Nielsen, *Hodayot*, p. 220 n. 5.

[134]The article with any form of עולם seems to be very rare in the non-biblical, Hebrew Scrolls; *cf.* for example, K. G. Kuhn, *Konkordanz zu den Qumrantexten*, (Göttingen: Vandenhoeck and Ruprecht, 1960), s.v. עולם.

[135]*E.g.*, 1QS 3:24; 1QM 13:2, 4, & 11/12; 4Q287 Ber^{b} 4, 3; 4Q491, 14-15, 10; 11QMelch 3 II 12; and 11QMelch 3 II 13.

[136]So Lohse, *Texte*, p. 162, who also translates "denn entsprechend den Geistern scheidet er sie zwischen dem Guten und dem Frevelhaften."

found in other places in the Scrolls in association (as here) with the prepositions בֵּין and ל.[137] The meaning of this verse, then, would be that God distinguishes between men on the basis of their good or evil religious dispositions.

We should note, finally, that if 1QH 14:11 were understood fully in the light of 1QS 3-4, this would still not mean that רוחות would have to be understood here as cosmic angels since the two spirits of 1QS 3-4 are themselves not angelic beings but essentially religious dispositions predestined by God which unconditionally determine the spiritual quality of a person's life (*cf.* chapter 8 below).[138] רוחות in 1QH 14:11, however, probably refers to religious dispositions in a less theoretical sense, *i.e.*, as involving God's help together with human effort in a daily process of change and growth. Thus, the psalmist confesses that his understanding of God has its source not in his own spirit but in God's holy Spirit (v. 13) and that as he grows in this understanding he also grows in zeal against the wicked (vv. 13-14). As a result of God's goodness, he determines within himself never to sin against God (vv. 17-18) or assign an improper rank to a community member (vv. 18-20) since it is untimately God Himself who is advancing or removing the members in their spiritual levels (v. 21). This view of a changing and fluctuating spirituality with the psalmist achieving a proper spiritual leadership of the sect at least in part through his own resolve (*cf.* v. 17), does not harmonize well with the view of 1QS 3-4 (or 1QH 15 & 4Q186) that the quality of a person's spirituality is determined unchangeably from birth.[139]

1QH 15:13, יצר כול רוח; and 1QH 15:22, רוח. Strictly speaking, *ruaḥ* in 1QH 15:13 does not belong in this category (*i.e.*, as an unqualifed use of *ruaḥ*) since its *nomen regens* כול does have a

---

[137]*E.g.*, 1QH 7:12; CD 6:17 and 12:19.

[138]This view is possible (although not characteristic) even for scholars who understand the two spirits as cosmic angels; *cf.* n. 113 above.

[139]*Cf.* H. W. Kuhn, *Enderwartung*, p. 121, who notes that 1QS 3-4 presents a spirituality "die dem Menschen schöpfungsmäßig gegeben ist und sein Handeln von vornherein festlegt."

qualifying effect on it.[140] It is treated here because of its close semantic and contextual relationship to the unqualified use of *ruaḥ* in v. 22.[141] Both v. 13 and v. 22, in fact, are immediately preceded by similar references having to do with man's inability to determine the nature of his own conduct (compare v. 13 לא יוכל אנוש להכין צעדו with v. 21 איך יוכל להכין צעדו). Both verses also describe the nature of *ruaḥ* with similar vocabulary (*cf.* the expression הכינותה in vv. 14 & 22 and the analogous concepts ברא in v. 14 and יצר in v. 22). Because of the similar contexts and vocabulary of *ruaḥ* in both passages, then, a conclusion about the meaning of *ruaḥ* in one passage will effect the assessment of its meaning in the other.

---

[140]*Cf.* Kautzsch, *Grammar*, §146c.

[141]This seems to be the view of most scholars; every scholar I know who analyzes *ruaḥ* in both v. 13 and v. 22 understands it as having the same meaning in both verses. It is also interesting to note that all these scholars except for one (*viz.*, Noll in "Angelology," pp. 84 & 136, who defines *ruaḥ* in both verses as "the motive principles of creation") understands *ruaḥ* here as referring in some sense to the spirit of man: *cf.* Brandenburger, *Fleisch*, pp. 86, 88-9 & 91; Coppens, "don," p. 218; Irwin, "Spirit-Dualism," pp. 54 & 193; Johnston, "Spirit," pp. 29 & 34; H. W. Kuhn, *Enderwartung*, pp. 123-6; Lichtenberger, *Studien*, p. 70; G. Maier, *Mensch*, p. 184; Nötscher, "Heiligkeit," pp. 337-8; and Schreiner, "Geistbegabung," p. 165 n. 19 and p. 166. Among those who have commented only on 1QH 15:13, only Holm-Nielsen in *Hodayot*, p. 230 n. 10 understands *ruaḥ* in this verse as a reference to the "spirits of the world" (*i.e.*, the two spirits of 1QS 3-4), while Huppenbauer in *Mensch*, p. 74 defines it as a reference to the "agierende Mächte des Bösen;" most scholars, however, have understood *ruaḥ* here as referring in some sense to man's spirit: *cf.* Betz, *Offenbarung*, pp. 129 & 147; Foerster, "Geist," p. 128; R. Murphy, "*Yeser* in the Qumran literature," *Biblica*, 39 (1958), p. 342; and Kurt Schubert, *The Dead Sea Community* (trans. by J. Doberstein; London: Adam & Charles Black, 1959), p. 60. Among those who have commented only on 1QH 15:22, only Hübner in "Dualismus," pp. 269-270 thinks that *ruaḥ* may refer to something other than man's spirit (*viz.*, "im Sinne der zwei-Geister-Lehre"); for those who understand *ruaḥ* here as man's spirit, *cf.* Anderson, "'Ruah'," p. 294; Kamlah, "Geist," p. 482; Osten-Sacken, *Gott und Belial*, p. 129; and Pryke, "'Spirit'," p. 345.

The most problematic use of *ruaḥ* syntactially in these two passages is in v. 13. Although most scholars agree that *ruaḥ* here refers to man's spirit,[142] others feel that it refers in some sense to angelic beings,[143] and there does seem to be some syntactical support for this view in the qualification of *ruaḥ* with כול.[144] This should not be considered decisive for its meaning. The phrase as a whole (יצר כול רוח) is a unique expression in the Scrolls and should be analyzed primarily on the basis of its own contextual and conceptual framework, and given this kind of analysis, two basic considerations point to *ruaḥ* as man's spirit both here and in v. 22. The first has to do with the immediate contexts of verses 13 and 22. In the context just preceding *ruaḥ* in v. 13, the psalmist notes that man cannot direct his own way, and just after *ruaḥ* here he identifies the reason for this inability in the fact that God alone creates the "righteous" and the "wicked" from the *womb* and alone establishes them either for salvation (v. 15) or destruction (v. 17). כול רוח יצר is thus preceded and followed by references not to angels but to human beings; furthermore, it is associated with much of the same vocabulary used in man's description.הכין and ברא are used with the "righteous" as their object in vv. 14-15 and ברא in v. 17 with the "wicked" as its object, and both of these verbs are used in v. 14 with יצר כול רוח as the object of ברא and probably the "works" of this "יצר" as the object of הכין. *Ruaḥ* in 1QH 15:13 therefore has to do with the spirit of man since it is within a context which has man as its theme and it is also described with the same vocabulary. The same kind of context is likewise found in v. 22 in which *ruaḥ* is directly preceded and followed by refer-

---

[142]*Cf.* n. 141 above.

[143]*Ibid.*

[144]In the four places in which כול רוח appears in the Scrolls (disregarding כול רוח ורוח in Temple Scroll 36:5 & 40:8 in which *ruaḥ* refers to "wind/ direction"), most scholars believe that it means "angel/demon"; *cf.* 1QH 1:9; 10:8 and 1Q36, 15, 5 in chapter 5 below; *cf.* also כול רוח עולה (1QS 4:20) in chapter 8 below in which *ruaḥ,* however, probably refers an evil disposition in man rather than to evil demons of some kind which are thought to live within him.

ences to man as the center of interest (*cf.* עפר and בשר in v. 21, and {probably} כול חי in v. 22; *cf.* the analysis of 4Q504, 6, 22 in section *3b3* above). The second consideration pointing to *ruaḥ* as man's spirit in both 1QH 15:13 & 22 has to do with the number of expressions these verses share with 1QS 3. This consideration is based, in turn, on the position that the two spirits of 1QS 3-4 are essentially dispositions within men rather than personal, angelic beings (*cf.* chapter 8 for the evidence of this). Given the validity of this position, then, the connections between 1QS 3 and 1QH 15 can be seen in their descriptions of God "establishing" (הכין, *cf.* 1QS 3:15 with 1QH 15:14 & 22) man's activity[145] before actually creating him with a good or evil spiritual nature (ברא, *cf.* 1QS 3:15-18 with 1QH 15:14-17) and, therefore, fixing unchangeably man's future activity (*cf.* פעולה in 1QS 3:16 and 1QH 15:22) so that it is in no sense under his personal control (compare 1QS 3:16: ואין להשנות ימלאו פעולתם) with 1QH 15:14: איכה יוכל כול להשנות את דבריך). Given the view that the two spirits of 1QS 3:13ff. are not personal, angelic creatures but essentially spiritual dispositions given to men at birth, it seems clear that *ruaḥ* in 1QH 15:13 & 22 has the same meaning. If a scholar is convinced of the angelic status of the two spirits, however, the kinds of connections noted above would be evidence that *ruaḥ* in 1QH 15:13 & 22, despite its predominant concern with man, is really referring to the cosmic angels of 1QS 3-4. Nevertheless, most scholars have not taken this position[146] even though most of them regard the two spirits of 1QS 3-4 as cosmic angels (*cf.* chapter two above).

We should note, finally, that *ruaḥ* in v. 22 is feminine and in an unqualified, singular form; this fact alone would indicate that the author is not thinking of a personal, angelic entity of some kind since an unqualified f. sg. of *ruaḥ* is never clearly

---

[145]The text is damaged at the end of v. 13, but with a comparison of v. 22 it is a resonable conjecture that it is man's פעולה or something analogous (*e.g.*, דרכי]ו[) which God establishes before creating man.

[146]*Cf.* n. 141 above.

used to refer to an angel or demon in the non-biblical, Hebrew Scrolls published so far.[147]

1QH 17:17; מרוחות. This is one of the most difficult occurrences of *ruaḥ* in the Scrolls to analyze since its expected form in association with the expression אשר נתתה בי is ברוח or מרוח.[148] Scholars seem to be almost equally divided over its meaning here with some suggesting that it refers to spiritual gifts or dispositions of some kind[149] or to angelic spirits (usually the two spirits of 1QS 3-4 viewed as angels)[150] or even to the Spirit of God.[151] The precise form of *ruaḥ* here (*i.e.*, an unqualified, feminine plural) is an additional problem for analysis since this form is rather rare in the non-biblical Scrolls[152] and never occurs with מ or מן. Nevertheless, *ruaḥ* here probably does not refer to God's Spirit or to angels but to various spiritual qualities associated with life in the Qumran community (as the recipient of the promise of Ezk. 36:26) for the following reasons: 1) there is no clear reference to the Spirit of God in the Scrolls

---

[147]*Cf.* n. 112 above.

[148]*Cf.* 1QH 12:11; 13:19; 16:11; and f 3:14.

[149]*Cf.*Dupont-Sommer, *écrits*, p. 263 n. 1; Irwin, "Spirit-Dualism," pp. 58, 193 & 225 n. 68; Johnston, "Spirit," p. 29; Licht, *Thanksgiving Scroll*, p. 38; Nötscher, "Heiligkeit," p. 337; and Pryke, "'Spirit'," pp. 345-6.

[150]*Cf.* Carmignac and Guilbert, *Textes*, p. 152 n. 40 & p. 175 n. 23; Ellis, "Gifts," pp. 136-7; Gaster, *Scriptures*, p. 253 n. 6; Holm-Nielsen, *Hodayot*, p. 247 n. 2 & p. 249 n. 22; Hübner, "Dualismus," p. 269; and J. Maier, *Texte*, vol. II, p. 206.

[151]*Cf.* Dietzel "Beten," p. 25; H. W. Kuhn, *Enderwartung*, p. 130; Schanckenburg, "'Anbetung'," p. 92; and Sjöberg, "Neuschöpfung," p. 135 n. 6. Leaney in *Rule*, p. 35 also defines *ruaḥ* here as God's Spirit, but he probably identifies God's Spirit with the good spirit of 1QS 3:18ff. (*cf. ibid.*, pp. 43-4); Hauschild in *Gottes Geist*, p. 251 interprets the plural of *ruaḥ* as a reference to both man's natural spirit and God's holy Spirit (*cf. ibid.*, p. 249 and n. 42).

[152]*Cf.* 1QH 1:29b; 14:11 and 1QM 10:12; *cf.* also 1QH 17:23 & 4Q511, 24, 2. Note, finally, that the number in שתי רוחות (1QS 3:18) qualifies *ruaḥ*; *cf.* Kautzsch, *Grammar*, §134c.

with any form of *ruaḥ* in the plural;[153] 2) there is rarely a reference to angels in the Scrolls with an unqualified use of *ruaḥ* in the plural;[154] 3) the closest clear syntactical parallel in the Scrolls to our expression is רוחות in 1QH 14:11, which appears to be a reference to no more than good and evil human dispositions (*cf.* the discussion of this verse above in this section); and finally, 4) the general context of this hymn seems to support the view that the psalmist is referring to spiritual dispositions and capacities which he has received not in birth but as a faithful member of the sectarian community. He notes that on his own he has only a "spirit of flesh" (v. 25) and that he has fallen into sin in the past (v. 18); he implores God not to let this happen again since he knows that God alone is the source of qualities such as צדקה and שכל (vv. 20-1). It is possible that the psalmist did not use the singular of *ruaḥ* in v. 17 since he wanted to make it clear that his reference was to spiritual dispositions and qualities rather than to the Spirit of God as such, and he may have used the phrase אשר נתתה בי (which is so characteristic in 1QH in referring to God's Spirit as an eschatological gift)[155] in order to make it clear that spiritual qualities such as righteousness and insight were *gifts* of God which he had received in his eschatological community rather than "natural," spiritual dispositions which had always been at his personal disposal from birth onward. This psalm, in fact, can be read as a protest against the implications of 1QS 3-4 and 1QH 15 that men are born with the ability (or inability) to keep the law and that nothing can alter this in the least (*cf.* 1QS 3:16 and 1QH 15:14).

e. The meaning of *ruaḥ* in the singular, followed by one or more participial adjectives: (8 times; *cf.* section 3a in this chapter above for references).

Except for the expression רוח נעוה in 1QH 13:15 and f 12:6, there is almost unanimous consensus among scholars that the oc-

---

[153]*Cf.* section *2a* in chapter 3 above.
[154]*E.g.*, 1QM 10:12; *cf.* also 1QH 17:23.
[155]*Cf.* section *2d2* in chapter 3 above.

currences of *ruaḥ* in the pattern above refer in some sense to the spirit of man,[156] and this consensus seems to be correct. Thus, רוח נשברה (*cf.* Ps. 51:19) is associated with יצר סמוך in 1QS 8:3 as a quality required of sectarian leaders, and in 1QS 11:1c it is conceptually parallel to ענוה as a quality of leadership sought by the psalmist. It is also clear that רוח נסוגה in 1QS 8:12 refers in some way to man (rather than to a demon) for the following reasons: 1) the context of this passage has to do primarily with the sectarians' fear of disloyalty in their new members rather than with a fear of demonic attack; 2) there is no difficulty in understanding *ruaḥ* in מיראת רוח נסוגה either as a human disposition ("because of a fear of disloyalty") or as a metaphorical reference to man ("because of a fear of a disloyal person");[157] and finally, 3) the feminine of *ruaḥ* is never used unambiguously in sectarian expressions to refer to an angel or demon. The expression רוח נבונה ואורה in 11QPsa DavComp 27 II 4, on the other hand, is more difficult to understand. Its context is less clear, and its position syntactically as the object of נתן reminds the reader of passages such as 1QH 12:11; 13:19; 16:11: and f 3:14 which refer to God's Spirit as a gift (*cf.* section *2d2* in chapter three above). But the expression is probably referring to a simple human disposition for the following reasons: 1) the verb נתן is followed not by ב but by ל, which is different from the regularity of expression in 1QH (נתן + ב) and may indicate a different meaning; 2) the immediate context of our expression (*cf.* vv. 2-3) is primarily interested in describing David's personal qualities (*i.e.*, he is חכם, נבון and תמים), and it is not until v. 11 of our text that a reference is made to David's gift of prophecy. This reference may have been necessary because nothing in vv. 1-4 expressly implied that David had the special charismatic

---

[156]I have found only two scholars who regard *ruaḥ* in any of these occurrences as referring to something other than the spirit of man: *cf.* Foerster, "Geist," p. 124, who thinks that *ruaḥ* in 1QH 8:12 could refer either to man's spirit or to one of the various spirits of Belial, and also Huppenbauer, "Belial," p. 84 and n. 22, who describes *ruaḥ* in 1QH 11:12 as an impersonal "*Macht*" which stands behind godlessness.

[157]*E.g.*, as in 1QH 1:22; 2:15; 3:21; 7:11; and 13:13.

presence of God's Spirit (and therefore the gift of prophecy),[158] and the author wished to make this point clear.

As noted above, רוח נעוה in 1QH 13:15 and f 12:6[159] has involved some disagreement among scholars.[160] Semantically, the status of נעוה as a participial adjective or a noun does not seem to make much difference[161] unless, of course, the four examples of this expression (1QH 3:21; 11:12; 13:15 and f 12:6) are not really identical in form (some having the noun and and some the participle). If as it seems, however, we are dealing with a single expression, the context of רוח נעוה in 1QH 3:21 and 11:12 (whether נעוה is regarded throughout as a noun or participial adjective) would indicate that the same expression in 1QH 13:15 (and f 12:6) is describing man rather than a demon. In 1QH 3:21 the sectarian refers to himself as a "perverted spirit" (*i.e.*, a perverted person) whom God has cleansed, and in 1QH 11:12 the same expression (this time with the meaning "perverted disposition") is presented as the opposite of בינת[כה] ("knowedge

---

[158]*Cf.* n. 32 in chapter 3 above.

[159]Sukenik in *אוצר המגילות* transcribes the letters in f 12:6 following נעוה as מעול (*cf.* this transcription *in loco*), but K. G. Kuhn believes that some form of the verb משל should be read; *cf.* K. G. Kuhn, *Kondordanz*, s.v. רוח in f 12:6. This would mean that 1QH 13:15 and f 12:6 have the same construction and probably the same meaning.

[160]Most scholars believe that *ruaḥ* in 1QH 13:15 is simply the human spirit (I have found no one except Huppenbauer who has commented on the meaning of *ruaḥ* in f 12:6), but some believe that it may refer to an evil spirit or demon: *cf.* Anderson, "'Ruah'," p. 298 (or possibly also man's spirit); W. H. Brownlee, "Anthropology and Soteriology in the Dead Sea Scrolls and the New Testament," *The Use of the Old Testament in the New and Other Essays*, Studies in Honor of W. F. Stinespring (ed. by J. E. Efird; Durham: Duke University Press, 1972), p. 229; Huppenbauer, "Belial,: p. 84 and n. 22 (for both 1QH 13:15 and f 12:6, but he regards these spirits as impersonal); *idem*, *Mensch*, pp. 74-5 and n. 304 (for both 1QH 13:15 and f 12:6 as "agierende Mächte des Bösen"); May, "Cosmological Reference," p. 5 n. 17; and Noll, "Angelology," p. 225. *Cf.* also Mansoor, *Hymns*, p. 179 n. 7.

[161]*Cf.* the discussion of this form in n. 23 above.

of [You]," *i.e.*, God).[162] In both cases, then, רוח נעוה is clearly descriptive of man, and this emphasis fits in well with the context of 1QH 13:15, which does not deal with the problem of demonic attack (*e.g.*, as in 4Q510, 1 and 4Q511,1) but with man's spiritual unworthiness from birth (vv. 13-15 and his own accountability before God's judgment (v. 16). A problem with this view of *ruaḥ* in 1QH 13:15, however, is the verb משל. In the only other use of משל with *ruaḥ* in the non-biblical Scrolls (*viz.*, CD 12:2), it clearly describes demonic activity[163] and this is true also of similar contexts in Jubilees.[164] But two basic syntactical considerations indicate that *ruaḥ* in 1QH 13:15 should not be read in the light of CD 12:2 or the analogous passages in Jubilees. The first is that CD 12:2 speaks of spirits in the plural while clearly associating them with Belial, which is characteristic of sectarian expression when referring to evil angels or demons,[165] whereas 1QH 13:15 has the singular of *ruaḥ* as part of an expression which is never found elsewhere as a clear reference to a demon (*viz.*, רוח נעוה; *cf.* above). But perhaps most importantly, *ruaḥ* in CD 12:2 is masculine in gender, which is characteristic for for its meaning as "angel/demon,"[166] whereas in 1QH 13:15 it is feminine, which is characteristic for its meaning as "man's spirit."[167]

f. Uses of *ruaḥ* which require special attention: הרוח, 4Q266 Da 1 XVII 6; רוח החיים, 4Q266 Da 1 XVII 12; יצר כול רוח, 1QH 15:13

---

[162]Note the similar contrasts between man's natural spirituality and divine knowledge in 1QH 1: 22-24 and 13:13-14

[163]*Cf.* chapter 5 below; I know of no scholar who disagrees with this view of *ruaḥ* in CD 12:2.

[164]*E.g.*, Jubilees 1:20; 10:3-6; 12:20 and 20:28.

[165]*Cf.* n. 43 above and 1QM 13:2, 4, & 11/12; 14:10; 4Q177, 1-4, 10; 4Q286Bera/287Berb 4,3; 4Q491, 14-15, 10; 11QMelch 3 II 12; and 11QMelch 3 II 13. In Jubilees also the "spirit" or "spirits" who rule over men are either expressly associated with Belial or clearly identified as demons; *cf.* the references in n. 164 above.

[166]*Cf.* section 1 in chapter 5 below

[167]*Cf.* section 2 in this chapter above.

(analyzed with רוח in 1QH 15:22 in section *3d* of this chapter above); and שתי רוחות, 1QS 3:18 (analyzed in chapter 8 below as part of the two-spirit Treatise).

According to Milik, 4Q266 Da 1 XVII is a fragment of a *halakhah* based on Lev. 13 & 15 which once belonged to CD but was not conserved by it.[168] The basic concern of 4Q266 Da 1 XVII in so far as this involves *ruaḥ* is the identification and ritual treatment of skin disease (lines 1-13). Its use of *ruaḥ* here requires special attention for two basic reasons: it is only in this fragment (line 6) in the non-biblical, Hebrew Scrolls published to date that הרוח (*i.e.*, unattached and with the article) ever appears in a context sufficient enough for analysis,[169] and it is only here that the Scrolls preserve a context (with the exception of the Aramaic 1QapGen 20) which closely relates *ruaḥ* to a disease process.[170] If *ruaḥ* in line 6 of this fragment is inter-

[168]J. T. Milik, "Fragment d'une source du psautier (4Q Ps 89) et fragments des Jubilés, du Document de Damas, d'un Phylactère dans la grotte 4 de Qumran," *Revue Biblique*, 73 (1966), p. 105.

[169]This appears otherwise only in the fragmentary context of 4Q178, 1, 6 and has no discernable meaning; *cf.* also 11QMelch 3 II 18 in section *2f* in chapter 3 above (with הרוח attached as a genitive to משיח).

[170]The idea that demons attack men was accepted at Qumran, but is is difficult to determine if these attacks were generally thought to involve disease. In van der Ploeg's analysis of the apotropaic, non-canonical matrerial attached to Ps. 91 found in Cave 11 (*cf.* J. van der Ploeg, "Un petit rouleau de psalmes apocryphes (11QPs Apa)," *Tradition und Glaube*, Festgabe für K. G. Kuhn (Göttingen: Vandenhoeck & Rupprecht, 1971), pp. 128-139), there does not seem to be a clear reference to demons as the *cause* of a disease process (although demons are mentioned and the psalmist seems to seek "healing" of some kind, *cf. ibid.*, pp. 130-1), and this is also true for the apotropaic literature analyzed by Baillet in *Discoveries*, VII, pp. 215-262 (4Q510 and 4Q511). Apparently, the main work of demons in sectarian thought (as seen in 4Q510 & 511) was to inspire fear (*cf. ibid.*, p. 225 line 4) and strike without warning at the sectarian's religious confidence and his capacity to obey the law (*cf.* 4Q511, 1, 6 in *ibid.*, p. 216: הפוגעים פתע פתאום לתעות רוח בינה ולהשם לבבם). Note also the Aramaic fragment 4QprNab, which speaks of an "exorcist"(?) (גזר) who healed Nabonidus of some sort of disease (שחנא באישא); the precise meaning of גזר, however, is not clear (*cf.* Kirch-

preted in the light of how most scholars interpret 1QapGen 20[171] (*cf.* also Jubilees 10),[172] it would seem to be clear that the

---

schläger, "Exorcismus," pp. 146-7), and there is no mention here of either a *ruaḥ* or demon. The status of this fragment as a sectarian composition is also unclear (*cf. ibid.*, p. 147).

Finally, we should note that the exact relationship between רוח טמאה in 11QPsa Plea 19:15 (probably a demon; *cf.* chapter 5 below) is ambiguous: the "pain" (and also "inclination to sin") here may not be the result of demonic activity as such but may themselves be personifications of evil which actively "possess" their victims (so Osten-Sacken, *Gott und Belial*, p. 143). Note, finally, that this is probably not a sectarian composition (*cf.* Sanders, *Discoveries*, IV, p. 76). *Cf.* also Tobit 6:7-8.

[171]The editors of the *Genesis Apocryphon* understood the destructive *ruaḥ* in column 20 as an "evil wind" (*cf.* Nahman Avigad and Yigael Yadin, *A Genesis Apocryphon, A Scroll from the Wilderness of Judaea* (Jerusalem: Magnes Press, 1956), pp. 43-44), and a number of scholars in the late 1950's followed their lead: *cf.* Burrows, *More Light*, pp. 389-390; Medico, *L'enigme*, pp. 521-2; and H. Michaud, "Un livre apocryphe de la Genèse en Araméen," *Positions Lutheriennes*, vol. 5 no. 2 (1957), pp. 96-97; *cf.* also Bardtke, *Handschriftenfunde*, p. 279, who translates *ruaḥ* here as "*Hauch*." In 1957, however, Flusser suggested that *ruaḥ* should be understood as a demonic spirit (*cf.* David Flusser, "Healing through the Laying-on of Hands in a Dead Sea Scroll," *Israel Exploration Journal*, 7 (1957), pp. 107-8), and most scholars have since agreed: *cf.* especially Fitzmyer, *Genesis Apocryphon*, pp. 131-2 for this view; *cf.* also Dupont-Sommer, *écrits*, pp. 300-1; *idem*, "Exorcismes et guérisons dans les écrits de Qoumrân," *Supplements to Vetus Testamentum*, VII (Leiden: Brill, 1960), p. 249; Joseph A. Fitzmyer and Daniel J. Harrington, *A Manual of Palestinian Aramaic Texts*, Biblica et Orientalia, 34 (Rome: Biblical Instutute Press, 1978), pp. 115-7; Gaster, *Scriptures*, pp. 266-7; P. Grelot, "Sur l'Apocryphe de la Gènese (col. XX, Ligne 26)," *Revue de Qumrân*, 2 (1958), pp. 274 & 276; Irwin, "Spirit-Dualism," pp. 73, 194 & 234 n. 70; B. Jongeling, C. Labuschagne and A. van der Woude, *Aramaic Texts from Qumran with Translations and Annotations*, Semitic Studies Series, 4 (Leiden: Brill, 1976), pp. 97-101; Kirchschläger, "Exorcismus," pp. 139-141; G. Lambert, "Une 'Genèse Apocrypha' trouvée à Qumran," *Recherches Bibliques*, 4 (1959), pp. 94-5; Lignée in Carmignac, Cothenet and Lignée, *Textes*, pp. 230-2; J. Maier, *Texte*, vol. I, pp. 160-1; Noll,

sectarians understood צרעת (and perhaps other physical afflictions) as the work of personal demonic forces, and the article on *ruaḥ* here would seem to underline this understanding.[173] It would also be clear that the sectarians could refer to a personal, demonic being with the feminine singular of *ruaḥ*. A number of considerations, however, indicate that *ruaḥ* here should not be understood as an evil angel or demon but as an abstract description of a disease process somewhat equivalent to נֶגַע in Leviticus 13, but with perhaps more emphasis on the disease as a virulent process drawing a person toward death rather than as a simple state of ill-health. Thus, 1) in the place in which נגע would be expected in 4Q266 Da 1 XVII, *ruaḥ* instead is found[174] and נגע otherwise never appears in the text.[175] 2) The counterpart of הרוח in 4Q266 Da 1 XVII 6 is not a personal angelic figure but rather the impersonal רוח החיים of Gen. 6:17, 7:15 & 22, an expression which in Genesis refers to the impersonal "breath of life" in both men and animals and is otherwise never found in Qumran's non-biblical literature. הרוח as the opposite of רוח החיים, then, would be the impersonal death/disease process which replaces man's רוח החיים.[176] 3) 1QapGen and Jubilees may not have been composed in sectarian circles and, therefore, should not be used uncritically as a background against which

"Angelology," pp. 31, 40 & 225; and Vermes, *Scrolls in English*, pp. 219-220.

[172]Russell notes in *Method*, p. 251, that the evil spirits in Jubilees 10 "make men suffer from all kinds of diseases."

[173]*Cf.* chapter one above on D. Lys' view of the effect of the article on *ruaḥ* in the Old Testament.

[174]*Cf.* Lev. 13:29 יהיה . . . נגע בראש או בזקן with line 6 of 4Q266 Da 1 XVII באה רוח ברוש או בזקן. Note that רוש is an alternate orthography in the Scrolls for ראש; *cf.* Baillet, *Discoveries*, VII, 251, note on line 3 of fragment 71.

[175]However, in line 16, which deals with the *halakhah* concerning discharges, the forms מגע and הנוגע) are found.

[176]*Cf.* the phrase (in various forms) in lines 1, 4-5, 10-11 and 11: נוסף אל המת מן החי (lit. "it has increased to the dead from the living").

to view 4Q266 Da 1 XVII.[177] Rather, the general lack of interest in the Scrolls in afflictions caused by demons or in rites of exorcism for healing these afflictions (as in col. 20 of 1QapGen)[178] points away from a view of הרוח in 4Q266 1 Da XVII 6 as a personal, demonic figure. Finally, 4) the consistency of the sectarians in using the feminine gender for man's spirit and the masculine gender for personal entities such as angels and demons in itself argues for an understanding of *ruaḥ* here as an impersonal disease process. It is difficult to say with certainly why the article is present on *ruaḥ* in both v. 6 and 12 of our fragment, but a possibility may be that both "spirits" were mentioned earlier in a section now lost.[179]

4. Conclusion.

For an analysis of this chapter and a comparison of its results with the results of chapters 3, 5 and 6 (*ruaḥ* as God's Spirit {ch. 3}, angel/demon {ch. 5}, and wind & breath {ch. 6}), see chapter 7 below.

---

[177]This is basically Lichtenberger's opinion on 1QapGen in *Studien*, pp. 40-2, citing Fitzmyer in *Genesis Apocryphon*, pp. 11-12; *cf.* also G. Nickelsburg, in Stone, *Writings*, p. 106, who notes that "indications of Essene beliefs are not demonstrable" in 1QapGen. The situation is more complex in the case of Jubilees. Nickelsburg reports (*ibid.*, pp. 101-2) that recent scholarship is divided over an Essene or pre-Essene date of composition and that those who favor an Essene date are divided on the question of Jubilee's origin in Qumran (*cf. ibid.*, p. 103 n. 74).

[178]*Cf.* n. 170 above and the observation of Kirchschläger in "Exorcismus," p. 151: "Eine Austreibungstätigkeit, wie sie uns in den synoptischen Evangelien für das Wirken Jesu bezeugt wird, hat es in Qumran nicht gegeben. Eine Durchsicht aller bisher aufgefundenen Texte gibt dafür nicht den geringsten Anhaltspunkt."

[179]*Cf.* Kautzsch, *Grammar*, §126d.

CHAPTER 5

RUAḤ AS ANGEL/DEMON

1. Basic syntactical charactersistics of *ruaḥ* as angel/demon.

Ruaḥ is found as angel/demon in the published,[1] nonbiblical Hebrew Scrolls 58 times, including 4 cases in which it is reconstructed (1QH 1:12; 1QM 19:1; 4Q511, 48-49+51, 2-3; and 4Q511, 182 1) and 9 cases in which it is partially reconstructed (1QH f 31:1; 4QSl 40, 24, 5; 4Q177, 1-4, 10; 4Q177, 12-13, I, 9; 4Q286Ber^a 10 II 7-8; 4Q287 Ber^b 4, 3; 4Q511, 15, 7; 4Q511, 81, 3; and 11QMelch 3, II, 13). It is usually found in the plural (51 times) and most often in a masculine form (31 times), although various forms of the feminine plural are also frequent (20 times). It also occurs 7 times in the singular in various patterns (1QH 1:9; 10:8; 1Q36, 15:5;[2] 4Q511, 15, 7; 4Q511, 81, 3; 4Q286Ber^a 10 II 7; and 11QPs^a Plea 19:15).[3]

Perhaps the most outstanding characteristic of *ruaḥ* as angel/demon is its consistently masculine gender. Thus *ruaḥ* is the subject of the masculine verbs יריבו (and possibly יתהלכו) in 1QS 4:23, יהיו in 1QH f 5:4, יושדו in 1QH f 5:6, ארורים in 1QM 13:4, יתהלכו (partially) in 1QM 13:11/12, ימשלו in CD 12:2, יצאו (partially) in

[1]*Cf.* John Strugnell, "The Angelic Liturgy at Qumran, 4Q Serek Šhîrôt ʿOlat Haššabbāt," *Supplements to Vetus Testamentum*, 7 (1959), pp. 32-3 who lists 18 unpublished forms of *ruaḥ* as angels (but *cf.* C. Newsom, *Songs of the Sabbath Sacrifice: A Critical Edition*, Scholars Press, 1985): רוחי דעת אמת : רוחי אלי עולמים : רוחות רוקמה : רוחות צדק : רוחות פלא :
רוחי צבאי : רוחי עולמים : רוחי כבוד : רוחי הוד והדר (אלוהים חיים) : רוחי הוד : רוחי דעת ובינה
רוחי ענן : רוחי משא : רוחי קורב קודש קודשים : רוחי קודש קודשים : רוחי קודש עולמים : פלא
: רוחי ממשלות and צירי רוחות:

[2]This form may not be singular or unattached to following modifiers due to its fragmentary context.

[3]For a complete listing of all the above forms, *cf.* section *2a* of this chapter below.

4QSl 40, 24, 5, מתהלכים in 4QSl 40, 24, 6, זעומים & ארורים in 4Q286 Bera/287 Berb 4, 3-4, משרתים in 4Q502, 27, 1, יתהלכו in 4Q511, 1, 3, and ה[יו [ה]ממרים ... (partially) in 11QMelch 3 II 12; it is referred to by masculine suffixes on מעשיהם in 1QH 1:9, ממשלתם in 1QH 1:11, טמאתם & רשעם in 1QM 13: 4-5, פקודתמה & טמאתמה, רשעמה in 4Q286 Bera/287 Berb 4, 3-4, and ממשלתם & להכניעם in 4Q511, 35, 7; finally, the masculine pronoun המה refers to *ruaḥ* twice in 1QM 13: 4-5, twice in 4Q286 Bera/287 Berb 4, 3-4, and once (partially) in 11QMelch 3 II 12. On the other hand, unambiguous references to *ruaḥ* as angel/ demon in the feminine are rare. A possible case is the expression רוח רעה in 4Q511, 15, 7 and 4Q511 81, 3, which may refer to a demon; but if so, it is unique and probably involves a special circumstance.[4]

2. Specific syntactical patterns of *ruaḥ* as angel/demon.

a. General observations

The most frequent use of *ruaḥ* as angel/demon is as a *nomen regens* in a masculine plural construct followed by one or more genitives and often preceded itself by the *nomen regens* כול (26 times): (כול) רוחי אמת (1QM 13:10), רוחי אמת ועול (1QS 4:23), (כול) רוחי אפעה (1QH 3:18), רוח[י ב]ליעל (4Q177, 1-4, 10), רוחי גורלו (11QMelch 3 II 12), (כול) רוחי גורלו (1QS 3:24; 1QM 13:2; 13:4; 13:11/12; 4Q286 Bera/287 Berb 4, 3; 4Q491, 14-15, 10; and 11QMelch 3 II 13), רוחי הבלים (4Q511, 15, 5), רוחי חבל (4Q511, 43, 6), רוחי [ח]בלו (1QM 14:10), (כול) רוחי מלאכי חבל (4Q510, 1, 5a), רוח]י ממזרי[ם (4Q511, 182, 1), (כו[ל]) רוחי ממזרים (4Q511, 35, 7), רוחי עולמים (4Q502, 27, 1), רו]חי צדק (1QH 2:4), רוחי רשע (4Q511, 1, 6), (כול) רוחי רש]עה (1QM 15:14), רוחי [?] (1QH 11:13), (כול) רוחי [?] (4Q510, 2, 3),(ריבי כול) רוחי [?] (4Q511, 48-49+51, 7-8), and רוח[י ?] (4Q511, 60, 2). The next most frequent pattern for *ruaḥ* as angel/demon is with *ruaḥ* as a *nomen regens* in a feminine plural form followed by a genitive and occasionally preceded itself by the *nomen regens* כול (16 times): רוחות [א]לוהים חיים (4QSl 40, 24, 6), רוחות בליעל (CD 12:2), רוחות דעת (1QH 3:22), רוחות ממזרים (4Q510, 1, 5b), [(כול) רוחות] ממזרים (4Q511, 48-49+51, 2-3), רוחות ממשלתה

[4]*Cf.* the analysis of this in section *2e3* of this chapter below.

(4Q511, 1, 3), רוחות עולה (1QH f 5:6), רוחות עולם 1QH 1:11), רוחות פשע (1Q36, 2:5), רוחות קודש (1QH 8:12), רוחו[ת] קודש קודשים (4QSl 40, 24, 5), רוחות רשעה (1QH f 5:4), רוחות[?] (1QH 17:23), (כול) רוחות[?] (1QH f 45:6). and (כול) רוחו[ת?] (4Q177, 12-13, I, 9); note, finally, the somewhat conjectural restoration (רוחות סערה) advocated by some some in 1QH 1:12.[5] The remaining forms of *ruaḥ* in the plural as angel/demon are less well represented and in some cases uncertain: *cf. ruaḥ* (masculine form) as a genitive in construct with the *nomen regens* צבא (3 times), צבא רוחיך (1QH 13:8), צבא רוחיו (1QM 12:9), and צ]בא רוחיו (1QM 19:1);[6] *ruaḥ* by itself with a suffix (3 times), (f. form) רוחתיו (4Q185, 1-2, I, 9), and (m. forms) רוחיכה (1Q36, 17:2) & ר]וחיך (1QH f 33:2);[7] *ruaḥ* (f. form) as a genitive with the article in construct with the *nomen regens* כול (2 times), כול הרוחות (4Q158, 14, I, 2 & 8Q5, 2, 6); and *ruaḥ* as an unqualified genitive in construct with משא (once), משא רוחות (1QM 10:12). Finally, *ruaḥ* occurs 7 times in the singular in the following forms: as the semantically plural[8] and qualified genitive of כול[9] (3 times), כול רוח (1QH 1:9; 10:8; and 1Q36, 15:5[10]); as a *nomen regens* of a genitive (2 times), רו]ח האב]דון (4Q286 Bera 10 II 7) and רוח טמאה (11QPsa Plea 19:15); and as qualified by the feminine adjective רעה (2 times), רוח רעה (4Q511, 15, 7 & 4Q511, 81, 3).

b. The meaning of *ruaḥ* as a *nomen regens* in a masculine plural construct form followed by one or more genitives: (16 times; *cf.* section 2a for references; note that 1QS 4:23 will be handled below in chapter 4).

Perhaps the best way to handle this pattern is to divide it into three categories: those occurrences over which there is no

---

[5]*E.g.*, Lohse, *Texte*, p. 112; *cf.* also Mansoor, *Hymns*, p. 99 n. 2.

[6]As restored on the basis of 1QM 12:9; *cf.* Lohse, *Texte*, p. 222.

[7]This form could also be a genitive with its *nomen regens* now lost due to its fragmentary context.

[8]*Cf.* n. 43 in chapter 4 above and also the plural suffix on מעשיהם in 1QH 1:9 referring back to כול רוח.

[9]*Cf.* Kautzsch, *Grammar*, §146c for this effect of כול on its genitive.

[10]*Cf.* n. 2 above.

apparent disagreement among scholars, those over which there is some disagreement, and those which have not been treated. We should note that even in the second category above a strong majority of scholars supports the meaning angel/demon for *ruaḥ* in every case.

1) Occurrences of *ruaḥ* over which there is no apparent disagreement among scholars:[11] רוח]י ב[ליעל (4Q177, 1-4, 10),[12] (כול) רוחי גורלו (1QM 13:2; 13:4; 13:11/12; & 4Q286 Ber^a/287Ber^b 4, 3), רו[חי צדק (1QH 2:4), and [?] רוחי (1QH 11:13).

This consensus seems to be essentially correct. Thus, the closest analogy syntactically to רוח]י ב[ליעל (or רוח]ות ב[ליעל ?) in 4Q177, 1-4, 10 is רוחות בליעל in CD 12:2, which clearly has to do with demons (*cf.* section 2*c* below), although the statement that Israel has "wallowed" (ה[ת]גוללו) in the spirits of Belial is similar to 1QS 4:22 which describes the sectarians as "wallowing"

---

[11]For *ruaḥ* as "angel" in 1QH 2:4, *cf.* Irwin, "Spirit-Dualism," p. 198 n. 17 & p. 199 n. 18 and Schweizer, "πνεῦμα," p. 390 n. 332; for 4Q177, 1-4, 10 & 4Q286 Ber^a/287 Ber^b 4, 3, *cf.* Noll, "Angelology," pp. 225-6; for (a) 1QH 11:13, (b) 1QM 13:2, (c) 1QM 13:4, and (d) 1QM 13: 11/12, *cf.* Anderson, "'Ruah'," pp. 297-8 (c & d); Betz, *Offenbarung*, p. 129 n. 3 (all); Böcher, *Dualismus*, p. 30, 47-8 & 75 (all); Coppens, "don," p. 119 (a only); Delcor, *Hymns*, p. 42 (a only);*idem*,"Doctrines," col. 964 (b, c & d); Hill, *Greek Words*, p. 235 (b, c & d); Holm-Nielsen, *Hodayot*, pp. 185 & 187 n. 26 (a only); Huppenbauer, *Mensch*, pp. 84-5 & 96 (all); Irwin, "Spirit-Dualism," p. 198 n. 17, p. 199 n. 18 & p. 194 (all); Johnston, "Spirit," p. 37 (b only); B. Jongeling, *Le rouleau de la guerre des manuscrits de Qumran*, Studia Semitica Neerlandica, 4 (Assen, 1962), p. 293 (b only); Leaney, *Rule*, p. 36 n. 1 (a only); Ross E. Lilly, "The Idea of Man in Qumran Literature," (dissertation; Boston University Graduate School, 1962), p. 70 (a, b & d); J. Maier, *Texte*, vol. II, pp. 204 & 206 (all); May, "Cosmological Reference," p. 2 (b, c & d); Noll, "Angelology," pp. 176 & 225-6 (all); Nötscher, "Geist," pp. 310 & 313 (a, b & c); Pryke, "'Spirit'," p. 345 (a & b); Ringgren, *Faith*, pp. 88 & 92 (a & d); Schreiner, "Geistbegabung," p. 162 n. 7 (all); Schweizer, "πνεῦμα," p. 390 nn. 331-2 (b & d); and Yadin, *Scroll of War*, p. 231 (b, c & d).

[12]This reading follows the reconstruction by John Strugnell, "Notes en marge du Volume V des 'Discoveries in the Judean Desert of Jordan'," *Revue de Qumrân*, 7 (1969-71), p. 238.

in a רוח נדה, which probably refers to a disposition rather than to a demon (*cf.* chapter 8 below). התגולל, however, is a traditional term (*cf.* 2 Sam. 20:12) which was often used by the sectarians metaphorically to describe man's involvement in impure attitudes and activities (*cf.* 1QS 4:19; 1QH 6:22; 17:19; CD 3:17; 8:5 & 19:17), but like most metaphors it was probably not limited to this. On the other hand, however, it is clear that the expression (כול) רוחי גורלו in 1QM 13:2, 13:4 & 13:11/12 refers to evil angels or demons since this is the way the author of 1QM defines them (*viz.*, כול רוחי גורלו מלאכי חבל, 1QM 13:11/12) and the same expression is given the same meaning by its context in 4Q286 Ber[a]/287 Ber[b] 4, 3, which handles the angelic followers of Belial separately from Belial's human followers.[13] This is in contrast to [?] רוחי in 1QH 11:13 which is more difficult to analyze since its genitive is not known and its context permits a reference to either men or angels. The general pattern of its construction, however, eliminates most of the ambiguity here since the masculine plural form of *ruaḥ* in the Hebrew Scrolls[14] never clearly refers to anything but angels or demons (*cf.* the lists in sections *2a* chapter 3, *3a* chapter 4, and the listings for "wind" and "breath" in chapter 6), and it is only in the unique two-spirit Treatise of 1QS 3-4 that any plural of *ruaḥ* in construct with any genitive ever refers to man's spirit (*cf.* 1QS 3:18-19 & 3:25; *cf.* also chapter 8 below and section *3a* in chapter 3 above). Finally, the expression רוחי צדק in 1QH 2:4 (the scribe originally wrote אמת but replaced it with צדק)[15] is difficult to analyze due to its fragmentary context, but it probably has to do with angels of some kind for the same reasons cited above in the analysis of *ruaḥ* in 1QH 11:13.[16]

---

[13]The human followers are called בני בליעל in line 6; for this as a description of men, *cf.* 4Q174, 1-2, 8.

[14]This form never occurs in the Hebrew Old Testament; *cf.* Mansoor, *Hymns*, p. 18 n. 7.

[15]*Cf.* Lohse, *Texte*, p. 116 note a.

[16]*Cf.* also רוחות צדק as "angels" in 4QSl (unpublished) in Strugnell, "Angelic Liturgy," p. 332.

2) Occurrences of *ruaḥ* over which there is some disagreement among scholars: (כול) רוחי אמת (1QM 13:10), רוחי אמת עולו (1QS 4:24, *cf.* chapter 8 below), (כול) רוחי אפעה (1QH 3:18), רוחי גורלו (11QMelch 3 II 12), (כול) ר]וחי גורל[ו (11QMelch 3 II 13; for 1QS 3:24, *cf.* chapter 8 above), רוחי [ח]בלו (1QM 14:10), and (כול) רוחי רש]עה (1QM 15: 14).[17]

1QM 13:10; כול רוחי אמת. According to Carmignac, this expression refers to the souls of the departed sectarians who fight on behalf of their earthly brothers,[18] but the context here does

---

[17]Most of the disagreement involves 1QH 3:18: for *ruaḥ* as man's spirit in this passage, *cf.* Ellis, "Gifts," p. 136 n. 6 and Pryke, "'Spirit'," p. 345; for *ruaḥ* here as either evil men or angels (or both), *cf.* Holm-Nielsen, *Hodayot,* p. 292 and n. 34, Barthélemy and Milik, *Discoveries,* I, p. 104 n. 5, Noll, "Angelology," pp. 84, 106 & 176, and Ringgren, *Faith,* p. 91. Dissenting views on other passages in this category can be found in Carmignac, *Règle,* pp. 18 & 192-4, who believes that 1QM 13:10 may refer to the souls of the departed sectarians, in Gaster, *Scriptures,* p. 435, who believes that 11QMelch 3 II 12 & 13 refers to elders who defy God's law, and in Noll, "Angelology," pp. 136, 212 & 226, who thinks that 1QM 14:10 and 15:14 may refer to men or angels. For the interpretation of *ruaḥ* as angel in 11QMelch 3 II 12, *cf.* Delcor , "Doctrines," col. 964 and in 11QMelch 3 II 12 & 13, *cf.* Noll, "Angelology," pp. 61 & 225; for *ruaḥ* as angel in (a) 1QH 3:18, (b) 1QM 13:10, (c) 1QM 14:10, and (d) 1QM 15:14, *cf.* Anderson, "'Ruah'," p. 298 (a & b), Betz, *Offenbarung,* p. 129 n. 3 (b & c); Böcher, *Dualismus,* pp. 30 & 48 (c & d); Carmignac and Guilbert, *Textes,* p. 198 n. 52 (a only); Delcor, *Hymns,* p. 39 (a only); Dupont-Sommer, *écrits,* p. 224 n. 4 (a only); Ellis, "Gifts," p. 136 (b only); Gaster, *Scriptures,* p. 566 (c only); G. S. Glanzman, "Sectarian Psalms from the Dead Sea," *Theological Studies,* 13 (1952), p. 523 n. 6 (a only); Hill, *Greek Words,* p. 235 (a & b); Huppenbauer, *Mensch,* pp. 74 & 84-5; Irwin, "Spirit-Dualism," p. 198 n. 17, p. 199 n. 18 & pp. 192 & 194 (all); Johnston, "Spirit," p. 37 (b & d); Jongeling, *rouleau,* p. 316 (c only); Licht, "Doctrine," p. 90 (a only); J. Maier, *Texte,* vol. II, pp. 204 & 206 (all); Mansoor, *Hymns,* p. 116 n. 1 (a only); Noll, "Angelology," pp. 176 & 226 (b only); Nötscher, "Geist," pp. 310 & 313 (a, b & d); Schreiner, "Geistbegabung," p. 162 n. 7 (b, c & d); Schweizer, "πνεῦμα," p. 390 and nn. 331 & 332 (all); and Yadin, *Scroll of War,* p. 231 (b only).

[18]*Cf.* n. 17 above.

not necessarily indicate this meaning for *ruaḥ*,[19] and in the only other place this expression occurs in the Scrolls (1QS 4:23) such a meaning would be difficult to support. The context of 1QM 13:10, on the other hand, is more ambiguous, but even if one accepts the existence of an earthly and heavenly division of sectarians, the heavenly group is never clearly described in 1QM (or anywhere else in the Scrolls) with any form of *ruaḥ*.[20] The close association in vocabulary and terminology between 1QS 3-4 and 1QM 13,[21] moreover, indicates that רוחי אמת in 1QS 4:23 and 1QM 13:10 should probably be interpreted in each other's light, and given this approach, the most suitable meaning for *ruaḥ* in both would be "angels."

1QH 3:18; כול רוחי אפעה. This expression is unique in the Scrolls and the precise meaning of אפעה is somewhat uncertain.[22] The context is also somewhat ambiguous and would seem to support equally well the meaning of *ruaḥ* here as either demons or evil men.[23] However, the form of *ruaḥ* as a masculine plural as well as its construction with a genitive indicates that it is referring to demons rather than to men (*cf.* the analysis of 1QH 11:13 in section *2b1* above).

11QMelch 3 II 12, רוחי גורלו; 11QMelch 3 II 13, כול ר]וחי גורל[ו. We should note, first of all, the identity of these expressions with those in 1QM 13:2, 13:4 & 13:11/12 and also that 1QM 13:10 expressly identifies these spirits as angels (מלאכי חבל), *cf.* the analysis of כול רוחי גורלו in section *2b1* above. This meaning also fits in well with the context of 11QMelch 3 II, which has to do with the angel Melchizedeq and his fellow angels (*cf.*

---

[19]*Cf.* n. 4 in chapter 4 above.

[20]Nötscher, "Heiligkeit," pp. 324-5.

[21]*Cf.* the chart of verbal relationships in Irwin, "Spirit-Dualism," p. 210 and note his comment on the style of the author of 1QM in *ibid.*, p. 30: "One is remined of a student writing a paper by copying the ideas of his source and using much of its vocabulary, but purposely juggling the terms in an attempt to conceal the close dependence."

[22]*Cf.* Mansoor, *Hymns*, p. 114 n. 7.

[23]*Cf.* the views on this in n. 17 above.

הצדק] אלי and בני אל in line 14)[24] who come to execute judgment against Belial and the "spirits of his lot" for rebelling against the law of God (*cf.* line 12; *cf.* also the idea of angelic rebellion against God in 4Q180 and 1 Enoch 6-10).

1QM 14:10; רוחי [ח]בלו.[25] This expression should be compared to כול רוחי גורלו מלאכי חבל in 1QM 13:11/12, in which the words רוח and חבל are associated in one way or another with the word מלאך; *cf.* Jubilees 10:5 and also רוחי חבל in the fragmentary context of 4Q511, 43, 6, which is the only other place in the non-biblical, Hebrew Scrolls in which a form of חבל is in construct with a form of *ruaḥ*. The meaning "destructive angel," however, fits the specific context of 1QM 14:10 well for two reasons: 1) the word גער, which is used here to describe God's opposition to the spirits, is closely associated with the rebuke of demonic figures in the Scrolls and in the Old Testament (*cf.* Zech. 3:2 with 1QH f 4:6 and the use of גער in 1QapGen 20:28-9); and 2) the idea that God rebukes the demons so that they do not molest his people fits in well with the sectarians' fear of demonic attack as seen especially in 4Q510, 1, and 4Q511, 10 in which the psalmist seeks divine protection from demons of various kinds through the recitation of God's praises;[26] *cf.* section *2b3* in this chapter below and also 1QS 3:24.

1QM 15:14; כול רוחי רש]עה.[27] The closest equivalent to the expression is רוחי רשע in 4Q511, 1, 6, which is difficult to analyze on the basis of context alone (*cf.* section *2b3* below), and the only other occurrence of a form of רשע as a genitive of *ruaḥ* is רוחות רשעה in 1QH f 5:4. In the specific context of 1QM 15:14, the meaning of *ruaḥ* as either demons or wicked men (or both) seems equally possible, but כול רוחי רשעה here probably has to do with wicked angels rather than with men for the reasons cited in section *2b1* above in the analysis of *ruaḥ* in 1QH 11: 13.

---

[24]*Cf.* Milik, "Milkî-sedeq," p. 107.

[25]This follows Baillet's reading; *cf.* Baillet, *Discoveries*, VII, p. 241, note on 4Q511, 43, 6.

[26]*Cf. ibid.*, p. 215.

[27]This follows Lohse's restoration in *Texte*, pp. 214-6; the reading, however, could be כול רוחי רשע .

3) Occurrences of *ruaḥ* which have not been defined by scholars: (כול) רוחי גורלו (4Q491, 14-15, 10), רוחי הבלים (4Q511, 15, 5), רוחי חבל (4Q511, 43, 6), (כול) רוחי מלאכי חבל (4Q510, 1, 5a), רוח]י ממזרי[ם (4Q511, 182, 1), (כול) רוחי ממזרים (4Q511, 35, 7), רוחי עולמים (4Q502, 27, 1), רוחי רשע (4Q511, 1, 6), רוח]י (4Q511, 60, 2), (כול) רוחי (4Q510, 2, 3), and (כול ריבי) רוחי (4Q511, 48-49+51, 7-8).

4Q491, 14-15, 10; כול רוחי גורלו. According to Baillet, 4Q491, 14-15, 10 is part of a variant recension of 1QM[28] and corresponds somewhat in content to 1QM 15:7ff.[29] The expression גורלו כול רוחי in this verse, then, should probably be understood in terms of the same expression found in 1QM 13:2, 13:4 & 13:11/12 (*cf.* the analysis of these verses in section *2b1* above).

4Q511, 15, 5; רוחי הבלים. This expression occurs only here in the Scrolls published so far and its context is too fragmentary for analysis. It probably refers to evil angels of some kind, however, for the reasons cited in section *2b1* above in the analysis of *ruaḥ* in 1QH 11:13.

4Q511, 43, 6; רוחי חבל. Compare this expression to רוחי חבלו in 1QM 14:10 analyzed above in section *2b2* and also to Jubilees 10:5. Although the specific context of 4Q511, 43, 6 is too fragmentary for analysis, it is still probable that *ruaḥ* here is referring to angels rather than to men because of its similarity of expression to 1QM 14:10 (and Jubilees 10:5) and also for the reasons cited in section *2b1* in the analysis of 1QH 11:13.

4Q510, 1, 5a; כול רוחי מלאכי חבל. This unique expression seems to be a variation of an expression found in 1 Enoch 19:1 ("the spirits of the angels"), which are said to defile the people and lead them into error. It is part of a story found in 1 Enoch 6-16 in which angelic spirits (or "watchers") come down to earth, consort with women who bear them giants, and as a result become the source of much of humanity's ills. It appears that these ideas were accepted at Qumran at least to some extent (*cf.* 4Q180, 7-8 with 1 Enoch 9:6-10) and evidently also by the author of this apotropaic canticle (*cf.* רוחות ממזרים, "spirits of bastards," with 1 Enoch 10:9 & 15:8-12). Note that our expression is

---

[28]Baillet, *Discoveries*, IV, p. 12.

[29]*Ibid.*, p. 314.

in apposition to five others all probably referring to various types of demons:[30] רוחות ממזרים (evil spirits that came forth from the dead bodies of the pre-flood giants, *cf.* 1 Enoch 9:6-10), שד-אים = (שדים, "demons"), לילית (a female demon), אחים (a howling demon?), and [ציים] (meaning imprecise, reconstructed from Isa. 13:21). Even without the mention of an "angel" in our expression, then, it is clear from this context and its conceptual ties to 1 Enoch 6-10 (in which evil, angelic beings victimize humanity) that the concern of 4Q510, 1, 1-9 is not to ward off evil men but rather to find protection against demons of various types.

4Q511, 182, 1, רוח]י ממזרי[ם; and 4Q511, 35, 7, כו[ל] רוחי ממזרים. Although the context of 4Q511, 182, 1 is too fragmentary for analysis, the reconstruction רוחי ממזרים offered by Baillet on the basis of 4Q511, 35, 7 seems to be certain enough[31] and it probably has the same meaning in both verses. 4Q511 35, 7, on the other hand, clearly belongs to the same type of context as 510, 1 (treated in the paragraph directly above) since the intent of each context is to exalt God (*cf.* 4Q511, 35, 6 with 4Q510, 1, 4) and in this manner to subdue or frighten away evil spirits (*cf.* 4Q511, 35, 6-7 with 4Q510, 1, 4-5). The genitive of our expression (ממזרים) is likewise another indication that evil spirits or demons are the concern here since it alludes directly to the context of 1 Enoch 10:9 and 15:8-12: *cf.* the comments on this in the analysis of 4Q510, 1, 5a above.

4Q502, 27, 1; רוחי עולמים. This expression is cited by Strugnell in "Angelic Liturgy," p. 332 as a term for angels in an unpublished fragment of 4QSl, and it may also be compared with עולם רוחות in 1QH 1:11 with which it shares a similar context, *viz.*, a description of nature as under the authority of various angelic spirits (*cf.* דגלי יר[חים and כוכב]י השמים in 4Q502, 27, 3-4[32] with מאורות and כוכבים in 1QH 1:11-12). The expression רוחי עולמים,

---

[30]What follows is basically Baillet's analysis; *cf. ibid.*, p. 217 note on line 5.

[31]*Ibid.*, p. 217 note on line 5.

[32]As reconstructed by Baillet in *ibid.*, p. 89.

then, probably has to do with angelic spirits in charge of natural phenomena.

4Q511, 1, 6; רוחי רשע. As noted in the analysis of 1QM 15:14 in section *2b2* in this chapter above, the meaning of *ruaḥ* in either 1QM 15:14 or 4Q511, 1, 6 could be understood as either demons or wicked men, but on the basis of the reasons cited in section *2b1* above in the analysis of *ruaḥ* in 1QH 11:13, *ruaḥ* here and in 1QM 14:10 probably refers to demons.

4Q511, 60, 2, רוח]י; 4Q510, 2, 3, כול רוחי]; and 4Q511, 48-49+51, 7-8, ...] ריבי כול רוחי. The fragmentary context of all these passages makes analysis difficult, but because of the reasons cited in section *2b1* above in the analysis of *ruaḥ* in 1QH 11:13, *ruaḥ* in all of these passages probably refers to demons. It should be noted, however, that the context just preceding ריבי כול רוחי in 4Q511, 48-49+51, 7-8 is the same as that in 4Q510, 1 (compare 4Q511, 48-49+51, 2-3 with 4Q510, 1, 4-5) and that 1QS 4:23 (which involves good and evil angels, *cf.* chapter 8 below) is the only other place in the Scrolls published so far in which a form of *ruaḥ* is directly engaged in the activity of ריב; note that in 1QS 4:18 the ריב is not between the "spirits" as such but between their משפתים.

c. The meaning of *ruaḥ* as a *nomen regens* in a feminine plural form followed by genitive: (15 times; *cf.* section *2a* for references).

Perhaps the best way to handle this pattern is to divided it into three categories: those occurrences of *ruaḥ* over which there is no apparent disagreement among scholars, those over which there is some disagreement, and those for the most part not treated. We should note that even in the second category above (except for 1QH 1:12, which requires conjectural restoration) a strong majority of scholars supports the meaning angel/demon for *ruaḥ* in every case.

1) Occurrences of *ruaḥ* over which there is no apparent disagreement among scholars:[33] רוחות אלוהים חיים (4QSl 40, 24, 6), רוחות בליעל (CD 12:2), רוחות קודש קדשים (4QSl 40, 24, 5), ?]רוחות (1QH 17:23), and [?]רוחות (כול) (1QH f 45:6).

The expression רוחות אלוהים חיים apparently occurs not only in 4QSl 40, 24, 6 but also throughout the unpublished fragments of 4QSl,[34] but so far it has not appeared outside of 4QSl in any other published Qumranian material. This is also true for רוחות קודש קדשים in the previous line[35] (5), but *cf.* the analogous רוחות קודש in 1QH 8:12. It is clear, however, that *ruaḥ* in both lines is referring to angelic beings of some kind since 4QSl 40, 24, 2-8 is describing the Divine Throne of God (*cf.* Ezk. 1) surrounded by the presence of various types of angels with their worship and ministry.[36] In support of Strugnell's translation of *ruaḥ* in line 6 as "the Spirits of the Living God," *cf.* Kautzsch, *Grammar*, §132h.[37]

The expression רוחות בליעל in CD 12:2 likewise refers to angelic beings (in this case the angels or demons of Belial) since

---

[33]For *ruaḥ* as angel in (a) 1QH 17:23, (b) 1QH f 45:6, (c) CD 12:2, (d) 4QSl 40, 24, 5, and (e) 4QSl 40 24, 6, *cf.* Betz, *Offenbarung*, p. 129 n. 3 (c only); Böcher, *Dualismus*, p. 48 (c only); Brownlee, "Anthropology," pp. 229-230 (a only); Delcor, *Hymns*, p. 52 (c only); Dupont-Sommer, "instruction," p. 20 (c only); Holm-Nielsen, *Hodayot*, p. 249 n. 22 (a only); Huppenbauer, *Mensch*, pp. 61-2 & 101 (c only); Irwin, "Spirit-Dualism," pp. 198-9 n. 17 & 199 n. 18 (c only); H. W. Kuhn, *Enderwartung*, p. 125 (a only); J. Maier, *Texte*, vol. II, p. 206 (a & c); Noll, "Angelology," pp. 125-6, 136 & 226 (b, c & d); Nötscher, "Geist,' p. 313 (c only); Pryke, "'Spirit'," p. 345 (c only); Ringgren, *Faith*, p. 91 (c only); Schreiner, "Geistbegabung," p, 162 n. 7 (c only); Schweizer, "πνεῦμα," p. 391 (c only); *idem*, "sieben Geister," p. 505, (c only); and Strugnell, "Angelic Liturgy,' pp. 332 (d & e).

[34]*Cf.* Strugnell, "Angelic Liturgy," p. 332, who describes this with the term *passim.* (But *cf.* n. 1 above on the 1985 work of Carol Newsom.)

[35]*Ibid.*, also with the term *passim.*

[36]*Ibid.*, pp. 335-6 & 342.

[37]*Cf. ibid.*, p. 337. Gaster in *Scriptures*, p.289, translates *ruaḥ* here as "live angelic spirits."

they are treated as masculine (*cf.* ימשלו) and are mentioned within the context of the occult (*cf.* v. 3). Compare also the similar expressions in Jubilees 1:20, 10:3 & 6, 12:20 and especially 20:28, which were probably well-known to the community.[38] Note, finally, that the only other occurrence of בליעל with a form of *ruaḥ* is in 4Q177, 1-4, 10 (*cf.* section *2b1* above), which refers to evil angels.

The form רוחות in 1QH 17:23, on the other hand, is more difficult to analyze because of its fragmentary context. However, if חזק is the correct transcription of the first legible word before על רוחות[39] and if רוחות is in construct with a word (now lost) such as פשע (*cf.* 1Q36, 2, 5) or רשעה (*cf.* 1QH f 5:4) or עולה (*cf.* 1QH f:6), then רוחות here would probably be referring to evil angels for the following reasons: 1) רוחות in construct with a genitive is a frequent pattern for referring to angels (*cf.* sections *2b* and *2c* above), whereas this pattern is clearly used for the human spirit or disposition only in the two spirit Treatise (*cf.* section *3a* in chapter 4 above); and 2) a reference to evil spirits or angels would fit this context well as part of the psalmist's request that God would keep him from sin (*cf.* vv. 21-23), *i.e.*, he would be asking God to strengthen him against the evil spirits who seek his spiritual downfall (*cf.* 1QS 3:24 and especially 4Q510, 1, 6 and 4Q511, 10, 2).[40]

The form כול רוחות in 1QH f 45:6 is in a context even more fragmentary than 1QH 17:23, but if כול רוחות is not followed by a suffix (*cf.* the only occurrences of this pattern with a suffix in Temple Scroll 30:10, 31:10 & 38:14 as "direction/side," a meaning which does not fit the available context of 1QH f 45:6), it

---

[38]*Cf.* Vermes, *Perspective,* p. 210: "Fragments [of Jubilees] representing no less than twelve manuscripts were found in Caves 1-4 and 11."

[39]The editor reads חוק, *cf.* Sukenik, *Dead Sea Scrolls,* plate 51, line 23; but *cf.* Lohse *Texte,* p. 172 and Vermes, *Scrolls in English,* p. 199.

[40]*Cf.* Vermes translation in *ibid.*: "Strengthen the loins of Thy servant that he may resist the spirits of falsehood." Note also the remarks of Baillet in *Discoveries,* VII, p. 220 on the close literary connection between 4Q510 & 511 and 1QH.

probably refers to either good or evil angels. The evidence for this is as follows: 1) whenever a feminine or masculine plural of *ruaḥ* (without an article or suffix) functions as a genitive in construct with כול, it is always itself in construct with a following genitive (when this can be checked) and its most probable meaning is always angels or demons (*cf.* 4Q511, 1, 3 for the only feminine form in this category and its analysis in section *2c3* below; for the masculine, *cf.* the numerous examples listed at the beginning of secion *2a* above and their analysis in section *2b*); 2) except for the two-spirit Treatise, רוחות in construct with a genitive never refers to man and when it does refer to man in this Treatise, it is not qualified with כול (*cf.* 1QS 3:18-19 & 3:25 and section *3a* in chapter 4 above); and finally, 3) only in 1QH 1:10 (רוחות עוז) and 1QM 9:13 (שלשת רוחות הפנים) does רוחות in construct with a genitive (outside of 1QS 3:18ff.) appear to refer to something other than angels (*viz.*, "wind," "direction"), but again, these expressions are not qualified by כול. It is most probable, then, that כול רוחות here is in construct with a following genitive now lost and that it is referring to evil angels or demons against which the psalmist is seeking help.

2) Occurrences of *ruaḥ* over which there is some disagreement among scholars: רוחות דעת (1QH 3:22), רוחות עולה (1QH f 5:6), רוחות עולם (1QH 1:11), רוחות פשע (1Q36, 2: 5), רוחות קודש (1QH 8:12), רוחות רשעה (1QH f 5:4);[41] note, finally that various

[41] A minority of scholars understands one or more or the above occurrences as possibly referring to something other than angels: Beaven, "Ruah," p. 103 believes that 1QH 8:12 may refer to "holy winds"; W. D. Davies, "Paul," p. 177 understands 1QH 3:22 as members of the community; Jean L. Duhaime, "La rédaction de 1QM and l'évolution du dualisme à Qumran," *Revue Biblique*, 2 (1977), pp. 575-6, understands 1QH f 5:4 & 5:6 as referring to internal dispositions; Holm-Nielsen, *Hodayot*, p. 22 n. 17 and p. 292 believes that 1QH 1:11 refers to forces of nature and that 1QH f 5:6 refers to ungodly people; Huppenbauer, "Belial," p. 84 understands 1QH f 5:4 & 5:6 as references to impersonal powers of evil standing behind godlessness; Irwin, "Spirit-Dualism," p. 192 believes that 1QH 1:11 could refer to wind; G. Maier, *Mensch*, p. 183, regards 1QH f 5:4 as a reference to men; Noll,

forms of *ruaḥ* have been suggested for 1QH 1:12, but this cannot be analyzed syntactically since there is not enough evidence in the Scrolls to conjecture what its actual form may have been.[42]

1QH 3:22; רוחות דעת. This expression appears to refer to angels rather than to men for the following reasons: 1) it is the third element in a series of expressions which probably refer to

---

"Angelology," p. 176, views 1QH 1:11 as describing the impersonal "motive forces" of creation; Nötscher, "Geist," p. 309 understands 1Q36, 2:5 a describing a spiritual disposition; and Schweizer, "Gegenwart des Geistes," p. 493 believes that 1QH 3:22 may refer to a member of the sectarian community in the sense of the Persian concept *daena*. For scholars who understand (a) 1QH 1:11, (b) 1QH 3:22, (c) 1QH 8:12, (d) 1QH f 5:4, (e) 1QH 5:6, and (f) 1Q36, 2:5 as references to angels or demons, *cf.* the following: Anderson, "'Ruah'," p. 298 (b, c, d & e); Betz, *Offenbarung*, p. 129 n. 3 (all); Böcher, *Dualismus*, pp. 36 & 75 (b & c); Brandenburger, *Fleisch*, p. 104 (b only); Carmignac and Guilbert, *textes*, p. 200 n. 11 and p. 239 n 22 (b & c); Coppens, "don," p. 212 (b only); Delcor, "Doctrines," col. 971 (b & c); *idem*, *Hymns*, pp. 42-44 (a, b & c); Ellis, "Gifts," p. 136 (b & c); Hill, *Greek Words*, p. 239 (c only); Holm-Nielsen, *Hodayot*, p. 68 n. 13 p. 291 n. 32 (b & c); Hübner, "Dualismus," pp. 269, 270 & 274 (a & b); Huppenbauer, *Mensch*, pp. 74 & 96 (b, d & e); Irwin, "Spirit-Dualism," pp. 52, 72, 192-4, 198 n. 17 & 199 n. 18 (b, c, d, e, & f); G. Jeremias, *Lehrer*, p. 251, n. 4 (c only); Johnston, "Spirit," p. 37 (a & d); H. W. Kuhn, *Enderwartung*, p. 146 (b only); Leaney, *Rule*, p. 36 n. 1. (c only); Licht, "Doctrine," p. 90 (b, d & e); Lichtenberger, *Studien*, p. 166 n. 8 (a only); Lilly, "Idea of Man," p. 70 (b only); G. Maier, *Mensch*, p. 183 (a, b, c, d & e); J. Maier, *Texte*, vol. II, pp. 204 & 206 (a, b, c, d, & e); Mansoor, *Hymns*, pp. 82, 98 and 117 n. 7 (a, b & c); May, "Cosmological Reference," p. 5 n. 17 (b only); Noll, "Angelology," pp. 91 & 225-6 (b, d, e, & f); Nötscher, "Geist," pp. 307 & 309-310 (b, c & f); *idem*, "Heiligkeit," p.323 n. 59 & p. 342 (b & c); Pryke, "'Spirit'," p. 345 (a, b, & c); Ringgren, *Faith*, pp. 57 & 88 (a & c); Schreiner, "Geistbgabung," p. 162 n. 7 (b & c); Schubert, *Community*, pp. 63-4 (b & c); Schweizer, "πνεῦμα," p. 390 (a, b, c & f); Strugnell, "Angelic Liturgy," p. 332 (a, b & c); Treves, "Two Spirits," p. 452 (a only); Wildberger, "Dualismus," p. 168 (b only); and Yadin, *Scroll of War*, pp. 231-2 (a,b & c).

[42]*Cf.* n. 5 above.

angels (*cf.* צבא קדושים and בני שמים in v. 22);[43] 2) the closest equivalents in form to רוחות דעת are two expressions from 4QSl, which refer according to Strugnell to angels (רוחי דעת אמת and רוחי דעת ובינה);[44] 3) and although *ruaḥ* in the plural can refer to men in the sense of "dispositions,"[45] it never refers to men's spirits as disembodied souls[46] nor is it ever used as a metaphor to mean "persons" (*e.g.*, "people of knowledge") as is the case occasionally with *ruaḥ* in the singular (e.g, רוח נעוה in 1QH 3:31 as a "perverted person").[47] Note, finally, that the plural of *ruaḥ* in construct with a following genitive never clearly refers to man in any sense in the Scrolls except for two occurrences in the unique two-spirit treatise of 1QS 3-4 in which it means "dispositions" (*cf.* the analysis of 3:18/19 and 3:25 in chapter 8 below and the list of forms for man's spirit in section *3a* of chapter 4 above). Given the observation, then that רוחות as the *nomen regens* of a genitive clearly refers to angels in a number of cases (*cf.* section *2c1* above) and except for 1QS 3:18-19 and 3:25 that it only rarely appears to refer to anything else (*cf.* the analysis of 1QH 1:10 and 1QM 9:13 as "winds/ directions" in section chapter 6 below), "angels" is probably also its meaning here.

1QH f 5:6, רוחות עולה; and 1QH f 5:4, רוחות רשעה. These two expressions are treated together here because of their similar context and syntax. Thus, both expressions are subjects of masculine verbs which follow them (יהיו following f 5:4 and יושדו in 5:6), and the devastation of the spirits in f 5:6 seems to be a continuation of the thought of f 5:4-5 in which God "terrifies" (תבית

---

[43]*Cf.* Mansoor, *Hymns*, p. 117 nn. 5, 6 & 7; *cf.* also Carmignac and Guilbert, *Textes*, p. 200 nn. 9 & 10 and Holm-Nielsen, *Hodayot*, p. 68 n. 11.

[44]*Cf.* Strugnell, "Angelic Liturgy," p. 332.

[45]*E.g.*, 1QS 2:20; 3:14; 1QH 14:11 and 17:17.

[46]*Cf.* n. 4 in chapter 4 above; the psalmist would then be thinking, perhaps, of the heavenly community of the departed.

[47]The psalmists would then be thinking of his fellow sectarians in the future (?), glorified community with whom he would praise God forever.

is probably a misspelling of תבעית)[48] the spirits and they cease to exist (ולא יהיו). With the observation that רוחות never refers to man in the Scrolls except in the sense of "dispositions" and that רוחות followed by a genitive refers to man only in the two-spirit Treatise (again, as "dispositions"; *cf.* chapter 8 below), it is probable here that *ruaḥ* in 1QH f 5:4 and 5:6 is referring to hostile demonic beings as is often clearly the case with this pattern (*cf.* section *2c1* above).

1QH 1:11; רוחות עולם. The question here is whether this expression refers to "spirit" in an impersonal sense such as "wind," or whether it refers to personal, angelic creatures. It probably means the latter for the following reasons: 1) רוחות עולם (ל) is in apposition to [מלאכי [קדשכה (ל) with the ל preceding both expressions referring back to היותם at the beginning of the verse as part of the verb "become"; 2) the closest analogy to רוחות עולם is רוחי עולמים in 4Q502, 27, 1 (*cf.* secion *2b3* above, understood as angels) and 4QSl (*cf.* n. 1 above), which Strugnell defines as "angels";[49] and 3) רוחות in construct with a genitive as "wind" is rare in the non-biblical Scrolls (1QH 1:9; *cf.* also 1QM 9:13). On the basis of these observations, then, and in the light of the clear use of רוחות with a following genitive to mean "angels" (*cf.* section *2c1* above), *ruaḥ* in 1QH 1:11 probably refers to angels rather than to wind.

1Q36, 2:5; רוחות פשע. This is a unique expression in the Scrolls and the context here is very fragmentary, but on the basis of its pattern (רוחות + a genitive), it probably refers to angels (*cf.* the analysis of 1QH 1:11 in the paragraph directly above). Note also the presence of the verb תריבו in line 1 (*cf.* 1QS 4:23 in chapter 8 below)

1QH 8:12; רוחות קודש. Almost all scholars understand this expression as referring to angels,[50] and this seems to be correct

---

[48]A characteristic of sectarian Hebrew is its elision of the gutturals as seen often in their writings; *cf.* Goshen-Gottstein, "Linguistic Structure," p. 107ff. *Cf.* also the analogous example in 1QH 11:32 (נשנתי for נשענתי). For a conceptual parallel to תבעית, *cf.* 4Q510, 1, 4-5.

[49]Strugnell, "Angelic Liturgy," p. 332.

[50]*Cf.* n. 41 above.

for the following reasons: 1) 1QH 8:12 is clearly alluding to the cherubim of Gen. 3:24,[51] and since רוחות קודש is parallel to גבורי כוח in 1QH 8:11 (which clearly refers to angels),[52] both terms can be seen as descriptions of the kind of angels that guard the community's "fruit" (v. 11); and 2) the term רוחות קודש is never clearly used to mean "winds" in the Scrolls (*cf.* chapter 6 below), whereas the varient expression רוחות קודש קודשים is a common term in 4QSl as "angels."[53]

3) Occurrences of *ruaḥ* which scholars have largely not treated: רוחות ממזרים (4Q510, 1, 5b), [(כול) רוחות] ממזרים (4Q511, 48-49+51, 2-3), (כול) רוחות ממשלתה (4Q511, 1, 3), and (כול) רוחו]ת (4Q177, 12-13, I, 9).

4Q510, 1, 5b, רוחות ממזרים; and 4Q511, 48-49+51, 2-3, [כול רוחות] ממזרים.[54] These two expressions are treated together here because of their similar syntax and context. Thus, they are both feminine plural forms of *ruaḥ* in construct with ממזרים and are both in apotropaic contexts as objects of the same verb (פחד) with the psalmist as the agent of this action. This apotropaic context together with the genitive ממזרים clearly points to these spirits as demonic beings; *cf.* the evidence for this view already given in section *2b3* above in connection with the following expressions: כול רוחי מלאכי חבל in 4Q510, 1, 5a, רוחי ממזרים in 4Q511, 35, 7 & 4Q511, 182, 1, and ריבי כול רוחי in 4Q511, 48-49+51, 7-8.

4Q511, 1, 3; כול רוחות ממשלתה. This expression does not occur elsewhere in the Scrolls published so far, although according to Strugnell, רוחי ממשלת is found in an unpublished fragment of 4QBerakot with the meaning "angels."[55] But even apart from this connection to 4Q Berakot, there seems to be enough evidence in the fragmentary context of 4Q511, 1 to indicate that

---

[51]As pointed out by Nötscher in *Terminologie,* p. 75.

[52]*Cf.* Mansoor, *Hymns,* p. 154 n. 7.

[53]*Cf.* Strugnell, "Angelic Liturgy," p. 332, who describes this with the term *passim.*

[54]This is Baillet's restoration on the basis of 4Q510, 1, 5b; *cf.* Baillet, *Discoveries,* IV, p. 244, note on lines 2-3.

[55]*Cf.* Strugnell, "Angelic Liturgy," p. 333.

רוחות here means angels. Thus, in line 1 of this text there is the mention of מ]משלחם (*cf.* רוחות עולם בממשלתם in 1QH 1:11), in line 2 there is the mention of the earth (בא]רץ) and just after this comes our expression with the feminine suffix on "dominion" (ממשלתה) referring back to ארץ. Given the background of Jubilees 2:2, which refers to classes of angels who have responsibility for various earthly and heavenly matters, it appears that Baillet is correct when he suggests that the expression in 4Q511, 1, 3 refers to angels who rule over earthly phenomena in contrast to those ruling in the heavens.[56]

4Q177, 12-13, I, 9; כול רוחו]ת. Although this text is somewhat fragmentary, this expression probably refers to evil spirits or angels for the following reasons: 1) the use of כול as the *nomen regens* of the form רוחות indicates that it is referring to angelic creatures (*cf.* the evidence for this in section *2c1* above in the analysis of כול רוחות in 1QH f 45:6, and 2) it is said that the mighty hand of God (יד אל הגדולה) is with His people to help them (לעוזרם) from "all" the spirits. This kind of language is reminiscent of 1QM 15:14 and 1QS 3:24 in which God "lifts up His hand in His marvelous might" (בג]בור[ת פלאו, 1QM 15:14) or "helps" (עזר, 1QS 3:24) His people against "all" the evil spirits (*cf.* section *2b2* above and chapter 8 below for an analysis of *ruaḥ* as evil angels in these passages).

d. Diverse patterns of *ruaḥ* in the plural: (9 cases; *cf.* section *2a* above for references).

1) *Ruaḥ*in a masculine plural form as a genitive with suffixes: צבא רוחיו (1QM 12:9); צבא רוחיך (1QH 13:8); and צ]בא רוחיו (1QM 19:1; reconstructed on the basis of 1QM 12:9, *cf.* n. 6 above). This pattern in these occurrences is regarded by almost all scholars as a reference to angels,[57] and this seems to be

---

[56]Baillet, *Discoveries*, VII, p. 220, note on line 3.

[57]I have found only two scholars who would disagree: *cf.* Carmignac, *Règle*, pp. 18 & 178, who believes that 1QM 12:9 refers to the souls of the dead, and Noll, "Angelology," p. 176, who believes that 1QH 13:8 refers to the impersonal motive forces of creation. For (a)

essentially correct. Thus, 1QH 13:8 is in a creation context and appears to reflect the view of Jubilees 2:2 in which a host of angels was created by God along with the heavens and earth in contrast to the creation of only two humans (*cf.* Jubilees 3:1ff.). A similar contrast between men and angels is also present in 1QM 12 in which the author as a member of the Qumran community notes that the host of spirits is with "our steps" (צעדינו). Perhaps within 1QM alone it is possible contextually to view these spirits as the disembodied souls of the sectarians,[58] but if 1QM 12:9 is taken together with 1QH 13:8, this view becomes less probable since it is doubtful that the sectarians believed that God created along with the heavens and earth a host of disembodied souls.[59] The common meaning which best fits both of these occurrences is "angels." It should also be noted that the only unambiguous meaning which *ruaḥ* has in the Scrolls in its masculine plural form is "angel" (*cf.* the list of forms in section *2a* above; *cf.* also section *2a* in chapter 3, *3a* in chapter 4 and the lists in chapter 6).

2) The masculine plural form of *ruaḥ* with a suffix (2 times): רוחיכה (1Q36, 17:2), and ר[וחיך (1QH f 33:2). The context

---

1QH 13:8 and (b) 1QM 12:9 as angels, *cf.* Anderson, "'Ruah'," pp. 294 & 298 (both); Betz, *Offenbarung*, p. 129 n. 3 (both); Böcher, *Dualismus*, pp. 36 & 47 (both); Delcor, *Hymns*, p. 41 (b only); Holm-Nielsen, *Hodayot*, pp. 277 & 212 n. 11 (a only); Huppenbauer, *Mensch*, p. 96 (b only); Irwin, "Spirit-Dualism," pp. 52, 192, 198 n. 17 and p. 199 n. 18 (both); Johnston, "Spirit," p. 34 (b only); Leaney, *Rule*, p. 36 n. 1 (a only); Lilly, "Idea of Man," p. 70 (b only); G. Maier, *Mensch*, p. 183 (a only); J. Maier, *Texte*, vol. II, pp. 204 & 206 (both); Manns, *symbole*, p. 92 (b only); Noll, "Angelology," p. 226, (b only); Nötscher, "Geist," pp. 310-311 (both); Schreiner, "Geistbegabung," p. 162 n. 7 (both); Schubert, *Community*, p. 63 (a only); Schweizer, "πνεῦμα," p. 390 n. 332 (b only); and Yadin, *Scroll of War*, p. 231 (both).

[58]*E.g.*, as Carmignac; *cf.* n. 57 above.

[59]*Cf.* the observation of Sjöberg, "πνεῦμα," pp. 379-380: "There can be no certainty when the idea of the pre-existence of the soul arose in Palestinian Judaism. In fact there are in the apocryphal and pseudepigraphical works of Palestine no unambiguous instances of the idea."

for both of these expressions is very fragmentary, and in the case of 1QH f 33:2 it is also possible that ר]וחיך is not alone but is in construct with a *nomen regens* now lost. Both of these expressions, however, probably refer to angelic beings of some kind since the masculine plural form of *ruaḥ* seems to have been used by the sectarians only for this purpose (*cf.* the comments on this in section *2d1* above). There is, however, some contextual evidence for רוחיכה in 1Q36, 17:2 as "demons" with the mention of the נפילים in the previous fragment (1Q36, 16:3), *i.e.*, the pre-flood giants from whose dead bodies came forth evil spirits.[60]

3) The feminine plural form of *ruaḥ* with a suffix: י[. . .] רוחתיו (4Q185, 1-2, I, 9). Although a suffixed f. pl. of *ruaḥ* is not unique in the Scrolls (*e.g.*, 1QS 2:20; 3:14; 4Q176, 21, 3; and Temple Scroll 30:10; 31:10 & 38:14), it is only here that a suffix on רוחות refers to God. The closest analogy to our expression, therefore, is not, *e.g.*, רוחותם in 1QS 2:20 (whose suffix refers to man) but rather patterns such as צבא רוחיך in 1QH 13:8 (whose suffix refers to God; *cf.* the analysis in section *2d1* above). Our expression, then, is probably referring to angels, and this understanding fits the available context best. Thus, in line 8 of the text God's מלאכים are mentioned, and it is possible to understand רוחותיו and whatever *nomen regens* might have been before it in line 9 (perhaps צירי; *cf.* צירי רוחות in Strugnell, "Angelic Liturgy" p. 333) as a further description of these מלאכים. The term צי[ר]י רוחתיו, then, would be the subject of the verb ישפט]ו and the translation of this section would be as follows: "Who can bear to stand before His angels? For like a flaming fire His spirit-messengers will execute judgment."

4) The feminine plural of *ruaḥ* with the article in construct with the *nomen regens* כול: כול הרוחות (4Q158, 14, I, 2; and 8Q5, 2, 6). This form occurs only in these two passages and in both cases in a very fragmentary context, but there does seem to be enough evidence in 8Q5, 2, 6, at least, to define כול הרוחות as "angels"

---

[60]*Cf.* the analysis of 4Q510, 1, 5a in section *2b3* of this chapter above.

since this passage talks about these spirits as "standing" before God (לפניכה ע] ומדים).[61] Thus, even though רוחות can refer to men, it is found in this form only with the meaning "dispositions";[62] and the meaning "winds," which רוחות may also have, is also difficult to harmonize with the concept of personal beings standing before God in attentiveness and worship.

5) The feminine plural of *ruaḥ* as an unqualified genitive of a *nomen regens*: משא רוחות (1QM 10:12). This form is essentially unique in the Scrolls. There are, of course, forms such as שתי רוחות (1QS 3:18) and ארבע רוחות (3Q15 VII 5), but the *nomen regens* in these cases (as a number) has a qualifying effect on רוחות,[63] and the genitive relationship in the only other comparable form (צירי רוחות in 4QSl unpub.) seems to be essentially different from that of משא רוחות.[64] Despite a lack of comparative forms, however, the meaning of *ruaḥ* in 1QM 10:12 as "angels" can still be seen in its parallel construction with ממשלת קדושים;[65] note especially the parallel between משא as angelic "responsibility" (*cf.* 1QSa 1:19f.) and ממשלה as angelic "authority."

e. Diverse patterns of *ruaḥ* in the singular: (7 cases; *cf.* section *2a* above for references).

1) The unqualified singular of *ruaḥ* as a genitive in construct with כול רוח: (אדון ל)כול רוח (1QH 10:8), כול רוח (1QH 1:9), and כול

---

[61]Baillet in *Discoveries*, III, p. 162, note on line 6, reconstructs the participle as feminine while also suggesting the reconstruction ע]מדו as an alternative reading.

[62]*Cf.* the listing of these form in section *3a* of chapter 3 above and their analysis in sections *3c* and *3d*.

[63]*Cf.* Kautzsch, *Grammar*, §134c.

[64]The genitive relationship of צירי רוחות seems to be like that of אהל ביתי, *i.e.*, the genitive is added to the *nomen regens* as a nearer definition; *cf. ibid.*, §128m. The genitive expression משא רוחות, on the other hand, seems to specify possession; *cf. ibid*, §128g.

[65]*Cf.* J. Maier, *Texte*, vol. II, p. 126 n. 8.

]רוח (1Q36, 15:5).[66] Except for the forms יצר כול רוח in 1QH 15:13 (as man's predestined being, *cf.* section *3d2* in chapter 4 above), כול רוח עולה in 1QS 4:20 (as "disposition," *cf.* chapter 8 below), and כול רוח ורוח in Temple Scroll 36:5 & 40:8 (as "side," *cf.* chapter 6 below), the above are the only verses with a singular *ruaḥ* as a genitive of כול in the non-biblical, Hebrew Scrolls, and with 1Q36, 15:5 this is not certain.[67] We include it here only because of its apparent relationship to 1QH 1:9 and 10:8. Yet even if this relationship were not valid and *ruaḥ* has another form

---

[66]A majority of scholars consider *ruaḥ* in (a) 1QH 1:9 and (b) 1QH 10:8 as a reference to angels (I know of only Noll in "Angelology," p. 225, who has commented on *ruaḥ* in 1Q36, 15:5, which he understands to be angels): *cf.* Anderson, "'Ruah'," pp. 294 & 298 (both); Betz, *offenbarung*, p. 129 n. 3 (b only); Böcher, *Dualismus*, p. 34 (both); Carmignac and Guilbert, *textes*, p. 179 n. 13 (a only); Delcor, "Doctrines," col. 970 (b only); *idem, Hymns*, p. 39 (b only) Dupont-Sommer, *écrits*, p. 217 n. 3 (a only); Hill, *Greek Words*, p. 235 (b only); Holm-Nielsen, *Hodayot*, p. 20 n. 10 (a only); Hübner, "Dualismus," pp. 269-270 (a only); Huppenbauer, *Mensch*, p. 74 (both); Irwin, "Spirit-Dualism," p. 192 (a only; he also considers "wind" a possibility); Johnston, "Spirit," p. 37 (both); J. Maier, *Texte*, vol. II, p. 206 (both); May, "Cosmological Reference," p. 6 n. 23 (a only); Merrill, *Qumran*, pp. 16-17 (a only); Nötscher, "Geist," p. 310 (b only); Pryke "'Spirit'," p. 345 (b only); Ringgren, *Faith*, pp. 57 & 84 (both); Schubert, *Community*, p. 63 (b only); Schweizer, "πνεῦμα," p. 391 n. 336 (b only); Treves, "Two Spirits," p. 452 (a only); and Yadin, *Scroll of War*, p. 231 (b only). A number of scholars consider *ruaḥ* in these passages to be a reference to man's spirit: *cf.* Brandenburger, *Fleisch*, p. 89 (a only); J. P. Hyatt, "The View of Man in the Qumran 'Hodayot'," *New Testament Studies*, 2 (1956), 280 (a only); Irwin, "Spirit-Dualism," p. 192 (b only); H. W. Kuhn, *Enderwartung*, pp. 124-6 (a only); G. Maier, *Mensch*, p. 184 (both); Medico, *énigme*, pp. 426 & 477 (both); Pryke "'Spirit'," p. 345 (a only); Schreiner, "Geistbegabung," p. 165 n. 19 (a only); and Schweizer, "πνεῦμα," p. 390 (a only). Finally, Lichtenberger, *Studien*, p. 166 n. 8 defines *ruaḥ* in 1QH 1:9 as "die von Gott gesetzte, jedes Schöpfungswerk bestimmende Kraft," and Noll in "Angelology," p. 80 defines it as referring to the impersonal motive principles of every living thing; he also doubts if *ruaḥ* in 1QH 10:8 refers to angels, (*cf. ibid.*, p. 84).

[67]*Cf.* n. 2 above.

here (*e.g.*, as a plural or modified with a genitive or adjective), it would still probably be a reference to angels since in most cases in the Scrolls and in a wide variety of contexts כול in construct with a form of *ruaḥ* means "angel"; compare the list in section *2a* above with the rare (1QS 4:20 & 1QH 15:13)[68] and specialized (Temple Scroll 30:10, 31: 10; 36:5; 38:14; & 40:8) contexts having other meanings. Finally, we should note that the fragment immediately following 1Q36, 15:5 contains a reference to the demonic נפילים (*cf.* 1Q36, 16:3 and the analysis of 1Q36, 17:2 in section *2d2* above), which indicates that this general context is concerned with evil spirits of various kinds. The syntactical pattern כול רוח in 1QH 10:8 and 1:9, on the other hand, is clear, and the contexts of both passages indicate that *ruaḥ* is referring at least in part to angelic creatures. Thus, כול רוח in 1QH 10:8 is third in a series of four descriptions all of which appear elsewhere to refer to angels (אלים,[69] נכבדים,[70] and מעשה[71]) and which belong to a context which seeks to contrast God's power to the weakness of mortal man (v. 22) by extolling God's rulership over the great, immortal powers of the universe, who in spite of their greatness (הגדולים), still cannot stand before His great glory (v. 11). It would be odd, then, to understand the phrase אדון לכול רוח in this context to mean "Lord over every (mere) man," although perhaps men may be included as humble members of the general world of "spirits."[72] The same emphasis on angelic powers also appears for כול רוח in 1QH 1:9 both from a syntactical and contextual standpoint. Thus, the masculine

---

[68]Both of these verses belong to the relatively rare conceptual context of the two-spirit pneumatology of 1QS 3-4 with its specialized vocabulary; *cf.* the analysis of 1QH 15:13 in section *3d2* of chapter 4 above and the analysis of 1QS 3-4 in chapter 8 below.

[69]*Cf.* Mansoor, *Hymns*, p. 163 n. 8.

[70]*Cf.* 1Q29, 4, 2 and especially 1Q19, 3, 3 in which the connection to 1 Enoch 106 (as noted by Milik) makes it clear that the נכבדים are angels; *cf.* Barthélemy and Milik, *Discoveries*, I, p. 85.

[71]*Cf.* 1Q34bis II 7 and Milik's comments on this in *ibid.*, p. 154, note on line 7.

[72]This seems to be Lichtenberger's opinion in *Studien*, p. 166 n. 8.

suffix on "their works" (מעשיהם) referring back to כול רוח is characteristic as a reference to angels (*cf.* section *1* above) but not as a reference to the spirits of men (*cf.* section 2 in chapter 4 above), and the primary interest of this author here contextually (as in Jubilees 2:1ff.) is to describe first the creation of the spiritual and earthly universe and then to describe man's creation in relationship to the earth.[73] Note that the description of man's creation does not happen until v. 15 of our text (*cf.* Jubilees 3:14).

2) The singular of *ruaḥ* as a *nomen regens* in construct with a genitive: רו[ח האב]דון (4Q286 Bera 10 II 7) and רוח טמאה (11QPsa Plea 19:15).[74]

4Q286 Bera 10 II 7 with its unique term רוח האבדון is interesting since this appears to be the only place in the Scrolls in which a *specific* angel (whether good or evil) is called a *ruaḥ*. It is also interesting to note that Belial is not called here either רוח (ה)עול or רוח חושך (*cf.* chapter 8 below for the distinction between the two spirits and two angels of 1QS 3:13-4:26).

As noted above in n. 74, there is some disagreement about the meaning of *ruaḥ* in 11QPsa Plea 19:15. According to Noll, the terms שטן and רוח טמאה appear in a list of psychological qualities (*viz.*, "a spirit of faith and knowledge" in line 14 and "pain" and "the evil inclination" following in line 15) and should be understood in the same manner.[75] Osten-Sacken, however, sees just the opposite happening with "pain" and the "evil inclination" acquiring in this context a kind of personal quality,[76] and it seems in this case that he is correct. The clos-

---

[73]*Cf.* Carmignac and Guilbert, *Textes*, p. 179 n. 13.

[74]Most scholars seem to agree that *ruaḥ* in 4Q286 Bera 10 II 7 refers to the evil angel Belial; as for *ruaḥ* in 11QPsa Plea 19:15, David Flusser in "Qumran and Jewish 'Apotropaic' Prayers," *Israel Exploration Journal*, 19 (1966), p. 205 and Osten-Sacken in *Gott und Belial*, p. 143 regard it as an evil angelic power; Noll, however, in "Angelology," p. 73 sees it as a disposition.

[75]*Ibid*, p. 72.

[76]Osten-Sacken, *Gott und Belial*, p. 143.

est analogy to שטן and רוח טמאה in this pre-Essene psalm[77] is not in the Qumran sectarian writings but in Zechariah 3 & 13 in which השטן (3:1ff.) and רוח הטמאה (13:2) are both found. The author of 11QPsa Plea 19, then, was probably thinking of שטן in the realistic terms of Zech. 3:1ff. when he wrote and probably also thought of רוח טמאה as a personal being since he put it in parallel with שטן. The lack of an article on שטן, in fact, may indicate that the author probably thought of this term as a personal name.[78]

3) The singular of *ruaḥ* modified by a feminine adjective: ר]וח רעה (4Q511, 15, 7; and 4Q511, 81, 3).

Both of these occurrences are in a very fragmentary context from which nothing can be gathered except the bare form רוח רעה itself. Nevertheless, it is possible that this expression is referring to an "evil spirit" or demon for the following reasons: 1) this form appears in Judges 9:23 and 1 Samuel 16:14 in a context which the sectarians could have easily understood as an attack of a demon (*cf.* 4Q510, I, 4-6), and 2) its Aramaic counterpart (רוח בעישא) appears in 1QapGen 20 as a demon.[79] If, then, רוח רעה is a demon, its feminine state would seem to conflict with the position that *ruaḥ* as a demon or angel is always found in the masculine (*cf.* section *1* above). Nevertheless, this appears to be an isolated case of direct borrowing from the Old Testament and nothing more. Thus, whenever *ruaḥ* is found in 1QapGen with the adjective בעיש, it is always feminine, but whenever it is without this adjective (and refers to a demon), it is always masculine.[80]

---

[77]*Cf.* Sanders, *Discoveries*, IV, p. 76.

[78]*Cf.* 1 Chron. 21:1 and Kautzsch, *Grammar*, §125b.

[79]*Cf.* n. 171 in chapter 4 above.

[80]*Cf.* Fitzmyer, *Genesis Apocryphon*, p. 91, who lists the relevant passages but does not notice the connection. To my knowledge, no other example appears in a Qumran Aramaic source published to date in which *ruaḥ* appears as a demon; *cf.* however Milik's reconstructions in J. T. Milik, *The Book of Enoch, Aramaic Fragments of*

3. Conclusion.

For an analysis of this chapter and a comparison of its results with the results of chapters 3, 4 and 6 (*ruaḥ* as God's Spirit {ch. 3}, man's spirit {ch. 4}, and wind & breath {ch. 6}), see chapter 7 below.

Qumrân Cave 4 (Oxford: Clarendon Press, 1976), p. 189 (4QEn^c 1 V 2) and p. 199 (4QEn^c 1 VI 20).

CHAPTER 6

OTHER USES OF *RUAḤ*: 1) WIND, 2) BREATH, AND 3) UNCERTAIN AND FRAGMENTARY TEXTS

1. *Ruaḥ* as "wind" with its related meanings "quarter/side" and "vanity."[1]

a. General observations.

Ruaḥ as "wind" or a related meaning is found 27 times in the published, non-biblical Hebrew Scrolls, including 14 times with the basic meaning "wind" (1QH 1:10; 6:23; 7:5; 7:23; f 3:6; 9:6; 19: 3; CD 8:13; 19:25; 4Q171, 1, 3-4 III 8; 4Q185, 1-2, I, 10; 4Q185, 1-2, I, 11; 4Q185, 1-2, I, 12; 11QPsa Crea 24 II 15 {recon.}), 12 times as "quarter/side" (1QM 9:13; 3Q15 VII 5; 4Q491, 1-3, 14; Temple Scroll 6:6; 30:10; 31:10; 36:5 {twice}; 38:13; 38:14; and 40:8 {twice}), and once as "vanity" (1QH 7:29). As in the Old Testament,[2] *ruaḥ* as wind can be either feminine (1QH 7:23, subject of חבלעני; 3Q15 VII 5, modified by ארבע; 4Q185, 1-2, I, 11, subject of חשא; and Temple Scroll 6:6, modified by ארבע) or masculine (1QH 1:9, referred to by the suffix on חוקידם and היותם; 1QM 9:13, modified by שלושה; and 4Q491, 1-3, 14, modified by ארבעה).

b. Specific patterns of *ruaḥ* as "wind."

1) The most frequent pattern of *ruaḥ* in this category is as an unqualified singular in the following expressions (10 times):[3] רוח כמוץ לפני (1QH 7:23), כול צב[י] רוח (1QH 7:29), בעבותי רוח (1QH f

---

[1]*Cf.* Brown, Driver and Briggs, *English Lexicon*, p. 924 for this category of meaning.

[2]*Cf.* Lys, *Ruaḥ*, p. 307 n. 2: "le genre de *ruaḥ* au sens de 'vent' est souvent flottant."

[3]Listed according to location.

9:6), כנפי רוח (1QH f 19:3), שוקל רוח ומתיף כזב (CD 8:13), הולך רוח ושקל סופות (CD 19:25), יובדו כענן האוד [בר]וח (4Q171, 1, 3-4 III 8), ציצו חשא רוח עד אייקום (4Q185, 1-2, I, 11), לא ימצא מרוח (4Q185, 1-2, I, 12), and ויוצא [רוח] מאוצרותיו (11QPsa Crea 24 II 15). In all these occurrences except three (*viz.*, 1QH 7:29; f 9:6; and CD 8:13),[4] I have found no one who disagrees with the definition of *ruaḥ* as wind or its related meanings, and this consensus seems to be correct. Thus, *ruaḥ* is found in these verses with vocabulary and concepts traditionally associated with wind (compare 1QH 7:23 with Is. 17:23; 1QH f 19:3 with 2 Sam 22:11; 4Q185, 1-2, I, 11 with Is. 41:16 & Ps. 103:15-16; 4Q185, 1-2, I, 12 with Dan. 2:35; and 11QPsa Crea 24 II 15 with Ps. 135:7) or its context is closely associated with a corresponding context in the Old Testament dealing with wind and its related concepts (compare CD 19:25 with Micah 2:11; and 4Q171, 1, 3-4 III 8 with Ps. 37:20). As for the three disputed texts, it is likely that they also refer to wind in one sense or another. This is especially true for CD 8:13 (parallel to CD 19:25 with both related to Micah 2:11) and also for 1QH f 9:6 in which עבותי is probably a reference to the

---

[4]For *ruaḥ* as "spirit" in 1QH f 9:6, *cf.* Holm-Nielsen, *Hodayot*, p. 268; as "wind," *cf.* Carmignac and Guilbert, *Textes*, p. 272. For *ruaḥ* as "spirit" in CD 8:13, *cf.* Irwin, "Spirit-Dualism," p. 69 (a possibility as a kind of manticism) and Molin, *Söhne*, p. 50 ("*Geisterverwirrer*"); as "wind," *cf.* Hill, *Greek Words*, p. 234, Johnston, "Spirit," p. 27, Lohse, *Texte*, p. 83 and Vermes, *Scrolls in English*, p. 105. The greatest difference of opinion is over the meaning of *ruaḥ* in 1QH 7:29: as "angel," *cf.* Johnston, "Spirit," p. 37 and Noll, "Angelology," p. 136 (as a possibility); as "man's spirit," *cf.* Betz, *Offenbarung*, p. 129, Leaney, *Rule*, p. 159, Nötscher, "Geist," p. 305, Pryke, "'Spirit'," pp. 345-6 and Schweizer, "πνεῦμα," p. 390; for "vanity" or "wind/breath" in the sense of vanity, *cf.* Hans Bardtke, "Considerations sur les Cantiques de Qumran," *Revue Biblique*, 63 (1956), p. 222, *idem*, *Handschriftenfunde*, p. 245, Carmignac and Guilbert, *Textes*, p. 233, Hill, *Greek Words*, p. 234, Holm-Nielsen, *Hodayot*, pp. 138 & 139 n. 8, Lohse, *Texte*, p. 141, Medico *énigme*, p. 464 and Schreiner, "Geistbegabung," p. 162 n. 7; finally, Irwin in "Spirit-Dualism," p. 192 believes that *ruaḥ* in 1QH 7:29 may refer to either "man," "wind" or "angel."

clouds[5] with the meaning "clouds carried along by the wind."[6] The interpretation of 1QH 7:29, on the other hand, is more difficult due to the uncertainty involved with the word צב[י];[7] its interpretation as "glory," however (*viz.*, "all glory is vanity"), is reminiscent of Is. 23:9, which describes God as bringing into dishonor כול צבי, and it fits in well with the thought of the verses just following our text (1QH 7:32-33) that man next to God is but emptiness and vanity.

2) A less frequent pattern for referring to wind is with the singular of *ruaḥ* as the *nomen regens* of a genitive (4 times): רוח עועיים (1QH 6:23 and 7:5), [. . .]רוח סוע (1QH f 3:6), and רוח הקדם (Temple Scroll 38:13). As for the last two examples, both the context and form of רוח הקדם in Temple Scroll 38:13 (*cf.* Ezk. 42:16) show that *ruaḥ* here means "wind" in the sense of its derivative meaning "quarter/side," and the context of 1QH f 3:6 with its reference to the author as a מקוי אפר ("heap of ashes") indicates that the *ruaḥ* before which the author cannot stand is a רוח־סוע]רה, *i.e.*, a "stormy wind."[8] The meaning of רוח עועיים in 1QH 6:23 and 7:5, however, is more difficult to determine. Some scholars regard this expression as a reference to man's spirit in some sense,[9] one regards it as a hostile angel,[10]

---

[5]For the strange plural, *cf.* Kautzsch, *Grammar*, §87s.

[6]*Cf.* Carmignac and Guilbert, *Textes*, p. 273 n. 9.

[7]*Cf.* Mansoor, *Hymns*, p. 152 n. 1.

[8]*Cf.* Ezk. 1:4; 13:11 & 13; Ps. 107:25 and 148:8 and also Holm-Nielsen, *Hodayot*, p. 263 n. 4; the word following *ruaḥ* could also be read as סועה, "raging" (*cf.* ps. 55:9). I know of no scholar who understands this as anything other than a reference to wind. Note that this expression is probably from רוח סערה in Ezk. 1:4, Ps. 107:25 and 148:8 (or רוח סערות in Ezk. 13:11 & 13); the genitive סוערה in our expression, then, would be an Aramaizing *qutl* form of סערה. *Cf.* Goshen-Gottstein, "Linguistic Structure," pp. 126-7.

[9]For *ruaḥ* in (a) 1QH 6:23 and (b) 1QH 7:5 as a reference to man's spirit or disposition, *cf.* Huppenbauer, *Mensch*, p. 74 (a only); May "Cosmological Reference," p. 5 n. 17 (a only, as a possibility); Nötscher, "Geist," p. 308 (b only); Pryke "'Spirit'," p. 345 (both); and Schweizer, "πνεῦμα," p. 391 (b only).

but most understand it as a reference to wind.[11] The feminine singular form of *ruaḥ* in 1QH 7:5 makes it unlikely that it is referring to a demon,[12] although a reference to the psalmist's disposition as confused or distorted seems possible by analogy with the same expression in Is. 19:14. Nevertheless, רוח עועיים in both 1QH 6:23 and 7:5 probably means "whirlwind" since in both contexts the psalmist describes himself as being caught in a violent storm at sea, and in 1QH 7:5 it is within this kind of a storm that the *ruaḥ* engulfs (בלע) him.

3) The feminine plural form of *ruaḥ* with suffixes occurs 5 times: ארבע רוח[ותיו] (3Q15 VII 5); ארבע רוחותיה (Temple Scroll 6:6), כול רוחותיו (Temple Scroll 30:10 & 31:10); and כול רוחותיה (Temple Scroll 38:14). As seen both from the form of these expressions (*cf.* Jer. 49:36 and Ezk. 42:20) and their context (all having to do with measurement or direction), these occurrences of *ruaḥ* are best translated as "sides."[13]

---

[10] *Cf.* May, "Cosmological Reference," p. 5 n. 17 (b only).

[11] For *ruaḥ* in (a) 1QH 6:23 and (b) 1QH 7:5 as "wind," *cf.* Bardtke, *Handschriftenfunde*, pp. 243-4 (both); Carmignac and Guilbert, *Textes*, pp. 224 & 228 (both); Dupont-Sommer, *écrits*, pp. 234 & 236 (both); Hill, *Greek Words*, p. 234 (both); Holm-Nielsen, *Hodayot*, p. 118 n. 143 and p. 123 n. 186 (a and possibly b); Irwin, "Spirit-Dualism," pp. 192 & 224 n. 58 (both); G. Jeremias, *Lehrer*, pp. 235 and 289 (both); Johnston, "Spirit," p. 27 (both); Lohse, *Texte*, pp. 137 & 139 (both); J Maier, *Texte*, vol. I, pp. 89 & 91 (both); and Vermes, *Scrolls in English*, pp. 171-2 (both).

[12] *Cf.* section *2a* of chapter 5 above. There could be, however, a metaphorical reference to the opposition of demonic power as a "stormy wind."

[13] Only the editors of these scrolls have commented on the meaning of *ruaḥ* here, and in every case they understand it as "side"; *cf.* Baillet, Milik and DeVaux, *Discoveries*, III, p. 292 for 3Q15 VII 5 and Yigael Yadin, *The Temple Scroll, Text and Commentary*, vol. II (Jerusalem: Israel Exploration Society, 1983), pp. 23, 132-3, 136 & 164 for Temple Scroll 6:6; 30:10; 31:10 & 38:14.

4) The feminine plural form of *ruaḥ* as the *nomen regens* of a genitive occurs 2 times: רוחות עוז (1QH 1:10), and שלושה רוחות הפנים (1QM 9:13).

Scholars are evenly divided over whether *ruaḥ* in 1QH 1:10 refers to angels or winds, while some are undecided between the two.[14] The masculine reference on חוקיהם might seem to point to רוחות as personal angelic beings,[15] but *ruaḥ* as wind can be masculine in the Old Testament[16] and in the Scrolls it appears as masculine with the related meaning "quarter/sides" (*cf.* 4Q491, 1-3, 14 and 1QM 9:13). It is in fact difficult to decide between the meaning "angels" or "winds" here, but it is possible that the psalmist had a literalistic understanding of Ps. 104:4 (upon which 1QH 1:10 seems to be based) and thought that there was a time when winds were simply "winds" until God made them into "angels." Nevertheless, רוחות followed by a genitive (especially a genitive indicating a quality) is a typical pattern for describing angelic beings at Qumran.[17] The only other pattern which even comes close to this as "wind" or a related meaning is in 1QM 9:13 above, and in this passage the genitive (הפנים) does not indicate a quality. Perhaps the author in using this pattern in 1QH 1:10 was effecting a deliberate ambiguity with *ruaḥ* as both "winds" and "angels."

---

[14]For *ruaḥ* as angels, *cf.* Delcor, *Hymns*, p. 44. Johnston, "Spirit," p. 37, Licht, "Doctrine," p. 90, J. Maier, *Texte*, vol, II, pp. 65 & 206; Mansoor, *Hymns*, p. 98, May, "Cosmological Reference," p. 6. n. 23, Pryke, "'Spirit'," p. 345 n. 10, Ringgren, *Faith*, p. 57 and Strugnell, "Angelic Liturgy," p. 333; for *ruaḥ* as wind, *cf.* Bardtke, *Handschriftenfunde*, p. 233, Carmignac and Guilbert, *Textes*, p. 178, Chavallier, *Souffle*, p. 52, Dupont-Sommer, *écrits*, p. 217, Hill, *Greek Words*, p. 234, Lichtenberger, *Studien*, p. 166 n. 8, Lohse, *Texte*, p. 113; Nötscher, "Geist," p. 305; Schweizer, "πνεῦμα," p. 390 n. 334 and Vermes, *Scrolls in English*, p. 150; for *ruaḥ* as either angel or wind, *cf.* Anderson, "'Ruah'," p. 302, Holm-Nielsen, *Hodayot*, pp. 16, 20 n. 14 and p. 277 and Irwin, "Spirit-Dualism," pp. 52 & 192.

[15]*Cf.* section *2a* in chapter 5 above.

[16]*Cf.* n. 2 above.

[17]*Cf.* the analysis of 1QH f 45:6 in section *2c1* of chapter 5 above.

Although most scholars understand שלושה רוחות הפנים in 1QM 9:13 as "the three sides of the front,"[18] some see it as referring to the "Angels of the Presence"[19] (*cf.* 1QH 6:13; 1QSb 4:26; and 3Q7, 5, 3). However, it is unlikely that this expression is referring to angels here since the Angels of the Presence are never called the "spirits of the Presence" at Qumran or in its related literature[20] and also because the word הפנים in the context of 1QM 9:13 seems to be referring to the three "fronts" of the tower which are to be protected with a barrier of 100 shields for each side for a total of 300 shields. The syntax and meaning of שלושה רוחות הפנים, then, is somewhat like that of Zech. 2:10 (ארבע רוחות השמים) "the four quarters of the heavens"; *cf.* also Ezk. 42:20.

5) Miscellaneous forms of *ruaḥ* (6 times): רוחו (4Q185, 1-2, I, 10), א]רבעת הרוחות (4Q491, 1-3, 14), and כול רוח ורוח (Temple Scroll 36:5 & 40:8).

The form רוחו in 4Q185, 12, I, 10 is the only example so far of a singular *ruaḥ* with a suffix in the published, non-biblical Hebrew Scrolls which does not refer to man's spirit. In this context it means a "breath" or wind from God and is based on the language and concepts of Is. 40: 6-8.

The form ארבעת הרוחות in 4Q185, 1-2, I, 10 is interesting for two reasons: it is one of the few times that *ruaḥ* has the article

---

[18]*Cf.* Anderson, "'Ruah'," p. 303; Bardtke, *Handschriftenfunde*, p. 224; Dupont-Sommer, *écrits*, p. 199; Hill, *Greek Words*, p. 234; Irwin, "Spirit-Dualism," p. 27 & 194; Jongeling, *rouleau*, p. 236; Lohse, *Texte*, p. 203; J. Maier, *Texte*, vol. I, p. 134; Medico, *énigme*, p. 394; J. van der Ploeg, *Le Rouleau de La Guerre, Traduit et annoté evec une introduction*, Studies on the Text of the Desert of Judah, 2 (Leiden: Brill, 1959), p. 44; and Vermes, *Scrolls in English*, p. 135.

[19]*Cf.* M. Delcor, "La guerre des fils de Lumiére contre des fils de tenebres," *La nouvelle Revue Theologique*, 77 (1955) p. 388 and Huppenbauer, *Mensch*, p. 84 n. 364.

[20]*Cf.* Jub. 1:27 & 29; 2:1, 2, & 18; 19:27; 31:14; *cf.* also Test. of Levi 3:5 {recension b}; 18: 5; Test. of Judah 25:2; and 1 Enoch 40 in which there are four rather than three angels of the presence as also in 1QM 9:15-16; *cf.* Irwin, "Spirit-Dualism," p. 27, who notes that four "spirits" rather than three would be expected in 1QM 9:13 if it were referring to angels.

in the published, non-biblical Hebrew Scrolls,[21] and it also belongs to a context like that of שלושה רוחות הפנים in 1QM 9:13 (*cf.* the analysis of this passage in paragraph 4 directly above) in which *ruaḥ* is referring together with פנים (*cf.* Baillet's reconstruction in *Discoveries*, VII, 18, note on line 14) to the four sides of a reassembled battle formation. The article on רוחות would be a reference to the previous mention of the left, right, back and front sides of this formation.

Finally, the form כול רוח ורוח in Temple Scroll 36:5 and 40:8 is the only distributive use of *ruaḥ* found in the non-biblical, Hebrew Scrolls so far, and in its contexts it means "each side."[22]

2. *Ruaḥ* as "breath."

a. General observations.

Ruaḥ as breath is found 5 times in the published, non-biblical Hebrew Scrolls. In the Old Testament *ruaḥ* with this meaning can be either masculine or feminine[23] but is not found in the plural; in the Scrolls it can be singular or plural, but there is no evidence for its gender.[24]

b. Specific patterns of *ruaḥ* as "breath."

1) The singular of *ruaḥ* used without qualification (2 times): רוח (1QH 1:28) and ארוכי רוח (1QM 6:12).

There is a difference of opinion among scholars on the exact meaning of ארוכי רוח in 1QM 6:12. Most understand *ruaḥ* here as

---

[21]*Cf.* כול הרוחות (angels) in 4Q158, 14, I, 2 and 8Q5, 2, 6; הרוח (sickness) in 4Q266 Da 1 XVII 6; and משיח הרוח (God's Spirit) in 11 QMelch III 2, 18; *cf.* also the fragmentary occurrence of הרוח in 4Q178, 1, 6.

[22]*Cf.* Yadin, *Temple Scroll*, vol. II, p. 153.

[23]For the masculine, *cf.* Ecc. 3:19 and Lam. 4:20; for the feminine, *cf.* Isa. 33:11 and Ps. 146:4.

[24]The suffix on דבריה in 1QH 1:28 probably refers back to לשון; *cf.* the translation of Dupont-Sommer in *écrits*, p. 219.

"breath,"[25] but some see this as a reference to the horse's disposition, *i.e.*, as "gentle" or "patient"[26] (*cf.* Ecc. 7:8). The author in this context, however, is probably more concerned with stamina in the cavalry rather than with gentleness or patience.

There is also a disagreement among scholars on the meaning of רוח in 1QH 1:28. Some understand it as referring simply to man's breath,[27] while others see it as pointing to a higher function in man such as a disposition or spiritual quality given to him by God.[28] The context, in fact, seems to indicate a divine inspiration of some sort since it is God himself who brings forth the "utterances of breaths" (מבעי רוחות, v. 29) so that man might make known His glory; nevertheless, there is still no essential connection between this process of inspiration and the three occurrences of *ruaḥ* in 1QH 1:28-29 since these verses depict *ruaḥ* more as a *tool* than as a source of inspiration. *Ruaḥ* in this context is no more a source of inspiration than is the tongue. The expression רוח in 1QH 1:28 along with מבע רוח שפתים in 1QH 1:29a and מבעי רוחות in 1QH 1:29b, then, should probably be understood in the sense of 1 Enoch 84:1, *i.e.*, that God has put "breath" in the mouth of all men. The author of 1QH 1:28-29, however, would also add that God foreordained the nature of this and all other aspects of human speech before they came

---

[25]*Cf.* Chavallier, *Souffle*, p. 52; Hill, *Greek Words*, p. 234; Irwin, "Spirit-Dualism," pp. 194 & 208 n. 13; Lohse, *Texte*, p. 195; Schreiner, "Geistbegabung," p. 162 n. 7; and Vermes, *Scrolls in English*, p. 132.

[26]*Cf.* Anderson, "'Ruah'," p. 296, who believes that ארוכי רוח can mean either long-winded or patient, and Burrows, *The Dead Sea Scrolls* (New York: Viking Press, 1955), p. 394, who translates this as "gentle."

[27]*Cf.* Anderson, "'Ruah'," p. 303; Bardtke, *Handschriftenfunde*, p. 234; Delcor, *Hymns*, pp. 88-9; Irwin, "Spirit-Dualism," p. 192 (may also refer to man); Lohse, *Texte*, p. 115; J. Maier, *Texte*, vol. I, p. 73; Schreiner, "Geistbegabung," p. 162 n. 7; Schweizer, "πνεῦμα," p. 390 n. 334; and Vermes, *Scrolls in English*, p. 152.

[28]*Cf.* Flusser, "Sect," p. 251; Holm-Nielsen, *Hodayot*, pp. 18 & 26 n. 54; Johnston, "Spirit," p. 36; Licht, *Thanksgiving Scroll*, p. 38; Merrill, *Qumran*, p. 16 n. 4; Pryke, "'Spirit'," p. 345.

into existence so that those who know Him would praise and exalt Him properly (*cf.* 1QH 1:28-31).

2) The singular of *ruaḥ* as a *nomen regens* of a genitive (2 times): מבע רוח שפתים (1QH 1:29a), and רוח שפתים (1QSb 5:24).

For the analysis of *ruaḥ* in 1QH 1:29a as "breath" see paragraph *1* directly above in connection with the analysis of *ruaḥ* in 1QH 1:28.

Scholars are somewhat divided on the meaning of רוח שפתים in 1QSb 5:24. The majority understand it as man's breath,[29] but a few see it as God's Spirit[30] or a human disposition.[31] The genitive שפתים, however, indicates that the basic meaning of *ruaḥ* here is simply "breath" as in Isaiah 11:4 from which this expression is taken. If this "breath" seems to have an extraordinary effect, it is not because it is really the *ruaḥ* of God but because it is the breath of the divinely authorized נשיא, just as the mouth of this leader remains his own even though it is exceptionally effective in leadership (*cf.* [וה]כיתה עמים בעז [פי]כה).

3) The feminine plural form of *ruaḥ* as an unqualified genitive (one time): מבעי רוחות (1QH 1:29b). There does not appear to be a plural form of *ruaḥ* in the Old Testament as "breath," but the close association of our expression with מבע רוח שפתים in the same verse indicates that its most likely meaning here is "breaths" (*cf.* the analysis in paragraphs 1 and 2 directly above).

---

[29]*Cf.* Bardtke, *Handschriftenfunde*, p. 288; Carmignac, Cothenet and Lignée, *Textes*, p. 40; Dupont-Sommer, *écrits*, p. 126; Gaster, *Scriptures*, p. 99; Irwin, "Spirit-Dualism," pp. 74, 187 & 192; Lohse, *Texte*, p. 59; Medico *énigme*, p. 337; Barthélemy and Milik, *Discoveries*, I, 128; and Vermes, *Scrolls in English*, p. 209.

[30]*Cf.* Foerster, "Geist," p. 119 and Irwin, "Spirit-Dualism," pp. 74-5 & 192 (as a possibility).

[31]*Cf.* J. Maier, *Texte*, vol. II, p. 206.

3. Fragmentary and uncertain uses of *ruaḥ* in the published, non-biblical Hebrew Scrolls.

a. The following occurrences of an unqualified use of *ruaḥ* in the singular (12 times) are in contexts too fragmentary for analysis: (occurrences undefined by scholars) (ו)רוח (4Q487, 4, 1; 4Q502, 238, 1; 4Q504, 4, 20; and 6Q18, 21, 2), ברוח (1Q69, 37, 1; 3Q9, 1, 1; and 5Q13, 23, 6), לרוח (5Q13, 4, 5), and מרוח (4Q513, 31, 2); (defined) מרוח (1QH 17:6 & 7; and f 14:1).[32]

b. The following diverse forms of a qualified or plural form of *ruaḥ* are in contexts too fragmentary for analysis (3 times, all undefined by scholars): הרוח (4Q178, 1, 6), רוחות (4Q511, 24, 2), and רוחותיהם (4Q176, 21, 3).

c. The following are possible occurrences of *ruaḥ* (2 times): ריח (4Q499, 6, 3), and ריח [אלוהים] (4Q511, 30, 6). In both of these verses it is possible, according to Baillet, that ריח should be read as רוח.[33] In the case of 4Q499, 6, 3 it seems that the form can be read either with a *yodh* or a *waw*, but the context is so fragmentary here that no significance can be attached to either reading. In the case of 4Q511, 30, 6 it appears that the reading ריח is certain, but from its context Baillet seems to be correct in seeing a scribal error here since it is based clearly on Is. 40:12-13, which reads רוח יהוה in this place. Baillet's suggestion that אלוהים follows ריח in this fragment, however, seems less likely since God's Spirit is never described in the non-biblical, Hebrew Scrolls published to date with the genitive אלוהים, just as יהוה is not used in this way. The only time, in fact, that אלוהים ever oc-

---

[32]*Ruaḥ* in 1QH 17:6 & 7 is defined by Pryke in "'Spirit'," p. 345 as man's spirit or disposition, and Carmignac in Carmignac and Guilbert, *Textes*, p. 173 n. 3 integrates f 14:1 into line 2 of 1QH 17 and defines *ruaḥ* in this context as the "esprit" which God places in His people through which they escape judgment. It seems impossible, however, to define *ruaḥ* in any of these initial verses of 1QH 17 due to the fragmentary context.

[33]*Cf.* Baillet, *Discoveries*, VII, 75, note on line 3, and p. 236, note on line 6.

curs with a form of *ruaḥ* in the Scrolls is with the phrase רוחות אלוהים (חיים), which is found in 4QSl in reference to the angels.[34] It is more likely that the expression following *ruaḥ* in 4Q511, 30, 6 was קודשך, since in the context of this fragment the psalmist is addressing God (*cf.* line 3) and a frequent way of referring to God's Spirit in the Scrolls (especially 1QH) while addressing Him is with the phrase רוח קודשך (*cf.* 1QH 7:6; 9:32; 12:12; *etc.*).[35]

4. Conclusion.

For an analysis of this chapter and a comparison of its results with the results of chapters 3, 4 and 5 (*ruaḥ* as God's Spirit {ch. 3}, man's spirit {ch. 4} and angel/demon {ch. 5}), see chapter 7 below.

---

[34] *Cf.* Strugnell, "Angelic Liturgy," p. 332.

[35] *Cf.* Baillet, *Discoveries*, VII, p. 220 on the close literary connection between 4Q510 & 511 and 1QH.

CHAPTER 7

ANALYSIS AND COMPARISON OF THE RESULTS OF CHAPTERS 3 - 6

1. General observations.

Perhaps the most significant syntactical characteristic of *ruaḥ* discovered in this study is its gender as this relates to its meanings as man's spirit and as angel/demon. As the spirit of man, *ruaḥ* is consistently feminine in the non-biblical Hebrew Scrolls (with the possible exception of 1QH 8:29), and as angel/demon, it is consistently masculine (with the possible exception of רוח רעה in 4Q511, 15, 7 and 4Q511, 81, 3). It is also important to note that although there is a considerable overlapping of the basic sytactical patterns used for *ruaḥ* in its five categories of meaning (*e.g.*, the singular of *ruaḥ* as the *nomen regens* of a genitive is found in all five categories), there is still very little semantic overlapping with the individual *expressions* of *ruaḥ* as listed at the beginning of chapters 3-5 and in the listings in chapter 6. The only real overlapping of individual expressions is found in the following cases: 1) with the unqualified and unattached singular of *ruaḥ* (*e.g.*, man's spirit in 1QH 15:22, wind in 4Q185, 1-2, I, 11 and breath in 1QH: 1:28), 2) with ברוח (*e.g.*, God's Spirit in 1QH 12:11 and man's spirit in 1QH 4:31), 3) with מרוח (*e.g.*, man's spirit in 1QH 9:16b and wind in 4Q185, 1-2, I, 12),[1] and 4) with רוחו (once for wind in 4Q185, 1-2, I, 10 and often for man's spirit, *e.g.*, 1QS 2:14). All the other individual expressions of *ruaḥ* (approx. 130) listed in chapters 3-6 have only one meaning within the five basic categories of God's Spirit, man's spirit, angel/ demon, wind and breath.

---

[1]The meanings of the preposition מ differ, however.

2. Analysis of specific categories of *ruaḥ*.

a. Syntactical patterns of *ruaḥ* associated with its meaning as God's Spirit; for the following references, *cf.* section *2a* of chapter 3 above.

The syntactical patterns of *ruaḥ* and the various expressions within these patterns used in the non-biblical, Hebrew Scrolls to refer to God are relatively few in number, especially in comparison with those used for man (*cf. 2b* below). Thus, the customary means for referring to God's Spirit (24 of 35 occurrences) is with the singular of *ruaḥ* as the *nomen regens* of a form of קודש in the singular as its genitive (*e.g.*, הקודש, קודשך/ו or קודש), and in the remaining 11 occurrences the variation of expression is not great. In most cases a simple, unqualified form of *ruaḥ* in the singular is used (*e.g.*, ברוח אשר נתתה בי, 4 times; משיחי רוח, once; סודי רוח, once; and [...]רוח, once), and in only 2 cases is a descriptive genitive other than קודש used (*e.g.*, רוח דעה, once; and רוח רחמיך, once) with one case of the root קדש as an adjective (רוח קדושה) and one case of *ruaḥ* as a genitive with the article (משיח הרוח). The gender of *ruaḥ* as God's Spirit is not clear, although the available evidence points to the feminine.[2] It should be noted, finally, that the individual expressions found in this category are for the most part contextually clear in their reference to God.

b. Syntactical patterns of *ruaḥ* associated with its meaning as man's spirit; for the following references, *cf.* section *3a* in chapter 4 above.

In contrast to the relatively few kinds of expressions used to describe God's Spirit in the Scrolls, those used for man's spirit are numerous and varied. Thus, the predominant pattern for describing the spirit of man is the use of *ruaḥ* in the singular with one or more genitives (37 times, plus 2 additional cases with *ruaḥ* in the plural), with 29 different genitives used and none over 3 times. This is in contrast to the same pattern for God's Spirit (which is also the most frequent pattern of its category),

---

[2]*Cf.* n. 1 in chapter three above.

which uses only 2 different genitives beyond the various forms of קודש which are normally used (24 times). Yet despite the variety of genitives which are used to describe man's spirit, none of these expressions ever overlaps with those of other meanings of *ruaḥ* using this pattern.[3]

A basic pattern of *ruaḥ* which belongs almost exclusively to the category of man's spirit is *ruaḥ* in the singular with a suffix of any kind (24 times). The only exception to this is 4Q185, 1-2, I, 10 in which *ruaḥ* refers to wind with its suffix referring to God.

As with the meanings "God's Spirit," "wind" and "breath," *ruaḥ* in a singular, unqualified form is also found for man's spirit (17 times). However, as a genitive following a *nomen regens* which, in turn, indicates a spiritual disposition or quality of character (8 times), *ruaḥ* refers only to man's spirit in the non-biblical, Hebrew Scrolls.

Another pattern which is used only to describe man's spirit is the singular of *ruaḥ* followed by one or more participial adjectives (8 times). There are only two other cases in the published, non-biblical Hebrew Scrolls in which *ruaḥ* is modified by an adjective, and in both cases the adjective is not a participle and its use involves a special situation.[4]

It is interesting to note that *ruaḥ* occurs in the plural only 7 times as man's spirit (all as a form of רוחות) with more than half of these occurring in the two-spirit treatise (4 times). Finally, as we noted above, all occurrences of *ruaḥ* as man's spirit are feminine with the possible exception of 1QH 8:29.

c. Syntactical patterns of *ruaḥ* associated with its meaning as angel/demon; for the following references, *cf.* section *4b* in this chapter above.

---

[3]*Cf.* however, the interesting attempt of the author(s) of 1QS 3:13-4:26 to redefine רוח קודש in terms of רוח אמת in 1QS 4:21; *cf.* the analysis of this in chapter 8 below.

[4]*Cf.* the analysis of 1QS 3:7 in section *2f* of chapter 3 above and also the analysis of 4Q511, 15, 7 and 4Q511, 81, 3 in section *2e3* of chapter 5 above. *Cf.* also n. 8 in chapter 6 above.

One of the most striking patterns of the word *ruaḥ* in the Scrolls is its masculine plural form, which is never found in the Hebrew Old Testament and which never unambiguously means anything other than angel/demon in its 31 occurrences in our material. It is found 4 times with a suffix (2 times as a genitive of צבא and twice by itself), but its most frequent pattern is as a *nomen regens* in construct with a genitive (26 times) often in turn preceded by the *nomen regens* כול (14 times).

The feminine plural form of *ruaḥ* is the next most frequent pattern in the Scrolls for describing angels or demons (20 times). There appears to be no difference of meaning between רוחות and רוחים as angels/demons since both forms can refer to both good and evil angels and in a number of expressions they seem to be interchangeable (*cf.* CD 12:2 with 4Q177, 1-4, 10; 4Q510, 1, 5b with 4Q511, 182, 1 & 4Q511, 35, 7; and 1QH f 5:4 with 4Q511, 1, 6 & 1QM 15:14; *cf.* also 1QH 1:11 with 4Q502, 27, 1). Also like רוחים, the form רוחות is found primarily as a *nomen regens* in construct with a genitive (16 times) and only 4 times in other patterns (twice with the article following כול, once with a suffix, and once as a genitive in construct with משא). Unlike רוחים, however, the form רוחות is found in the Scrolls not only as angel/demon but also as wind, breath and man's spirit (disposition). Yet as a *nomen regens* followed by a genitive, רוחות seems to be used primarily to refer to angelic beings since 1) this pattern is found in relationship to men only in the two-spirit Treatise of 1QS 3-4 as part of a pneumatology almost unique to this Treatise (*cf.* chapter 8 below) and 2) the only other occurrences of this pattern are in 1QH 1:9 as "wind" (which may intentionally be mixing the concepts "winds" and "angels") and in 1QM 9:13 as "quarter/side" in which the genitive has to do with direction (פנים) rather than with a quality or spiritual character as is usually the case with this pattern when it means "angel/demon."

We should note, finally, that *ruaḥ* as angel/demon is almost always plural with a masculine gender in the sectarian writings. The exceptions to this are more apparent than real. Thus, 1) רוח טמאה in 11QPsa Plea 19:15 was probably not composed by a sectarian, 2) כול רוח in 1QH 1:9, 10:8 and possibly

1Q36, 15, 5 is semantically plural, 3) רוח האבדון in 4Q286 Bera 10 II 7 is a unique reference to Belial as a *ruaḥ*, and 4) רוח רעה in 4Q511, 15, 7 & 4Q511, 81, 3 is a term directly borrowed from the Old Testament by the sectarians and otherwise avoided by them despite its biblical origin and their interest in demonology.

d. Syntactical patterns of *ruaḥ* associated with its meaning as "wind" (with the associated meanings "quarter/side" and "vanity"); for the following references *cf.* the listings in chapter 6 above.

An unqualified *ruaḥ* in the singular is the most frequently used pattern of *ruaḥ* in the non-biblical, Hebrew Scrolls for referring to "wind" and its related meanings (10 times). This syntactical pattern is also used to refer to God's Spirit, man's spirit, and breath, but the context and vocabulary related to *ruaḥ* as wind in these 10 occurrences usually remove most ambiguity.

A less frequent pattern of *ruaḥ* in the singular as wind is *ruaḥ* as the *nomen regens* of a genitive (4 times). This pattern is also found for God's Spirit, man's spirit, breath and (in non-sectarian authorship) for angel/demon. In the four cases of *ruaḥ* as wind above, however, the vocabulary and context surrounding *ruaḥ* indicate its meaning as "wind."

Ruaḥ as "quarter/side" appears 5 times as a feminine plural form with suffixes. Although this pattern is used also for man's spirit and for angels, the context in all 5 occurrences above indicates the meaning of *ruaḥ* as "sides."

There are two occurrences of *ruaḥ* in a feminine plural form as the *nomen regens* of a genitive, once as "winds" and once as "sides." This form is a frequent pattern for describing angels/demons and is used twice in the two-spirit Treatise to describe man. In one of the above cases (1QM 9:13), the genitive of *ruaḥ* (הפנים) and the context identify it as "sides," but in the other case (1QH 1:10), the psalmist may have used this pattern to create an intentional ambiguity between "winds" and "angels."

The miscellaneous forms of *ruaḥ* (6 times, *cf.* 4Q185, 1-2, I, 10 רוחו; 4Q491, 1-3, 14 א]רבעת הרוחות; and Temple Scroll, 36:5 & 40:8 כול רוח ורוח) are all within contexts which clearly identify them as either wind (once) or sides (5 times).

We should note, finally, that 1) *ruaḥ* as wind or a related meaning can be either masculine or feminine with no apparent effect on its meaning and that 2) it shares its basic syntactical patterns with other meanings of *ruaḥ* while relying on its context and surrounding vocabulary (*e.g.*, כנפי, לפני + מוץ, הקדם) to remove most ambiguity.

e. Syntactical patterns of *ruaḥ* associated with its meaning as "breath"; for the following references, *cf.* the listings in chapter 6 above.

Ruaḥ is found twice as an unqualified, singular noun as "breath." Although it shares this pattern with *ruaḥ* as God's Spirit, man's spirit and wind, its context in both cases (*viz.*, its association with war horses in 1QM 6:12 and man's tongue in 1QH 1:28) identifies it as "breath."

Ruaḥ as breath also appears two times in the singular as a *nomen regens* of a genitive, and although it also shares this pattern with *ruaḥ* as God's Spirit, man's spirit, angel/demon (in a non-sectarian writing) and wind, the two cases above are identified as "breath" by their context and characteristic vocabulary (both in construct with the genitive שפתים).

There is only one case of *ruaḥ* in a feminine plural form as "breaths" (1QH 1:29b), but its context and associated vocabulary (*viz.*, מבעי, also used in this context with *ruaḥ* as "breath") identify it as "breaths" rather than man's spirit, wind or angels.

We should note, finally, that there is no evidence for the gender of *ruaḥ* as "breath" in the non-biblical, Hebrew Scrolls so far and that *ruaḥ* as breath shares its syntactical patterns with the other categories of *ruaḥ* while depending on its context and associated vocabulary to resolve most ambiguity. In this respect, then, *ruaḥ* as "breath" is like the categories of "God's Spirit" and "wind," neither of which depend on gender or special syntactical patterns for communicating meaning but on context and characteristic vocabulary (*e.g.*, a form of the genitive קודש in the singular following *ruaḥ* in the singular is often used for "God's Spirit"). However, *ruaḥ* as "breath" is unlike the categories of "man's spirit" and "angel/demon" since both of these depend on their gender as important elements in communicating their meaning and both have a number of syntactical patterns which are either strongly or exclusively confined to their use (*e.g.*, the use of *ruaḥ* in the singular with a suffix to refer to man's spirit, or the use of רוחים to refer to "angels/demons").

CHAPTER 8

THE MEANING OF *RUAḤ* IN 1QS 3:13-4:26

1. Initial observations.

Ruaḥ appears 16 times[1] in the two spirit Treatise of 1QS 3:13-4:26 and is implied an additional 4 times.[2] One of its most striking features is the number of its forms which appear only here or very rarely in other parts of the Scrolls. Thus, the phrase לכול מיני רוחותם is found only here, and the only other occurrence of רוחות with a suffix in the Scrolls as a reference to man is in 1QS 2:20 (רוחותם). Most importantly, however, the key expressions שתי רוחות (3:18), רוחות האמת והעול (3:18/19), רוחות אור וחושך (3:25) and רוחי אמת ועול (4:23) never occur elsewhere at Qumran in the Scrolls published so far and, in fact, the only occurrences of any form of *ruaḥ* with any form of אמת, עול, אור or חושך outside of the two-spirit Treatise are with רוח אמת[3] in 4Q177, 12-13, I, 5, רוחי אמת in 1QM 13:10, רוח עצת אמת in 1QS 3: 6, רוחות עולה[4] in 1QH f 5:6 and רוח נבונה ואורה in 11QPsa DavComp 27 II 4 (*cf.* also 1QH 2:4). Other expressions unique to 1QS 3:13-4:26 are רוח זנות in 4:10 (*cf.* Hos. 4:12 and 5:4) and רוח נדה in 4:22; *cf.* also רוח ענוה in 4:3 (found elsewhere only in 1QS 3:8 as רוח יושר וענוה) and סודי רוח in 4:6 (also found as סוד רוחו in 1QH f 31:1). Out of the total of 16 expressions involving *ruaḥ* in the Treatise, then, 5 of the most important to its thesis (3:14, 18, 18-19, 25 & 4:23) are never found elsewhere in the Scrolls and most of the others appear only rarely or in variant forms with different meanings. Only

---

[1] 1QS 3:14, 18, 18/19, 24 & 25; 4:3, 4, 6, 9, 10, 20, 21a, 21b, 22, 23 & 26b.

[2] 1QS 4:15, 16, 25 & 26a.

[3] The same form is found in the Treatise in 4:21b; but *cf.* also ch. 5. n. 1.

[4] A similar form (רוח עולה) is found in the Treatise in 4:9 &4:20; *cf.* n. 3 above.

four expressions, in fact, are found with any frequency with the same form and basic meaning outside of the Treatise: רוחי גורלו in 3:24 (*cf.* 1QM 13:2, 4, & 11/12; 4Q287 Berb 4, 3; 4Q491, 14-15, 10 and 11QMelch 3 II & 13), רוח דעת in 4:4 (*cf.* 1QSb 5:25b and 6Q18, 5, 3), רוח קודש in 1QS 4:21a (*cf.* 1QSb 2:24; 4Q177, 3-10 IV 25; and 4Q504, 4, 5), and רוחו in 1QS 4:26 (*cf.* 1QS 2:14; 7:18 & 23; 9:15 & 18, *etc.*). All of this creates the impression of a literary and conceptual[5] isolation of the two-spirit Treatise within sectarian literature and tends to support Osten-Sacken's view that the two-spirit dualism of 1QS 3-4 is a secondary and later development in the evolution of sectarian thought.[6]

2. An exegetical analysis of *ruaḥ* in 1QS 3:13-4:26 on the basis of its use in the rest of the non-biblical, Hebrew literature of Qumran.

a. 1QS 3:14 כול מיני רוחותם.

Most scholars understand this expression as referring to man's spirit in one sense or another[7] although a significant minority sees it as a reference to the two spirits[8] (understood as cosmic beings) and others think that it includes these and other

---

[5]Only 1QH 15 and 4Q186 seem to share the basic idea of 1QS 3:13-4:26 that man's good or evil spiritual nature is given to him at birth; *cf.* also 4Q177, 12-13, I 5.

[6]*Cf.* Osten Sacken, *Gott und Belial*, pp. 165-9.

[7]*Cf.* Böcher, *Dualismus*, p. 73; Brandenburger, *Fleisch*, p. 88; Dupont-Sommer, "instruction," p. 13; H. W. Kuhn, *Enderwartung*, p. 122; K. G. Kuhn, "Πειρασμός," p. 214 n. 1; Leaney, *Rule*, p. 147; Lilly, "Idea of Man," p. 68; J. Maier, *Texte*, vol. II, p. 206; Noll, "Angelology," p. 135, Nötscher, "Geist," pp. 306 & 309; Pryke, "'Spirit'," p. 345; Treves, "Two Spirits," p. 450; and Wernberg-Møller, "Reconsideration," p. 419.

[8]Johnston, "Spirit," p. 30; Ehrhard Kamlah, *Die Form der katalogischen Paränese im Neuen Testament*, Wissenschaftliche Untersuchungen zum Neuen Testament, 7 (Tübingen: Mohr, 1964), p. 42 (he also includes the numerous angels/demons under the two spirits); Licht, "Doctrine," p. 90 n. 7: May, "Cosmological Reference," p. 2; Schweizer, "πνεῦμα," p. 390 (he seems to include the numerous angelic spirits here also); and Wernberg-Møller, *Manual* p. 67.

possible meanings.[9] It seems, however, that the majority is correct in this case. One reason is in the phrase כול מיני itself ("all the varieties of"), which one would expect to read שני מיני ("the two kinds of") if it were referring primarily to the two cosmic spirits. A second reason is that the closest analogy syntactically and semantically to our expression is רוחותם in 1QS 2:20, which is used in that context to refer to the varieties of spiritual perfection among the Essene priests which serve as the basis for their rank.[10] Such a use of רוחותם just before our expression in 1QS 3:14 (*i.e.,* after the two-spirit Treatise was incorporated into 1QS as we now have it) must have created an expectation in the sectarian reader of 1QS 3:13-15 that he would now receive instruction not only on the spiritual differences between the pious and wicked but also on the reason for the spiritual differences between sectarians. A final reason for viewing our expression as referring to a variety of spiritual dispositions is that the context of 1QS 3-4 itself ultimately envisions a wide variation of spirituality among men in proportion to their inheritance in a lesser or greater amount of the two "divisions" of the spirits (*cf.* 1QS 4:16 & 24 and the analysis of these verse in section 3 below). This would probably remain true whether 1QS 3:13-4:26 has one author or several[11] since its last author or redactor could have easily edited the opening statement of the treatise to fit its concluding views.[12]

---

[9]*Cf.* Irwin, "Spirit-Dualism," pp. 8 & 191 ("a generalized term including all the other meanings"); Licht, *Rule,* p. 90 (may refer either to the two spirits or to man's character; *cf.* n. 8 above); and Shaked, "Qumran," pp. 435-6 (has both a psychological and cosmic sense).

[10]I have found only one scholar who thinks that *ruaḥ* in 1QS 2:20 may refer to something more than man's spirit; *cf.* Shaked, "Qumran," p. 436, who believes that it has both a psychological and cosmic sense.

[11]For a single author, *cf.* Licht, "Analysis," pp. 88-100; for several stages of composition and probable multiple authorship, *cf.* Osten-Sacken, *Gott und Belial,* pp. 17-27.

[12]*Cf.* Noll, "Angelology," p. 131, who sees evidence of a literary interrelationship with the beginning of 3:13ff and expressions in 4:15-26.

b. 1QS 3:18 שתי רוחות and 3:18/19 רוחות האמת והעול.

These expressions together with רוחות אור וחושך in 1QS 3:25 and רוחי אמת ועול in 1QS 4:23 are at the heart of a complex and involved debate on the meaning of *ruaḥ* in 1QS 3:13-4:26. The fundamental difference of opinion is whether the "spirits" in these four passages denote personal, angelic powers external to man (as well as spiritual forces influencing him internally)[13] or are simply spiritual dispositions and nothing more.[14] Additional areas of debate involve the meanings of *ruaḥ* in these passages in relation to each other[15] and to the two angels (the Prince of Light and Angel of Darkness) also mentioned in this context (1QS 3:20ff.).[16]

---

[13]I have not found any scholar who denies the psychological function of these spirits in these passages; *cf.* Charlesworth, "Comparison," p. 82 and the discussion in chapter 2 above.

[14]*Cf.* n. 16 below.

[15]*E.g.*, Nötscher, in "Geist," p. 310 believes that 3:18-19 is referring to opposite spiritual orientations whereas 3:25 and 4:23 refer to numerous, angelic spirits. For scholars who see two cosmic spirits in 3:18-19 but see a plurality of angelic spirits in 3:25, *cf.* Baumbach, *Qumran*, pp. 14 & 47, Flusser, "Dualism," p. 164 and Huppenbauer, *Mensch*, p. 27 n. 82 & p. 31 n.100; for those who see a plurality in 4:23, *cf.* Irwin, "Spirit-Dualism," p. 198 n. 17 and H. W. Kuhn, *Enderwartung*, p. 121; *cf.* also Yadin, *Scroll of War*, p. 231. Most scholars, however, believe that *ruaḥ* in 3:25 and 4:23 refer to the same two spirits of 3:18-19; *cf.* nn. 17, 31, 32, and 77 below.

[16]*Cf.* Betz, *Paraklet*, pp. 67-68, who views 1QS 3:18/19, 25 & 4:23 as referring to the two spirits and distinguishes them from the two angels of 3:20ff. A number of scholars distinguish *ruaḥ* in (a) 3:18 & 18/19, (b) 3:25 and (c) 4:23 from the two angels by regarding *ruaḥ* in one or more of these passages as no more than dispositions in man: *cf.* F. M. Braun, "arrière-fond," p. 13 (a only); Coppens, "don," p. 210 (c only); Graystone, "Scrolls," vol. 22, pp. 227-8 (a only); Johnston, "Spirit," p. 30 (c only); K. G. Kuhn, "Sektenschrift," p. 301 n. 4 (a & c); Noll, "Angelology," pp. 135-7 & 176 (he resists the identification of the two spirits in a & b with the two angels and prefers to regard them as "ethical principles"); Nötscher, "Geist," p. 310 (a only); Pryke, "'Spirit'," pp. 345-6 (a & b); Treves, "Two Spirits," p. 450 (c only) and Wernberg-Møller, *Manual*, p. 67 (c only). Note that later Wernberg-Møller in "Reconsideration," pp.

Most scholars who offer clear opinions on the two spirits in 1QS 3:18 & 18/19 tend to identify them with the two (good and evil) angels mentioned in 3:20-25[17] with a few of them understanding these expressions as involving not just the two angelic leaders but also their angelic followers as two groups or armies of angelic spirits.[18] Some scholars, however, understand *ruaḥ* here as simple human dispositions with no essential connection

---

422 & 425 also identified 3:18 & 18/19 as dispositions, and in the same work he redefined the two angels of 3:20ff. as no more than personifications of these dispositions, *cf. ibid.*, p. 426 n. 30. Most scholars identify the two spirits in 3:18 & 18/19 (and wherever else they may find them) with the two angels of 3:20ff.: *cf.* nn. 17 and 31 below.

[17]Some scholars are ambiguous on this relationship, but *cf.* Anderson, "'Ruah'," pp. 298-9; Becker, *Heil Gottes*, pp. 85-86 & 89; Betz, *offenbarung*, pp. 58, 129 n. 3 & pp. 143-4 (*cf.* Betz in n. 16 directly above); Böcher, *Dualismus*, pp. 36, 38, 77 & 101; Burrows, *More light*, pp. 280, 283, & 287; Charlesworth, "Comparison," pp. 77-8; Chevallier, *Souffle*, p. 52; Cross, *Library*, pp. 210 & 213; W. D. Davies, "Paul," pp. 167 & 173; Jean Daniélou, "Une source de la spiritualité chrétienne dans le Manuscrits de la Mer Morte: la doctrine des deux Esprits," *Dieu Vivant*, 25 (1953), p. 128; Driver, *Scrolls*, p. 537; Dupont-Sommer, "instruction," p. 18; Ellis, "Gifts," pp. 135-6; Hill, *Greek Words*, p. 236; Huppenbauer, *Mensch*, p. 19; Johnston, "Spirit," p. 39; Leaney, *Rule*, p. 43; Lichtenberger, *Studien*, p. 191; May, "Cosmological Reference," p. 5; Montague, *Holy Spirit*, pp. 117-8; Murphy, *Scrolls*, pp. 65-66; Ringgren, *Faith*, pp. 78-79 & 82; and Schweizer, "πνεῦμα," p. 390. For those who see the two spirits as cosmic or angelic beings but are ambiguous about how the two angels relate to them, *cf.* Brandenburger, *Fleisch*, pp. 97-98; Irwin, "Spirit-Dualism," p. 191; Licht, "Analysis," pp. 91-92; G. Maier, *Mensch*, pp. 234-6; Osten-Sacken, *Gott und Belial*, p. 141; Shaked, "Qumran," pp. 435-6; and Wernberg-Møller, *Manual*, p. 67. Note, finally, that Baumbach in *Qumran*, pp. 14-16, Licht in *Rule*, p. 82 and Schubert in *Community*, p. 62 seem to distinguish the two spirits (understood as angelic beings) from the two angels.

[18]*Cf.* J. T. Milik, *Ten Years of Discovery in the Wilderness of Judea*, Studies in Biblical Theology (trans. by J. Strugnell; Naperville: Alec R. Allenson, Inc., 1959), p. 118; Nötscher, *Gotteswege*, p. 92; and J. van der Ploeg, *The Excavations at Qumran, A Survey of the Judaean Brotherhood and its Ideas* (trans. by K. Smyth; London: Longmans Green and Co., 1958), pp. 98 & 101.

to personal, angelic figures[19] and in this opinion they seem to be basically correct. The key evidence for this is the feminine gender of *ruaḥ* in both verses, which can be seen in its modification by שתי in v. 18 and its connection to הנה in vv. 18/19. The use of the masculine suffix (בם) in reference to *ruaḥ* in v. 18 is semantically neutral since בהן is rare (if it exists at all) in the non-biblical Scrolls with בם or בהם replacing it (*cf.* 1QS 5:12 with בם in relationship to הנסתרות and אלות; *cf.* also CD 3:4 & 14, 4:16, and also Kautzsch, *Grammar*, §135c). If the author had wished to indicate personal, angelic beings with רוחות in these verses, especially following his announced intent in v. 14 to talk about the varieties of human dispositions, he almost certainly would have used the masculine gender as is customary everywhere in the sectarian, Hebrew Scrolls in talking about angels.[20] As it is, he used the feminine gender, which is almost always used in the sectarian Scrolls in reference to man's spirit.[21] His main point in 3:15-19a is that man's inner spirituality does not have its origin in his own autonomy or free will but in God's power of predetermination and creation (vv. 15-17). It is God alone who creates man (ברא v. 17) and then situates him (וישם לו v. 18) in relationship to the good or evil spiritual disposition in which he is to carry out all of his predetermined, good or evil conduct (להתהלך בם v. 18) with no possibility of change (אין להשנות v. 16).

It is clear, however, that a cosmic significance is not entirely absent for *ruaḥ* in 1QS 3:18 & 18/19 despite the author's primary interest in it as a human disposition. This can be seen in two respects: 1) the author uses a pattern of *ruaḥ* (רוחות with a genitive indicating a quality) which is usually used to describe angels,[22] and 2) he refers to a "Spring of Light" and a "Well of Darkness" from which come the "natures" or "origins"[23] of truth and iniquity[24] (v. 19). In this way the au-

---

[19]*Cf.* n. 16 above.

[20]*Cf.* section *1* in chapter 5 above.

[21]*Cf.* section 2 in chapter 4 above.

[22]*Cf.* section *2c* in chapter 7 above.

[23]תולדות in 3:19 has been translated variously as "generations," "succeeding generation," "origins," "history" and "nature"; *cf.* Osten-

thor indicates that a man's good or evil spiritual disposition cannot be regarded as simply a personal or individual matter between himself and others (or even God) but is deeply involved in a cosmic Good or cosmic Evil. Good and Evil far transcend human limitations, and it is precisely here that the two, cosmic angels are introduced.[25] Unlike the notion of the "two spirits," however, which is probably original with this author,[26] the concept of a good angel ruling over the pious and an evil angel ruling over the wicked was probably already a traditional idea in sectarian thought at the time 1QS 3:13-4:26

Sacken, *Gott und Belial*, p. 19 n. 1. Osten-Sacken (citing J. Maier) seems to be correct in noting that the context supports the translation "Herkunft. . . im Sinn der Wesensbestimmtheit" (*ibid.*); but *cf.* Licht "Analysis," pp. 89-90 n. 5. For מעין (rather than מעון) as symbolic for God, *cf.* Lichtenberger, *Studien*, p. 127 n. 22.

[24]*Cf.* Lichtenberger, *Studien*, pp. 127-8, who notes that there is no hint of the mythological or cosmic proportions of the two spirits as powers outside of man until verse 19: "Der Übergang dazu [*i.e.*, to a view of the two spirits as forces outside of man] wird freilich im folgenden Satz Z. 19 angebahnt, wenn mit Wahrheit und Frevel nunmehr Licht und Finsternis in Bezug gesetzt werden. . . . 'Wahrheit' entstammt dem göttlichen Bereich, 'Frevel' dem widergöttlichen. . . ." Lichtenberger seems to be correct here, but not in the sense that the two spirits attain a personal angelic status; verse 19, rather, is indicating that the good and evil "spirits" are not simply individual or personal characteristics in men but are intimately connected to vast sources of cosmic Good and Evil, which flow from a cosmic "Spring of Light" or godless "Well of Darkness," respectively. Lichtenberger also points to 1QS 10:12 and other verses which show that God Himself may have been thought of as the "Spring of Light" and suggests that the "Well of Darkness" may have been Belial (*cf. ibid.*, p. 127 n. 22).

[25]Wernberg-Møller in "Reconsideration," p. 425 n. 30 is the only scholar I know who clearly regards the two angels as no more than personifications of good and evil dispositions in man.

[26]*I.e.*, within the Qumran community; *cf.* Test. of Judah 20:1-5. This seems to be a reasonable conjecture since the two-spirit teaching as such with its distinctive vocabulary (*e.g.*, שתי רוחות, רוחות האמת והעול, רוחות אור וחושך) is never otherwise clearly found in Qumran, although some sources (*e.g.*, 1QH 15 and 4Q186) share similar concepts of *ruaḥ*.

was written[27] and was probably also understood in a non-deterministic way.[28] The author of this Treatise introduced the two angels in 3:20ff. because he wanted to relate his new pneumatology to the traditional and popular view that the pious and wicked walk in righteousness and in sin (respectively) because of their voluntary submission to their good and evil angelic leaders. His goal was to teach his listeners that a person falls under the authority of either the good or evil angel not because of his own good or evil "decision" but because he is predestined and created by God with a good or evil spiritual disposition which unchangeably determines the angel under whose personal authority he is to submit. This pneumatology has no essential connection to the two angelic figures, however, as can be seen in the absence of these angels in 1QH 15 and 4Q186.

We should note, finally, that the articles in the expression רוחות האמת והעול in v. 18/19 refer back to שתי רוחות in v. 18.[29]

c. 1QS 3:24 כול רוחי גורלו.

Almost all scholars are agreed that this expression refers to demons or evil angels of some kind[30] and this view seems to

---

[27]*Cf.* the Vision of 'Amram, in which two angels (good and evil) claim to have authority over "all the sons of men" (4Q'Amram^{b} 1, 12) and dispute with each other over who will control 'Amram (lines 10-11). Noll notes in "Angelology," p. 44 that Milik dates manuscript b to the mid- or early 2nd century B.C. and that the five copies of this work at Qumran attest to its popularity there.

[28]*Cf. ibid.*, p. 45: "The most unusual feature of the vision of 'Amram is that the patriarch is given a choice between the two angels." *Cf.* also CD 5 and 1QM 13.

[29]*Cf.* Kautzsch, *Grammar*. §126d.

[30]I have found only three scholars who believe that *ruaḥ* here refers to something other than evil angels or demons: *cf.* K. G. Kuhn in "Πειρασμός," p. 207 n. 2, who believes that it refers to the human enemies of the sect, Schweizer in "Gegenwart des Geistes," p. 493, who believes that it may refer to the spirits of men as "daena," and Treves in "Two Spirits," who doubts that 3:24 refers to angels but is unclear in his alternative view. For scholars who consider רוחי גורלו to be a reference to evil angels or demons, *cf.* nn. 11 and 17 in chapter 5 above.

be correct; see the analysis of this expression in section *2a* of chapter 5 above.

d. 1QS 3:25 רוחות אור וחושך.

The majority of scholars interpret this expression as a reference to the two spirits of 3:18-19 (seen as cosmic beings) with most identifying these spirits with the two angels of 3:20-25[31] while others are more ambiguous about how these spirits (although cosmic in nature) relate to the two angels;[32] some scholars, however, see *ruaḥ* here as a plurality of good and evil angelic spirits[33] or as referring to something other than angels.[34] It appears that the majority is correct in identifying *ruaḥ* in 3:25 with the two spirits of 3:18-19 (*cf.* the numerical identity between 3:18 & 3:25 with the spirits of 3:25 being defined by אחת אהב and אחת תעב in 3:26 and 4:1), but the feminine gender of *ruaḥ* in 3:18-19 and 3:25[35] indicates that *ruaḥ* in both verses refers not to personal angelic beings but to two opposed

---

[31]*Cf.* Anderson, "'Ruah'," pp. 298-9; Betz, *Offenbarung*, p. 129 n. 3 & pp. 143-4; Böcher, *Dualismus*, pp. 36, 38, 77 & 101; Burrows, *More Light*, p. 280; Charlesworth, "Comparison," p. 80; Chevallier, *Souffle*, p. 52; Daniélou, "spiritualité," p. 128; Dupont-Sopmmer, "instruction," pp. 16 & 18; May, "Cosmological Reference," pp. 2 & 5; Montague, *Holy Spirit*, pp. 117-8; Murphy, *Scrolls*,pp. 65-66; Ringgren, *Faith*, pp. 69, 78-79 & 92; and Schweizer, "πνεῦμα," p. 390. Note, finally, that Betz in *Paraklet*, pp. 67-68 and Schubert in *Community*, p. 62 distinguish the two spirits from the two angels of 3:20-25.

[32]*Cf.* Flusser, "Sect," p. 246; Irwin, "Spirit-Dualism," pp. 198-9 n. 17 & p. 191; Licht, "Analysis," p. 92; G. Maier, *Mensch*, p. 249 and Wernberg-Møller, *Manual*, p. 67.

[33]*Cf.* n. 18 above and also Baumbach, *Qumran*, p. 47; Flusser, "Dualism," p. 164; Huppenbauer, *Mensch*, p. 27 n. 82; Nötscher, "Geist," p. 310 and *idem*, *Terminologie*, p. 96.

[34]*Cf.* Pryke, "'Spirit'," pp. 345-6 (two dispositions) and Noll, "Angelology," p. 176 (ethical principles).

[35]*Cf.* the feminine references to *ruaḥ* in 3:25 with the suffixes on עלילותיה in 4:1, סודה in 4:1, דרכיה in 4:1, and the references with אחת in 3:26 and 4:1. For the unusual form עליהון, *cf.* Lohse, *Texte*, p. 10 note g, who equates it with עליהן.

spiritual dispositions in man. As in 3:18 & 18/19, however, the author in 3:25 is describing more than simply good and evil personal attitudes, but with the pattern רוחות in construct with a genitive descriptive of a spiritual quality[36] and with the statement that these dispositions had their own special creation (with no mention of man), the author seems to give the impression of good and evil entities existing beyond the confines of the individual man and his existence. Again, however, the feminine gender shows that the author's intent is not to describe personal, angelic beings which exist alongside of man, but to show that the dispositions which spiritually define man are not merely individual or personal matters but are intimately related to a cosmic good and cosmic evil which transcend man. A refusal of those outside the community to follow sectarian law, therefore, is evidence to the author of this treatise of more than simply a mistaken decision on their part or even of the effect of Belial's personal rule over them. It shows that their innermost religious life, *i.e.*, their religious identity as human beings, has its primary source in a great cosmic Well of Darkness (3:19) which totally and unchangeably defines who they are spiritually according to the predetermining and creative act of God. This is quite a harsh view of the non-sectarian and may indicate that it arose (or became accepted in the community) at a time in which the conflict between sectarian and non-sectarian was so intense that the community felt the need to isolate itself as much as possible not only physically but also spiritually from the outside world.

e. 1QS 4:3 רוח ענוה.

A majority of scholars views this expression as no more than a disposition in man,[37] although one sees it as a definite

---

[36]This pattern is characteristically used in the sectarian writings to describe angels, *cf.* section 2c in chapter 7 above.

[37]*Cf.* Anderson, "'Ruah'," p. 295; Coppens, "don," p. 210; W. D. Davies, "Paul," p. 176; Driver, *Scrolls*, p. 538; Duhaime, "rédaction," pp. 575-6; Irwin, "Spirit-Dualism," p. 191 G. Maier, *Mensch*, p. 187; Manns,

reference to the "spirit of truth"[38] another as a "personified power" (but only as a possibility)[39] and two others as the Spirit of God.[40] The majority seems to be correct in this case, however, since רוח ענוה is part of a series of expressions all referring to human qualities which, in turn, are said to describe the "ways" of the two spirits (*cf.* אלה דרכיהן in 4:2). Note that the closest analogy to this expression in the Scrolls is וענוה רוח יושר in 1QS 3:8, which was analyzed in chapter in section *3b2* of chapter 4 above as man's spirit or disposition.

f. 1QS 4:4 רוח דעת.

A significant majority of scholars regards this expression as a simple disposition in man,[41] although some understand it as God's Spirit[42] or as the good spirit of 3:18-19.[43] Like *ruaḥ* in 4:3, however, רוח דעת is part of a series of expressions all referring to qualities in men which, in turn, are descriptive of the "ways" of the two spirits (4:2). Note also that the closest analogies in the Scrolls to our expression are רוח דעת in 6Q18, 5, 3, which is in a context too fragmentary for analysis (*cf.* section *3b3* in chapter 4 above) and רוח דעת in 1QSb 5:25b, which is an allusion to Is 11:2 and probably refers in the context of 1QSb to no more than a disposition in man (*cf.* the analysis of this verse in section *3b2* of chapter 4 above).

---

symbole, p. 87; Nötscher, "Geist," pp. 306 & 309-10; Pryke "'Spirit'," p. 345; Schweizer, "Gegenwart des Geist," p. 492; and *idem*, "πνεῦμα," p. 390. *Cf.* also Seitz, "Two Spirits," p. 93 (an attribute of the spirit of truth).

[38]Lichtenberger, *Studien*, p. 134.

[39]Chevallier, *Souffle*, p. 54.

[40]Flusser, "Sect," p. 249 and Osten-Sacken, *Gott und Belial*, p. 152.

[41]*Cf.* Anderson, "'Ruah'," p. 296; Böcher, *Dualismus*, p. 75; Burrows, *More Light*, p. 295; Driver, *Scrolls*, p. 538; Duhaime, "rédaction," pp. 575-6; Irwin, "Spirit-Dualism," pp. 9 & 191, G. Maier, *Mensch*, p. 187; Nötscher, "Geist," p. 306 & 309; and Pryke, "'Spirit'," p. 345; *cf.* also Seitz, "Two Spirits," p. 93 (an attribute of the spirit of truth).

[42]*Cf.* Flusser, "Sect," p. 249; Manns, *symbole*, pp. 77-78; and Nötscher, *Terminologie*, p. 42 (*cf.* Nötscher, in n. 41 directly above).

[43]Schweizer, "πνεῦμα," p. 390; *cf.* also Chevallier, *Souffle*, p. 54.

g. 1QS 4:6 סודי רוח.

For the analysis of this use of *ruaḥ*, see section *2d2* in chapter 3 above and also section *3* of this chapter below for its place in the two-spirit treatise.

h. 1QS 4:9 רוח עולה.

Most scholars see this expression as a specific reference to the evil spirit of 3:18-19 (sometimes identified with the Angle of Darkness[44] and sometimes not[45]) while a few regard this as no more than a human disposition.[46] The identification of this spirit as the evil spirit of 3:18-19 seems to be correct since it is presented as being the source of the numerous evil qualities in the wicked (vv. 9-11) and seems to reflect the expression רוחות (האמת) והעול in 3:18-19. However, as in 3:18, 18/19 and 25 (*cf.* the analysis of these passages in section *2b* and *2d* above), *ruaḥ* here is not a personal, angelic figure but rather a fundamentally perverse spiritual disposition with an intimate connection to cosmic evil, *i.e.*, it defines human spirituality, but it is not simply one human characteristic or disposition among others (*e.g.*, such as קצור אפים in 4:10). It is a fundamentally perverse spirituality proceeding from a Well of Darkness (3:19). As in 3:18, 18/19 and 25, however, the impersonal, non-angelic nature of this "spirit" is reflected in its feminine gender (*cf.* בה in v. 12 referring back to רוח עולה in v. 10). A further indication that the author is referring to a disposition in man (although intimately related to cosmic evil) is the pattern of *ruaḥ* in the singular followed by a genitive indicating a quality: in Qum-

---

[44]*Cf.* Böcher, *Dualismus*, p. 36; Charlesworth, "Comparison," p. 78; Daniélou, "spiritualité," p. 128; May, "Cosmological Reference," pp. 3 & 5; Montague, *Holy Spirit*, pp. 117-8; and Ringgren, *Faith*, p. 71 (*cf.* also p. 82)

[45]*E.g.*, Delcor in "Doctrines," col. 973; Irwin in "Spirit-Dualism," p. 191 and J. Maier ln *Texte*, vol. II, p. 206 are ambiguous on this possible identification; Licht in *Rule*, pp. 62 & 97 seems to view them as separate angelic spirits. *Cf.* also Baumbach in *Qumran*, p. 14, who seems to regard *ruaḥ* here as only one angelic spiritual power among others.

[46]Coppens, "don," p. 210; Duhaime, "rédaction," pp. 575-6; and Wernberg-Møller, "Reconsideration," p. 431.

ran's sectarian Hebrew literature this syntactical pattern is never used to refer to an angel or demon but is the most frequent means of referring to man's spirit or disposition.[47]

i. 1QS 4:10 רוח זנות.

I have found only one scholar who thinks that this expression may refer to something other than a human disposition.[48] The majority view seems to be correct here, however, since this expression is found as part of a series of descriptions which refer to human qualities (vv. 9-11) and its syntactical pattern is the one most frequently used by the sectarians to refer to man's spirit or disposition.[49] Its closest parallel is the expression רוח זנונים in Hosea 4:12 and 5:4, which probably also refers to a human disposition.[50]

j. 1QS 4:20 כול רוח עולה.

A number of scholars understand this expression as either a reference to the evil spirit of 3:18-19 (usually also identified with the Angel of Darkness)[51] or as a reference to evil angels in general,[52] but others understand it as no more than a disposition

---

[47]*Cf.* n. 60 in chapter 4 above.

[48]*Cf.* Baumbach, *Qumran*, p. 14, who believes that this is an individual, angelic spirit. For this expression as a human disposition, *cf.* Anderson, "'Ruah'," p. 296; Burrows, *More Light*, p. 295; Duhaime, "rédaction," p. 576; Irwin, "Spirit-Dualism," pp. 9 & 191; Licht, *Rule*, p. 98; Murphy, *Scrolls*, pp. 82-83; Nötscher, "Geist," p. 309; and Schweizer, "πνεῦμα," p. 390 n. 329 (metaphorical use); *cf.* also Seitz, "Two Spirits," p. 93 (an attribute of the spirit of perversity).

[49]*Cf.* section *3a* in chapter 4 above.

[50]*Cf.* Lys, *Ruaḥ*, p. 75 and Imschoot, *Theology*, p. 183 n. 23.

[51]*Cf.* Charlesworth, "Comparison," p. 78 and Dupont-Sommer, "instruction," pp. 18 & 32; *cf.* also Driver, *Scrolls*, p. 537.

[52]*Cf.* Baumbach, *Qumran*, p. 40; W. D. Davies, "Paul," p. 161; Irwin, "Spirit-Dualism," pp. 8-9 (he also believes that *ruaḥ* here may refer to an element in man's character, *cf. ibid.*, p. 191); H. W. Kuhn, *Enderwartung*, p. 121; and Otzen, "Sektenschriften," pp. 138-9.

in man.[53] It seems reasonable to understand כול רוח עולה here as a reference to the evil spirit of 3:18-19 since the same expression (except for כול) occurs in 4:9 as the evil spirit of 3:18-19 (*cf.* the analysis of 4:9 in section *2h* above), and the context just preceding (4:16) and following (4:24-25) our expression indicates that individuals are influenced to some extent by both the good and evil spirit (*cf.* section *3* below). As with רוח עולה in 4:9, however, the expression in 4:20 is essentially a human disposition (with cosmic overtones) rather than one or more angelic beings. The correct translation of כול רוח עולה is probably not "every spirit of perversity"[54] (indicating a plurality) but "all spirit of perversity"[55] (indicating a single, perverse disposition).[56] We should note, finally, that although the construction of כול רוח in at least two cases in the Scrolls is clearly used as a description of angelic beings (*cf.* 1QH 1:9 & 10:8 and the analysis of these passages in section *2e1* of chapter 5 above), it can also be used to describe man's spirit (*cf.* 1QH 15:13 and the analysis in section *3d2* of chapter 4 above); also, the singular of *ruaḥ* with a genitive indicating a quality is never clearly used by the sectarians to describe an angel,[57] whereas this is the most frequently used pattern in the non-biblical, Hebrew Scrolls for describing man's spirit or disposition.[58]

---

[53]*Cf.* Coppens, "don," p. 210; Licht, *Rule*, p. 103; Manns, *symbole*, p. 88; Pryke, "'Spirit'," p. 345; and Wernberg-Møller, "Reconsideration," p. 423. Note that K. G. Kuhn in "Sektenschrift," pp. 301-2 relates *ruaḥ* in 4:20 to the evil spirit of 3:18-19, but at this time he regarded the two spirits as no more than human dispositions (*cf.* n. 18 in chapter 2 above); *cf.* also Nötscher, "Geist," pp. 307-8 & 310, who seems to hold a similar view at that time.

[54]*E.g.*, as in W. D. Davies, "Paul," p. 161 and H. W. Kuhn, *Enderwartung*, p. 121.

[55]*E.g.*, as in Dupont-Sommer, *écrits*, p. 97; Leaney, *Rule*, p. 154; Vermes, *Scrolls in English*, p. 77; and Wernberg-Møller, *Manual*, p. 27.

[56]The lack of the article is probably because the author is treating this expression as a proper name; *cf.* Kautzsch, *Grammar*, § 125f.

[57]*Cf.* section *2a* in chapter 5 and n. 60 in chapter 4 above.

[58]*Cf.* section *3a* of chapter 4 above.

k. 1QS 4:21a רוח קודש.

A majority of scholars understands this expression as referring to the Spirit of God with some of them equating it with the spirit of truth in 3:18/19[59] and a few equating it further with the angelic Prince of Lights.[60] Others are silent or non-committal on these possible relationships[61] while some doubt that *ruaḥ* here has much to do with either the spirit of truth or Prince of Lights.[62] A minority, on the other hand, understands רוח קודש as a sanctified, human disposition and nothing more.[63]

It seems that the majority is correct in this case, however, especially those who do not identify רוח קודש here with the spirit of truth in 3:18-19. Thus, although רוח אמת just following רוח קודש in the same line appears because of its parallel construction to define רוח קודש as the spirit of truth of 3:18/19 (*cf.* רוח אמת with {רוחות האמת {והעול), both of these expressions in 4:21 are in a conceptual context fundamentally different from that of *ruaḥ* in 3:18-19 and as a result must be analyzed on a different

---

[59]*Cf.* Delcor, "Doctrines," col. 972-3; *idem, Hymns*, pp. 45 & 47; Flusser, "Sect," pp. 246 & 256; Foerster, "Geist," p. 131; Jaubert, *notion*, pp. 239 & 244; Nötscher, "Heiligkeit," pp. 340-1; and Seitz, "two Spirits," p. 93.

[60]*Cf.* Anderson, "'Ruah'," pp. 298-9 & 302; Böcher, *Dualismus*, pp. 38-9 & 77; Cross, *Library*, pp. 210 & 213; Leaney, *Rule*, pp. 43 & 158-9; and Ringgren, *Faith*, pp. 82 & 89.

[61]*Cf.* Carmignac and Guilbert, *Textes*, p. 37 n. 76 & p. 155 n. 9; Dietzel, "Beten," p. 19; Graystone, "Scrolls," vol. 23, pp. 33-34; G. Maier, *Mensch*, pp. 189-190; J. Maier, *Texte*, vol. II, p. 206; Manns, *symbole*, p. 88; Montague, *Holy Spirit*, p. 118; Schnackenburg, "'Anbetung'," p. 89; and Sjöberg, "Neuschöpfung," p. 135 n. 3; *cf.* also Chevallier, *Souffle*, pp. 54-6.

[62]Baumbach, *Qumran*, pp. 13-14; Beaven, "Ruah," pp. 90-91; Betz, *Offenbarung*, p. 148; Bruce "Holy Spirit," pp. 50 & 53; Coppens, "Documents," p. 37 n. 46; Irwin, "Spirit-Dualism," p. 191(he also thinks that *ruaḥ* here may be the same as the spirit of truth, *cf. ibid.*, p. 10); Johnston, "Spirit," p. 39; and H. W. Kuhn, *Enderwartung*, p. 137 (*cf.* also pp. 120-1).

[63]Burrows, *More Light*, p. 295; Licht, *Rule*, pp. 38 & 28; and Wernberg-Møller, "Reconsideration," pp. 423 & 440.

basis. From the beginning of the Treatise, *ruaḥ* has been presented within a creation context in which men are understood as created with a good or evil spirit as a result of God's foreordaining will (3:15-18). In 4:18ff., however, the author now speaks of *ruaḥ* not as a spiritual capacity unchangeably conditioning man's religious life from birth but as an eschatological gift of God which is to cleanse him from all evil deeds and to effect a radical change in his inherited spiritual nature (4:20-21). The author of 4:21a, then, is dealing with a traditional, biblical concept based on passages such as Is. 44:3, Joel 3:1 and Ezk. 36:25-27, and even though it may have been his intent to redefine רוח קודש fully within the sense of the spirit of truth in 3:18/19 (*cf.* section 3 below), this was not the traditional meaning of this expression among the sectarians from whom he received it.

There are two additional points of evidence which show that רוח קודש refers to God's Spirit: 1) there is no unambiguous use of the singular of *ruaḥ* in the Scrolls in construct with any form of קודש in the singular which means anything other than God's Spirit, whereas this basic pattern is often clearly used to refer to God's Spirit (*cf.* sections *2b*, *2c* and *2e* of chapter 3 above), and 2) the רוח קודש of our passages "cleanses" (טהר) man from sin of a moral nature, and this kind of cleansing is never attributed in the sectarian literature to man or man's spirit but is always the work of God or His Spirit.[64]

l. 1QS 4:21b רוח אמת.

Because of the similarity of expression, most scholars understand רוח אמת as a reference to the good (cosmic) spirit of 3:18/19 with some identifying it further as the angelic Prince of Lights[65] and the rest ambiguous or non-commital on this identification;[66] a few scholars, however, view this expression as no

---

[64]*Cf.* n. 65 in chapter 3 above.

[65]*Cf.* n. 60 above and also Ellis "Gifts," pp. 135-6 and Montague, *Holy Spirit*, p. 118.

[66]*Cf.* n. 59 above and also Irwin, "Spirit-Dualism," pp. 8 & 10; Licht, "Analysis," p. 97; and Manns, *symbole*, p. 88.

more than a human disposition[67] or (it appears) as God's holy Spirit separate from the good spirit of 3:18-19.[68] The author's intent is probably to refer to the good spirit of 3:18/18 (as a disposition), but note the basically different change in conceptuality here from that of 3:18/19 (*cf.* the comments on this in the analysis of רוח קודש in section *2k* above and the analysis of the author's purpose here in section *3* below).

m. 1QS 4:22 רוח נדה.

Scholars seem to be divided over the meaning of this expression. Some understand it as a reference to the (cosmic) evil spirit of 3:18-19[69] with one identifying it further as the Angel of Darkness[70] and another as a demon separate from the evil (cosmic) spirit of 3:18-19,[71] while others see it as a simple human disposition.[72] It seems, however, that רוח נדה is an alternate term for רוח עולה in 4:20 which, in turn, refers to the evil spirit or disposition of 3:18-19 (*cf.* the analysis of this in section *2j* above). Although it is true that the pious are described as "wallowing" (התגוללו) in the "spirits" (*i.e.* evil angels) of Belial in 4Q177, 1-4, 10,[73] this metaphor is most often used in the Scrolls to describe an involvement not with evil spirits but with impure spiritual dispositions and conduct (*cf.* 1QH 6:22; 17:19; CD 3:17; 8:5 & 19:17) as is also the case in the immediate context of our expression (*viz.*, 4:19 אמת תבל . . . התגוללה בדרכי רשע). As

---

[67]*Cf.* Coppens, "don," p. 210; Nötscher, "Geist," p. 309 (*cf.* n. 59 above); Pryke, "'Spirit'," p. 345; and Wernberg-Møller, "Reconsideration," p. 423; *cf.* also Treves, "Two Spirits," p. 450.

[68]*Cf.* Chevallier, *Souffle*, pp. 55-56 and Huppenbauer, *Mensch*, p. 17.

[69]*Cf.* Delcor, "Doctrines," col. 973 and Schubert, "Sektenkanon," p. 505 n. 33.

[70]Dupont-Sommer, "instruction," p. 33 (*cf.* also p. 18).

[71]Baumbach, *Qumran*, p. 14; *cf.* also J. Maier, *Texte*, vol. II, p. 204.

[72]*Cf.* Irwin, "Spirit-Dualism," pp. 9 & 191; Licht, *Rule*, p. 104; Manns, *symbole*, p. 88 and Wernberg-Møller, "Reconsideration," p. 423.

[73]This follows Strugnell's reconstruction in "Notes," p. 238; *cf.* the discussion of this verse in section *2b1* in chapter 5 above.

with *ruaḥ* in 3:18-19, 25 and 4:20, however, *ruaḥ* in 4:22 involves more than simply a man's individual or private spiritual conduct but is intimately related to evil on a cosmic scale which totally conditions his religious life and which can be overcome only by an act of God himself.

We should note, finally, that at least one scholar understands רוח נדה here as the spirit *for* impurity (*i.e.*, "the spirit of purification") by analogy with מי נדה ("purifying waters").[74] It seems, however, that Dupont-Sommer is correct in his observation that the idiomatic force of מי נדה should not be extended to רוח נדה,[75] since התגולל, whenever it appears in the Scrolls, always has a negative meaning.[76]

n. 1QS 4:23 רוחי אמת ועול.

A majority of scholars understands this expression as a reference to angelic beings with most identifying them as the two (cosmic) spirits of 3:18-19[77] and others as a plurality of angelic and demonic beings;[78] a minority, on the other hand, understands the spirits here as no more than good and evil dispositions within men.[79] It seems, however, that the majority is correct in this case, especially those who understand רוחים as refer-

---

[74]*Cf.* Vermes, *Scrolls in English,* p. 78.

[75]Dupont-Sommer, "instruction," p. 33.

[76]*Cf.* 1QH 6:22; 17:19; CD 3:17; 8:5; 19:17; and 4Q177, 1-4, 10; *cf.* also 4Q177, 19, 4.

[77]*Cf.* Anderson, "'Ruah'," pp. 298-9; Betz, *Offenbarung,* p. 146; Böcher, *Dualismus,* pp. 38-39 & 77; Brandenburger, *Fleisch,* pp. 97-98; Charlesworth, "Comparison," p. 89; Cross, *Library,* pp. 210-211; Licht, "Analysis," p. 98; Montague, *Holy Spirit,* p. 117; Ringgren, *Faith,* p. 72; and Schweizer, "πνεῦμα," p. 390. For the additional question of the relationship of the two spirits to the two angels, see n. 17 in this chapter above.

[78]*Cf.* Irwin, "Spirit-Dualism," pp. 8-9 & 198 n. 17; H. W. Kuhn, *Enderwartung,* p. 121; Nötscher, "Geist," pp. 310 & 313; and Yadin, *Scroll of War,* p. 231.

[79]Coppens, "don," p. 210; Johnston, "Spirit," p. 30; Wernberg-Møller, *Manual,* p. 67; and *idem,* "Reconsideration," p. 422. *Cf.* also Treves, "Two Spirits," p. 450.

ring to a plurality of good and evil angelic beings. The basic evidence for this is: 1) the masculine plural form of *ruaḥ*, which often means "angels/demons" in the Scrolls and never unambiguously has a meaning other than this[80] and 2) the masculine reference (as we would expect) to רוחים (יריבו in v. 25 and possibly יתהלכו in v. 24),[81] normal for *ruaḥ* as angel/demon but not as a reference to man's spirit.[82] The author's intent, then, is to expand on the thought already expressed in 3:24 that the pious must deal not only with their own sinful nature but also with the problem of demonic attack, which has the potential of making them fail in their religious lives (להכשיל בני אור). The same thought is also found in 4Q510, 1, 6 in which the demons attempt to destroy the heart of the faithful (להשם לבבם)[83] and so lead them astray and in 4Q511, 48-49+51, 4 in which the

---

[80]*Cf.* section *2c* in chapter 7 above.

[81]There is a question as to whether בלבב גבר in 4:23 goes with יריבו preceding it (*e.g.*, Wernberg-Møller, *Manual*, p. 27) or with יתהלכו following it in v. 24 (*e.g.*, Licht, "Analysis," p. 98). If the spirits in 4:23 are identical to the two spirits of 3:18-19 and בלבב גבר is understood as going with יריבו, this produces a conceptual tension in the Treatise since the two spirits are no longer seen as dividing mankind into two clearly defined groups (as in 3:18ff.) but as dividing the spirituality of the individual into two conflicting elements (*cf. ibid.*, p. 91 n.13). Given the definition of *ruaḥ* in 3:18ff. as "dispositions" and רוחים as numerous angelic spirits, however, this is no longer as much of an issue, although it would probably make the most sense in the light of passages such as 4Q510, 1 and 4Q511, 48-49+51 to view גבר here as referring to individual men (especially sectarians) who must contend with the strife of demonic attacks (*cf.* also 1QS 3:24 and 1QM 13:10ff.). The expression בלבב גבר, then, should probably be read with יריבו, with the "spirits" as its subject and with men as the subject of יתהלכו (as in K. G. Kuhn, "Epheserbrief," p. 341) since the chief interest of this treatise is men's conduct.

[82]*Cf.* section *3a* of chapter 5 above. 1QS, however, seems to prefer the masculine to the feminine in the imperfect plural; *cf.* 2:15-16 and 4:17-18. For the feminine imperfect plural in the other Scrolls (although not in connection with *ruaḥ*), *cf.* 1QH 7:11; 18:15; 1QM 8:1; 4QpPs 37 II, 16.

[83]*Cf.* the analysis of this context in section *2b3* of chapter 5 above.

psalmist mentions "wars" (מלחמות) within his "body" (גויה) apparently because of the רוחות ממזרים (lines 2-3) which are attacking his spiritual life.[84]

We should note, finally, that the feminine references beginning in 4:25 (*cf.* the suffixes on שמן, מעשיהן and ינחילן) do not refer to the רוחים of 4:23 but to the two spirits or dispositions which are the subject of the whole Treatise. Verses 25-26, then, are a restatement or summary of the most important points of the essay, especially those from 4:15 onward (*cf.* 4:16 with 4:25).

o. 1QS 4:26 רוחו.

Most scholars understand רוחו here as referring to man's spirit,[85] which seems to be correct. The immediate context of this expression involves the statement that man's wickedness is proportionally related to his participation in the "lot" (גורל) of wickedness (4:24), and directly before רוחו in 4:26 the author says that God causes the "lots" (גורלות) to fall for "all the living" (כול חי, to which the suffix on רוחו refers). The context here, then, shows that "all the living" with its "lots" refers primarily to man, whose "lot" is the primary interest of this Treatise. The same meaning for כול חי can be seen in 1QS 9:12, whose context is also primarily interested in men and how the משכיל is to deal with them. An additional indication that רוחו refers to man's spirit in 4:26 is its subordination to the preposition לפי, which is used with *ruaḥ* in the Scrolls only to indicate a relationship involving the human spirit or disposition (*cf.* 1QS 2:20; 9:15; and CD 20:24).

---

[84]*Cf.* Baillet in *Discoveries*, VII, p. 244, note on line 4, who draws attention to this parallel with 1QS 4:23.

[85]Except for Ringgren in *Faith*, p. 72 (who renders רוחו somewhat ambiguously as "His (its) spirit"), almost every one understands *ruaḥ* here as man's spirit in one sense or another: *cf.* Irwin, "Spirit-Dualism," p. 191; K. G. Kuhn, "Πειρασμός," p. 214; H. W. Kuhn, *Enderwartung*, p. 122; Licht, *Rule*, p. 76; J. Maier, *Texte*, vol. II, p. 206; Molin, *Söhne*, p. 24; Nötscher, "Geist," p. 309; *idem*, *Terminologie*, p. 180; Pryke, "'Spirit'," p. 345; Schweizer, "Gegenwart des Geistes," p. 492; and *idem*, "πνεῦμα," p. 391; and Wernberg-Møller, *Manual*, p. 27.

3. Conclusion.

A basic problem in the definition of *ruaḥ* in 1QS 3:13-4:26 which has occupied scholars from the beginning of the study of 1QS has been the relationship of the two spirits in 3:13-4:14 to their function in 4:15-26.[86] In 3:13-4:14 the two spirits divide *humanity* into two opposed spiritual groups of good and evil, but in 4:15-26 they divide the *individual* into two opposed spir-

---

[86]*Cf.* K. G. Kuhn, "Sektenschrift," p. 301 n. 4 for the first extensive discussion of this problem. Kuhn's position here is that these two sections involve only a terminological difference (*cf.* section *2a* of chapter 2 above), but in not making it clear that the *sharp* division of humanity rests primarily on the leadership of the two angels rather than on the two opposite "spirits" in man, Kuhn is subject to the kind of criticism found in Osten-Sacken, *Gott und Belial*, p. 24 n. 2: "Diese einheitliche Interpretation verkennt die unterschiedliche Stellung diesen Motive in S III, 13ff. und IV, 23bff. In III, 13 bis IV, 14 dominiert die Tendenz der Trennung in Menschengruppen, die Bemerkung über die verführung der Lichtsöhne durch den Finsternisengel wird ferner sofort abgeschwächt durch die Zusicherung der Hilfe Gottes und des Engels seiner Wahrheit und nicht in dualistischen Sinne ausgewertet. In IV, 23ff. dagegen ist der Widerstreit thematisch behandelt. Eine exakte Scheidung zwischen Licht- und Finsternissöhnen, wie sie die Darstellung III, 13 bis IV, 14 durchzeiht, ist nach diesem Abschnitt wie auch in IV, 15ff. unmöglich." However, if the two angels are presupposed in 4:15-26, an exact division of humanity into two, good and evil, warring groups can also be understood there with the individual members of each group being in more or less agreement with their respective angelic rulers. On the other hand, if the two spirits are regarded as cosmic beings ruling over humanity and identified as the two angels of 3:20ff. (so most scholars), the tension between 3:13-4:15 and 4:15-26 would seem to be irreconcilable. Licht in "Analysis," pp. 88-100 has made the most convincing attempt within a view of the two spirits as angelic in nature for understanding 3:13-4:26 as a conceptual unity, but this has involved the view that 4:16 & 24 are not referring to the participation of the individual in both the good and evil spirits, (*cf.* the discussion of this in n. 87 below).

itual dispositions of good and evil.[87] The problem, then, is one of consistency: if the two spirits are to be regarded as influencing to one extent or another each individual (4:15-26), how can they be understood as also giving rise to two sharply distinguished groups of humanity? If both spirits influence each individual, it would be more logical to expect a sliding scale of good and evil in humanity (with most people in the middle) rather than two sharply distinguished groups with one confined to a realm of spiritual darkness and the other to a realm

---

[87]Licht maintains in "Analysis," p. 91 n. 13 that the Treatise throughout never presents the two spirits as competing for the soul of the individual person since the notion "is quite incompatible with the main argument, *viz.* the division of mankind" (*ibid.*). He understands passages such as 4:16 & 24, therefore, as referring to the greater or lesser participation of the individual in one spirit or the other, but not in both (*ibid.*, pp. 95 & 98). There are varying levels of righteousness in the Qumran community, then, not because of a greater or lesser influence of the spirit of iniquity in the individual sectarian, but because each has a different level of inheritance in the one good spirit. This view, however, does not sufficiently take into account the positive presence of spiritual evil in the sectarian as seen in 3:21-23 and especially in 4:20, which is probably referring to the Qumranian faithful when it says that God will destroy "all spirit of iniquity from the bounds (?) (מתכמי) of his flesh;" *cf.* note 97 below and passages such as 1QS 11:9-12, 1QH 13:13-16 and 17:25 in which the secarian is accutely aware of his inward, spiritual sinfulness. *Cf.* also Lichtenberger, *Studien*, p. 137 and especially Osten-Sacken, *Gott und Belial*, p. 24, who notes that 4:16 in the context of 4:18-22 "erscheint nur dann als sinnvoll, wenn ausgedrückt werden soll, daß der Mensch in unterschiedlichem Grad an beiden Geisterklassen Anteil hat und entsprechend dieser Erbschaft handelt." Note, finally, that 4Q186 understands the spirit of the individual as being conditioned by both "darkness" and "light"; *cf.* Allegro, "Cryptic Document," pp. 291-4. Nevertheless, the conflict of the two spirits in the soul of the individual is not *personal* in nature since these "spirits" are not personal, angelic beings; they clash only as two fundamentially different spiritual dispositions in men's hearts. The personal dimention in this conflict is only in the numerous good and evil angels who either attack or aid the spiritual life of the sectarian (*cf.* 1QS 3:24; 4:23; 1QM 12:8-9; 13:10; 4Q Sl 40)

of light. Moreover, the consensus that the two spirits should be identified with the two angels (the Prince of Lights and Angel of Darkness)[88] further intensifies this problem since each angel would have his "dominion" to one extent or another over each individual rather than over a clearly defined, good or evil group of people. As a result of this conceptual tension, then, as well as considerations based on vocabulary, style and literary structure, Osten-Sacken has disagreed with the predominant view (reflected especially in Licht)[89] that 3:13-4:26 is a literary unity and sees rather three distinct stages in its production (3:13-4:14; 4:15-23a; and 5:23b-26).[90] The general reaction to Osten-Sacken's position here seems to be mixed: one scholar accepts his analysis entirely,[91] another only in respect to a division between 3:13-4:14 and 4:14-26,[92] and two others are willing to accept 3:13-4:14 and 4:15-26 as two distinguishable sections (while maintaining the possibility of one author) but resist the view that these sections contain pneumatologies which are in essential tension with each other.[93]

It is possible that Osten-Sacken is correct in his analysis of 1QS 3:13-4:26 (especially in his distinction between 3:13-4:14 and 4:15-26), but it seems clear that the meaning of *ruaḥ* in this treatise should not be used as evidence to prove that 3:13-4:26 had two or three different authors or stages of composition. Although the two spirits are closely related to good and evil of a cosmic nature, they manifest themselves throughout the two-spirit treatise essentially as dispositions in man and are always sharply distinguished from the two cosmic angels (3:20ff.) whose leadership divides humanity into two distinct

---

[88]*Cf.* n. 17 above.

[89]*Cf.* Licht, "Analysis," pp. 88-100 and also the comments of Noll in "Angelology," p. 131 and n. 6.

[90]Osten-Sacken, *Gott und Belial*, pp. 17-27.

[91]Murphy-O'Connor, "genése," pp. 541ff.

[92]Delcor, "Doctrines," col. 963-4.

[93]*Cf.* Lichtenberger, *Studien*, pp. 139 & 141 and Noll, "Angelology," pp. 131-3.

realms of spiritual light and darkness.[94] It is possible that 3:13-4:14 intends to describe the pious as entirely good (sinning only because of demonic attack, *cf.* 3:24) and the wicked as entirely evil, and if this is the case, 3:13-4:14 would be in conceptual tension with 4:15-26 since the latter clearly envisions the individual as participating in both the good and evil spirit.[95] But 3:13-4:14 does not clearly say that the pious have no involvement with the spirit of iniquity, and the demonic temptations to which they are subject (3:21ff.) may involve a tacit assumption of underlying sinful propensities on their part.[96] In fact, 3:21-24 creates the problem of how spiritually perfect people, influenced only by the spirit of truth and under the protection of the Prince of Lights, can yet be brought into sin by the Angel of Darkness and his demons. It difficult to know how the author of 3:21-24 would have handled this problem if he did not anticipate the kind of solution found in 4:15-26 (as most scholars understand this).[97] On the other hand, it is reasonable to suppose that whoever wrote 4:15-26 would have expected his teaching to have been read in the light of 3:13-4:14. This would mean, then, that although the angels of 3:20-25 are not mentioned in 4:15-26, the author would still view those who had sufficient spiritual light as being fully under the authority of the Prince of Lights (despite their darkness, *cf.* CD 16:4-5) with the Angel of Darkness fully dominating the "sons of iniquity"

---

[94]This is accomplished primarily by the use of gender: *cf.* the transition from feminine to masculine in 3:20ff., from masculine to feminine in 3:25ff., from feminine to masculine in 4:23ff. (to indicate personal angelic and demonic forces), and from masculine to feminine in 4:25f.

[95]*Cf.* n. 87 above.

[96]*Cf.* K. G. Kuhn, "Sektenschrift," p. 301 n. 4, who notes that demonic attack against the sectarian is possible because his "flesh" (*i.e.*, the conceptual equivalent to the evil spirit of 3:18/19) makes him vulnerable to this. Kuhn cites 1QS 11 (*cf.* v. 9) which talks about the sectarian's "iniquitous flesh" (עול בשר) as the underlying thought of 3:24.

[97]*Cf.* Lichtenberger, *Studien*, p. 141, who notes that "der Hinweis in 1QS 3:21ff. auf die Sünde der Frommen [machte] de Fortsetzung in 1QS 4:15-26 grundsätzlich notwendig."

despite any small portion of genuine spirituality they might have. There would still exist, therefore, two distinct divisions of humanity in 4:15-26, but with the added clarification that individuals within these divisions have dispostions of varying amounts of both good and evil. This additional clarification would be especially helpful to the sectarian who felt himself led into sin not only by external, demonic forces (3:24 & 4:23) but also by his own internal desires (*cf.* 1QS 11:9-12).

We should note, finally, the attempt in this Treatise to relate the two-spirit doctrine to two traditional views in sectarian pneumatology. One has to do with God's Spirit[98] and the other with the problem of demonic influence.[99] Both are closely related to a view that God's eschatological Spirit is not a present reality in the community's spirituality. In the first case the author tries to reinterpret the traditional view of the sect that God through His Spirit will deliver His people from sin in the last days by describing the eschatological רוח קודש as the

---

[98]*Cf.* 4Q504, 1-2, 15 which speaks about God as pouring out His holy Spirit on His people. According to Baillet, this is a pre-Essene writing which prefigures the spirituality adopted by the sectarians; *cf.* Baillet, *Discoveries,* VII, p. 137.

[99]A concern about demons leading people into sin can be seen in Jubilees 10 and 11 (fragments of this book were found at Qumran), whose date of composition should probably be set before 140 B.C.; *cf.* the recent work of O. S. Wintermute in Charlesworth, *Pseudepigrapha,* vol. II, pp. 43-44. *Cf.* especially 1 Enoch 15 and 16 (fragments of this book were also discovered at Qumran) and the comments of E. Isaac in Charlesworth, *Pseudepigrapha,* vol. I, p. 7, who notes that the consensus of critical scholarship on 1 Enoch 12-16 (before Qumran) is that these chapters were written in early pre-Maccabean times. According to J. T. Milik, *The Books of Enoch, Aramaic Fragments of Qumran Cave 4* (Oxford: Clarendon Press, 1967), p. 25, "the dates of our manuscripts of 4Q allow us to establish that from the first half of the second century B.C. onwards the Book of Watchers [*i.e.,* 1 Enoch 1-36] had essentially the same form as that in which it is known through the Greek and Ethiopic versions." Milik also adds that the author of the Book of Watchers "used an early written source which he incorporated without any great changes in his own work (6-19)."

רוח אמת of 3:18/19.[100] In this way the author indicates that the "holy Spirit" which will come from God in the future is really none other than the good spirituality given to the sectarian at his creation. This means, then, that the author is not comfortable with the idea that the community is already enjoying an eschatological outpouring of God's Spirit: he confines its decisive work to the future while redefining it as essentially no more than the spirit/disposition of truth (3:18/19) possessed by all good men to one extent or another in all ages. This view, in turn, is related to the second, traditional sectarian concern, *viz.*, the fear of demonic attack (3:24 and 4:23). All things being equal, the sectarian's predominantly good spirituality would presumably keep his evil nature in check (*cf.* 1QH 15:14-16), but with the external and unpredictable (*cf.* 4Q510, 1, 6) attacks of demons, this "natural" balance is threatened, and the sectarian is in danger of committing sins which may even cost him his membership in the community itself (*cf.* 1QS 6:27-7:2). The answer to this traditional concern would be assurance of an external, spiritual help of some kind beyond the natural capacities of the sectarian; but unlike the author of 1QH 7:7-8, the author(s) of the Treatise cannot assure the sectarian of God's help through the presence of His eschatological Spirit but only of the help given by God through His Angel or angels (*cf.* 3:24 & 4:23). There is only one verse in the Treatise, in fact, which may indicate that God's eschatological Spirit is already present among the sectarians (*cf.* סודי רוח in 4:6 and the analysis of this verse in section 2*d*2 of chapter 3 above), but this is probably a traditional expression within traditional materials (especially 1QS 4:2-6 and 4:9-11) which circulated independently before they were incorporated into the two-spirit

[100]*Cf.* K. G. Kuhn, "Sektenschrift," p. 302. n.4: ". . . der aus der iranischen Religion in die Sektentexte übernommene Dualismus der beiden Ur-Geister der Wahrheit und des Frevels in Sekt. 4, 20ff. *verbunden* ist mit den alttestamentlichen Gedanken von dem "neuen Geist," dem "Heiligen Geist" . . . den Gott dem Frommen ins Herz geben wird . . . Gedanken vor allem aus Ez. 36, 25ff. . . ." [emphasis his].

Treatise as such.[101] The author or redactor of 4:6, then, would have made use of סודי רוח as part of his effort to reinterpret the more traditional pneumatology of the sect in the light of his two-spirit doctrine, but he found this goal difficult to accomplish probably due to the inertia of the traditional views (expressed especially in 1QH) and also because of the continuing influence of the Old Testament itself. Thus, the author(s) of the Treatise would wish to redefine both רוח קודש and סודי רוח as the spirit of truth of 3:18/19, yet 1) the traditional and biblical view that God is to shed *His* Spirit upon man to deliver him from sin (rather than sprinkling on man an additional amount of man's own "spirit of truth," *cf.* Ezk. 36:27) and 2) the conviction of the sectarians (from their origins; *cf.* 4Q504, 1-2, 15) that they were already living in the final age with its promise of God's Spirit (*cf.* Ezk. 36 & 37) would have prevented a new understanding of either of these expressions much beyond the author(s) of this Treatise as, in fact, the conceptual and literary isolation of this Treatise demonstrates (*cf.* section *1* of this chapter above).

---

[101]The promise of reward and threat of punishment in 4:2-14 are more at home in a less deterministic context which has room for an appeal to the hearers' will; *cf.* Lichtenberger, *Studien*, pp. 135-6. Note especially that Osten-Sacken, *Gott und Belial*, p. 157 on the basis of Foerster's comparisons of 1QS 4:2-6 (*cf.* Foerster, "Geist," p. 129f.) understands the pneumatology of 4:2-6a as being essentially that of 1QH: "In den Tugendkatalog [*i.e.* 1QS 4:2-6a] sind überwiegend Verhaltensweisen aufgenommen, die in den Lobliedern als Wirkungen des heiligen Geistes erscheinen, der den Frommen mit dem Eintritt in die Gemeinde geschenkt ist." This relationship between 1QS 4: 2-6 and 1QH led Foerster to identify *ruaḥ* (*ibid.*) in 1QS 4:6 as God's holy Spirit and then to identify this Spirit with the spirit of truth in 1QS 3:18/19 because of the position of 4:6 within the two-spirit Treatise.

CHAPTER 9

CONCLUSION

Almost from the beginning of Qumranian studies a key issue in the analysis of sectarian religion has been the meaning of *ruaḥ*. As parts of 1QH and other scrolls became available in 1950, K. G. Kuhn concluded that a major theme in sectarian religion was a belief in a spiritual *Neuschöpfung* comparable to that of early Christianity. With the publication of 1QS 3-4, however, he revised this opinion in adopting a view of sectarian religion which taught that men are born with a good or evil spiritual disposition which remains essentially unchanged throughout life. Most scholars followed him on this except that the majority of them also tended to identify the two spirits of 1QS 3-4 as angelic, cosmic beings (often equated with the Prince of Lights and Angel of Darkness). This consensus continued into the 1960's when it became increasingly clear that 1QS 3-4 should not be used as a basis on which to understand all the rest of sectarian pneumatology. A number of studies beginning with E. Sjöberg's article "Neuschöpfung" in 1955 were already leading in this direction, but the 1966 publication of H. W. Kuhn's *Enderwartung* on the eschatological expectations of the sect seems to mark a decisive turning point; since his study, most of the literature dealing with sectarian pneumatology agrees that 1QS 3-4 should not be used uncritically as Qumran's standard pneumatology, and there has been more interest in tracing its origins in the Old Testament.

The general results of chapters 3-7 have confirmed this trend since Kuhn. In chapter 3 we noted that the expressions in the Scrolls dealing with *ruaḥ* as God's Spirit are related conceptually and syntactically much more closely to the Old Testament than to 1QS 3-4. The closest conceptual parallels were found with eschatological passages in the Old Testament such as Is. 44:3, Joel 3:1-2 and especially Ezk. 36:27, 37:6 & 14.

An especially close syntactical parallel was found between Ezekiel and the Scrolls in the unqualified use of *ruaḥ* to describe God's Spirit. In chapter 4 on man's spirit, *ruaḥ* was again found to reflect the basic categories of the Old Testament, but with a more negative emphasis on man's spirit as sinful at birth and with the tendency not only to describe man as having a spirit but also as *being* a spirit. There was very little evidence found of man's spirit as a predestined spirituality given to him at birth (with the exceptions of 1QS 3-4, 1QH 15 and 4Q186), but a number of instances of *ruaḥ* were seen to reflect the conceptions of Ezk. 36:26 in which God promises to give His people a new "spirit" (*i.e.*, disposition) in the future. In chapter 5 on *ruaḥ* as angel/demon, the use of the masculine gender to indicate a personal entity (as in the Old Testament, *cf.* 1 Kgs. 22:21ff.) was seen as a key semantic marker throughout its various contexts in the Scrolls, and in chapter 6 expressions for *ruaḥ* as "wind" and "breath" were seen to be basically reflective of the Old Testament and 1 Enoch 84:1, respectively, except for the plural רוחות in 1QH 1:29b as "breaths," which is not found in the Old Testament. In the comparison of chapters 3-6 in chapter 7, we found that there were no particular syntactical characteristics associated with *ruaḥ* as "God's Spirit," "wind" and "breath" which would aid in determining its meaning but rather that *ruaḥ* in these cases depends primarily on its context and characteristic surrounding vocabulary for resolving most ambiguity. *Ruaḥ* as "man's spirit" and "angel/demon," however, was found to depend on a number of syntactical patterns for communicating its meaning, chief of which is the use of the feminine gender for man's spirit (as is primarily the case in the Old Testament) and the masculine gender for angel/demon (to indicate a personal entity as in 1 Kgs. 22:21ff.). This discovery was seen to be especially helpful in the interpretation of 1QS 3-4, since the two spirits here are consistently described with the feminine gender, thus indicating that the author does not wish to describe personal, angelic beings existing independently of man but rather the "spirits" or dispositions which condition his religious activity.

A basic result of the present study, then, is to confirm the general direction of scholarship since the late 1960's as described above. It has shown that the expressions and syntactical patterns of *ruaḥ* in 1QS 3-4 (especially those directly related to its two-spirit pneumatology) are essentially confined to 1QS 3:13-4:26 and that expressions more common in the non-biblical Hebrew Scrolls (*e.g.*, רוח קודש in 1QS 4:21 and רוחי גורלו in 3:24) are present in the Treatise as part of an attempt to integrate its relatively novel two-spirit teaching into the traditional pneumatology of the sect. The same isolation can be seen for 1QS 3-4 conceptually: its view of *ruaḥ* as a spiritual disposition inherited at birth seems to be clearly present only in 1QH 15 and 4Q186. On the other hand, the basic pneumatology of the rest of the non-biblical, Hebrew Scrolls has its origin in the Old Testament, especially in eschatological passages such as Ezk. 36-37. The extensive use of *ruaḥ* to designate angels/demons and the concept of two cosmic angels ruling over all men are, of course, developments beyond the Old Testament itself. But their presence in sectarian thought also has nothing essentially to do with the two-spirit pneumatology of 1QS 3-4: the two spirits are consistently presented throughout the Treatise as impersonal dispositions within men (although closely related to cosmic Good and Evil), and the two angels of 3:20-25 (seen also in 1QM 13, CD 5 and 4Q'Amram) are throughout the Treatise carefully distinguished from them. It appears that the author introduced the two angels into the pneumatology of the Treatise because they were already an important element in sectarian theology which he could not afford to ignore.

The evidence, then, points to Qumran as an eschatologically oriented community which saw itself as the heir of God's eschatological Spirit and regarded this Spirit as the basis and source of its spirituality. As noted above, however, exceptions to this view can be seen in 1QS 3:13-4:26, lQH 15 and 4Q186 in which the spirituality characteristic of the sect is given to the sectarian at birth. How or why these alternate and conflicting pneumatologies arose is difficult to determine, but it seems clear from a literary standpoint, at least, that they remained isolated and secondary in Qumranian thought.

INDEX TO *RUAḤ* IN THE NON-BIBLICAL, HEBREW SCROLLS OF QUMRAN PUBLISHED TO DATE

CITATION	EXPRESSION	MEANING	PLACE TREATED
1QS 2:14	נספתה רוח	man's spirit	ch. 4, sec. 3c
1QS 2:20	לפי רוחותם	man's spirit	ch. 4, sec. 3c
1QS 3:6	ברוח עצת אמת	man's spirit	ch. 4, sec. 3b2
1QS 3:7	ברוח קדושה	God's Spirit	ch. 3, sec. 2f
1QS 3:8	ברוח יושר וענוה	man's spirit	ch. 4, sec. 3b2
1QS 3:14	לכול מיני רוחותם	man's spirit	ch. 8, sec. 2
1QS 3:18	שתי רוחות	man's spirit	ch. 8, sec. 2
1QS 3:18/19	רוחות האמת והעול	man's spirit	ch. 8, sec. 2
1QS 3:24	כול רוחי גורלו	demons	ch. 8, sec. 2
1QS 3:25	רוחות אור וחושך	man's spirit	ch. 8, sec. 2
1QS 4:3	רוח ענוה	man's spirit	ch. 8, sec. 2
1QS 4:4	רוח דעת	man's spirit	ch. 8, sec. 2
1QS 4:6	סודי רוח	God's Spirit	ch 3, sec. 2d
1QS 4:9	לרוח עולה	man's spirit	ch. 8 sec. 2

1QS 4:10	ברוח זנות	man's spirit	ch. 8, sec. 2
1QS 4:15	implied	man's spirit	ch. 8
1QS 4:16	implied	man's spirit	ch. 8
1QS 4:20	כול רוח עולה	man's spirit	ch. 8, sec. 2
1QS 4:21a	רוח קודש	God's Spirit	ch. 8, sec. 2
1QS 4:21b	רוח אמת	man's spirit	ch. 8, sec 2
1QS 4:22	ברוח נדה	man's spirit	ch. 8, sec. 2
1QS 4:23	רוחי אמת ועול	demons	ch. 8, sec. 2
1QS 4:25	implied	man's spirit	ch. 8
1QS 4:26a	implied	man's spirit	ch. 8
1QS 4:26b	לפי רוחו	man's spirit	ch. 8, sec. 2
1QS 5:21	רוחום	man's spirit	ch. 4, sec. 3c
1QS 5:23/24	רוחם	man's spirit	ch. 4, sec. 3c
1QS 5:25/26	בקנאת רוח רשע	man's spirit	ch. 4, sec. 3b1
1QS 6:17	לרוחו	man's spirit	ch. 4, sec. 3c
1QS 7:18	רוחו	man's spirit	ch. 4, sec. 3c
1QS 7:23	רוחו	man's spirit	ch. 4, sec. 3c
1QS 8:3	רוח נשברה	man's spirit	ch. 4, sec. 3e
1QS 8:12	מיראת רוח נסוגה	man's spirit	ch. 4, sec. 3e

1QH 1:22	רוח התועה	man's spirit	ch. 4, sec. 3b1
1QH 1:28	רוח בלשון	breath	ch. 6, sec. 2b1
1QH 1:29a	מבע רוח שפתים	breath	ch. 6, sec. 2b2
1QH 1:29b	מבעי רוחות	breath	ch. 6, sec. 2b3
1QH 1:32	רוח אנוש	man's spirit	ch. 4, sec. 3b1
1QH 2:4	רוחי צדק	angels	ch. 5, sec. 2b1
1QH 2:15	לרוח קנאה	man's spirit	ch. 4, sec. 3b1
1QH 3:18	כול רוחי אפעה	demons	ch. 5, sec. 2b2
1QH 3:21	רוח נעוה	man's spirit	ch. 4, sec. 3e
1QH3:22	רוחות דעת	angels	ch. 5, sec. 2c2
1QH 4:31	כי אם ברוח יצר לו	man's spirit	ch. 4, sec.3d2
1QH 4:36	רוחי	man's spirit	ch. 4, sec.3d2
1QH 5:28	להכשיל [רוח]	man's spirit	ch. 4, sec.3d1
1QH 5:36	להכשיל רוח	man's spirit	ch. 4, sec.3d1
1QH 6:23	רוח עועיים	wind	ch. 6, sec. 1b2
1QH 7:5	רוח עועיים	wind	ch. 6, sec. 1b2
1QH 7:6/7	רוח קודשכה הניפותה בי	God's Spirit	ch. 3, sec. 2b
1QH 7:11	אין פה לרוח הוות	man's spirit	ch. 4, sec. 3b2
1QH 7:23	כמוץ לפני רוח	wind	ch. 6, sec. 1b1

1QH 7:29	כול צבי רוח	wind/vanity	ch. 6, sec. 1b1
1QH 8:12	רוחות קודש	angels	ch. 5, sec. 2c2
1QH 8:29	יחפש רוחי	man's spirit	ch. 4, sec. 3c
1QH 8:36	רוח כושלים	man's spirit	ch. 4, sec. 3b1
1QH 9:12a	רוחי	man's spirit	ch. 4, sec. 3c
1QH 9:12b	רוחי	man's spirit	ch. 4, sec. 3c
1QH 9:16 (2X)	רוח מרוח תגבר	man's spirit	ch. 4, sec.3d2
1QH 9:32	רוח קודשכה	God's Spirit	ch. 3, sec. 2b
1QH 10:8	אדון לכול רוח	angels	ch. 5, sec. 2e1
1QH 10:22	אתה ירצתה [רוח עבדכה]	man's spirit	ch. 4, sec. 3b1
1QH 11:12	מרוח נעוה	man's spirit	ch. 4, sec. 3e
1QH 11:13	רוחי [דעת]	angels	ch. 5, sec. 2b1
1QH 12:11	ברוח אשר נתתה בי	God's spirit	ch. 3, sec. 2d
1QH 12:12	ברוח קודשכה	God's Spirit	ch. 3, Sec. 2b
1QH 13:8	צבא רוחיך	angels	ch. 5, sec.2d1
1QH 13:13	רוח בשר	man's spirit	ch. 4, sec. 3b1
1QH 13:15	רוח נעוה משלה בו	man's spirit	ch. 4, sec. 3e
1QH 13: 18/19	ברוח אשר נתתה בי	God's Spirit	ch. 3, sec. 2d

1QH 14:3	ענוי רוח	man's spirit	ch. 4, sec.3d1
1QH 14:11	לפי רוחות [יבד]ילם	man's spirit	ch. 4, sec.3d2
1QH 14:13	ר]וח קודשך	God's Spirit	ch. 3, sec. 2b
1QH 14:25	חנותני ברוח דעה	God's Spirit	ch. 3, sec. 2f
1QH 15: 13/14	יצר כול רוח	man's spirit	ch. 4, sec.3d2
1QH 15:22	אתה יצרתה רוח	man's spirit	ch. 4, sec.3d2
1QH 16:2	ברוח קו[דשך ...]	God's Spirit	ch. 3, sec. 2b
1QH 16:3	רוח קוד[שך ...]	God's Spirit	ch. 3, sec. 2b
1QH 16:6	לבקש רוח[...]	God's Spirit	ch. 3, sec. 2d
1QH 16:7	רוח ק[דשך]	God's Spirit	ch. 3, sec. 2b
1QH 16:9	ותחונני ברוח רחמיך	God's Spirit	ch. 3, sec. 2c
1QH 16:10	רוח צדיק	man's spirit	ch. 4, sec. 3b1
1QH 16:11	ברוח אשר נתתה בי	God's Spirit	ch. 3, sec. 2d
1QH 16:12	ברוח קודשך	God's Spirit	ch. 3, sec. 3b
1QH 16:14	ברוח עבדך	man's spirit	ch. 4, sec, 3b1
1QH 17:6	מרוח	?	ch. 6, sec. 3a
1QH 17:7	מרוח	?	ch. 6, sec. 3a
1QH 17:17	מרוחות אשר נתתה בי	man's spirit	ch. 4, sec.3d2

1QH f 33:2	...ר]וחיך	angels/demon	ch. 5, sec.2d2
1QH f 45:6	כול רוחות[. . .	demons	ch. 5, sec. 2c1
1QM 6:12	ארוכי רוח	breath	ch. 6, sec. 2b1
1QM 7:5	תמימי רוח ובשר	man's spirit	ch. 4, sec.3d1
1QM 9:13	לשלושת רוחות הפנים	wind/sides	ch. 6, sec. 1b4
1QM 10:12	משא רוחות	angels	ch. 5, sec.2d5
1QM 11:10	נכאי רוח	man's spirit	ch. 4, sec.3d1
1QM 12:9	צבא רוחיו	angels	ch. 5, sec.2d1
1QM 13:2	כול רוחי גורלו	demons	ch. 5, sec. 2b1
1QM 13:4	כול רוחי גורלו	demons	ch. 5, sec. 2b1
1QM 13:10	כול רוחי אמת	angels	ch. 5, sec. 2b2
1QM 13: 11/12	כול רוחי גורלו מלאכי חבל	demons	ch. 5, sec. 2b1
1QM 14: 7	בענוי רוח[...]	man's spirit	ch. 4, sec.3d1
1QM 14:10	רוחי [חב]לו	demons	ch. 5, sec. 2b2
1QM 15:14	[על] כול רוחי רש[עה...]	demons	ch. 5, sec. 2b2
1QM 19:1	צ[בא רוחיו...]	angels	ch. 5, sec.2d1
CD 2:12	ביד משיחו (משיחי) רוח קדשו	God's Spirit	ch. 3, sec. 2b
CD 3:3	לא בחר ברצון רוחו	man's spirit	ch. 4, sec. 3c
CD 3:7	רוחם	man's spirit	ch. 4, sec, 3c

4Q158, 14, I, 2	כול הרוחות	angels/demons	ch. 5, sec.2d4
4Q171, 1, 3-4 III 8	יובדו כענן האוד [בר]וח	wind	ch. 6, sec. 1b1
4Q171, 3-10 IV 25	רו]ח קודש	God's Spirit	ch. 3, sec. 2e
4Q176, 21, 3	רוחותיהם	?	ch. 6, sec. 3b
4Q177, 1-4, 10	הת]גוללו ברוח[י ב]ליעל	demons	ch. 5, sec. 2b1
4Q177, 12-13, I, 5	רוח אמת	man's spirit	ch. 4, sec. 3b3
4Q177, 12-13, I,9	לעוזרם מכול רוחו[ת...	demons	ch. 5, sec. 2c3
4Q178, 1, 6	הרוח	?	ch. 6, sec. 3b
4Q183, 1 II 6	תועי רוח	man's spirit	ch. 4, sec.3d1
4Q184, 4, 4	בן אדם רוחו	man's spirit	ch. 4, sec. 3c
4Q185, 1-2, I, 9	כאש להבה ישפט[ו]י רוחתיו	angels	ch. 5, sec.2d3
4Q185, 1-2, I, 10	נצב[ה] רוחו	wind	ch. 6, sec. 1b5
4Q185, 1-2, I, 11	ציצו תשא רוח	wind	ch. 6, sec. 1b1
4Q185, 1-2, I, 12	לא ימצא מרוח	wind	ch. 6, sec. 1b1

4Q499, 6, 3	רוח	?	ch. 6, sec. 3c
4Q502, 27, 1	רוחי עולמים	angels	ch. 5, sec. 2b3
4Q502, 238, 1	רוח	?	ch. 6, sec. 3a
4Q504, 1-2 V 15	יצקתה את רוח קודשכה עלינו	God's spirit	ch. 3, sec. 2b
4Q504, 4, 5	(חנו)את[(נו] רוח) ק[ודש	God' Spirit	ch. 3, sec. 2e
4Q504, 4, 20	את רוח	?	ch. 6, sec. 3a
4Q504, 6, 22	רוח כול חי	man's spirit	ch. 4, sec. 3b3
4Q506, 131-132, 11(parallel to 4Q504, 4, 5)	[חנו]את[(נו) רוח] הק(ודש	God's Spirit	ch. 3, sec, 2c
4Q510, 1, 5a	כול רוחי מלאכי חבל	demons	ch. 5, sec. 2b3
4Q510, 1, 5b	רוחות ממזרים	demons	ch. 5, sec. 2c3
4Q510, 1, 6	ל)תעות רוח בינה	man's spirit	ch. 4, sec. 3b3
4Q510, 2,3	כול רוחי[...	angels/ demons	ch. 5, sec. 2b3
4Q511, 1, 3	בכול רוחות ממשלתה	angels	ch. 5, sec. 2c3
4Q511, 1, 6	רוחי רשע	demons	ch. 5, sec. 2b3
4Q511, 10, 2 (perhaps a longer recension of 4Q510, 1)	ל]תעות רוח [בינה	man's spirit	ch. 4, sec. 3b3

6Q18, 21, 2	ורוח[...	?	ch. 6, sec. 3a
8Q5, 2, 6	כול הרוחות	angels	ch. 5, sec.2d4
11QMelch 3 II 12	רוחי גורלו	demons	ch. 5, sec. 2b2
11QMelch 3 II 13	כול ר[וחי גורל]ו	demons	ch. 5, sec. 2b2
11QMelch 3 II 18	משיח הרוח	God's Spirit	ch. 3, sec. 2f
11QPsa Plea 19:14 (11QPsb Plea 2-3 is parallel)	רוח אמונה ודעת חונני	man's spirit, disposition	ch. 4, sec. 3b2
11QPsa Plea 19:15	אל תשלט בי שטן ורוח טמאה	demon	ch. 5, sec. 2e2
11QPsa Crea 24 II 14-15	ויוצא [רוח] מאוצרותיו	wind	ch. 6, sec. 1b1
11QPsa DavComp 27 II 4	ויתן לו יהוה רוח נבונה ואורה	Man's spirit, disposition	ch. 4, sec. 3e
Temple Scroll 6:6	לארבע רוחותיה	wind/sides	ch. 6, sec. 1b3
Temple Scroll 30:10	לכול רוחותיו	wind/sides	ch. 6, sec. 1b3
Temple Scroll 31:10	לכול רוחותיו	wind/sides	ch. 6, sec. 1b3
Temple	לכול רוח ורוח	wind/side	ch. 6, sec. 1b5

CLASSIFIED BIBLIOGRAPHY

1. REFERENCE WORKS FOR THE OLD TESTAMENT AND QUMRAN

Brown, F.; Driver; S. R.; Briggs, C. A. *A Hebrew and English Lexicon of the Old Testament*. Oxford: Clarendon Press: 1906.

Fitzmyer, J. A. *The Dead Sea Scrolls, Major Publications and Tools for Study*. Sources for Biblical Study, 8. Missoula: Scholars Press, 1975.

Kautzsch, E., ed. *Gesenius's Hebrew Grammar*. Translated by A. E. Cowley. 2nd ed. Oxford: Clarendon Press, 1910.

Kuhn, K. G., ed. *Konkordanz zu den Qumrantexten*. Göttingen: Vandenhoeck & Rupricht, 1960.

________. "Nachtrage zur 'Kondordanz zu den Qumrantexten'." *Revue de Qumrân*, 4 (1963-1964), 163-234.

________. *Rückläufiges Hebräisches Wörterbuch*. Göttingen: Vandenhoeck & Rupricht, 1958.

Mandelkern, S. *Veteris Testamenti Concordantiae, Hebraicae atque Chaldaicae*. Tel Aviv: Schocken Publishing House Ltd., 1967.

2. TEXTS, EDITIONS, AND SOURCES FOR *RUAḤ* AT QUMRAN

Allegro, J. M. "An Astrological Cryptic Document from Qumran." *Journal of Semitic Studies*, 9 (1964), 291-4.

_________. *Discoveries in the Judaean Desert of Jordan*, V: *Qumrân Cave 4, I (4Q158-4Q186)*. Oxford: Clarendon Press, 1968.

Avigad, Nahman, and Yadin, Yigael. *A Genesis Apocryphon, A Scroll From the Wildernes of Judaea*. Jerusalem: The Magnes Press of the Hebrew University and Heikhal Ha-Sefer, 1956.

Baillet, M. *Discoveries in the Judaean Desert*, VII: *Qumrân Grotte 4, III (4Q482-4Q550)*. Oxford: Clarendon Press, 1982.

Baillet, M.; Milik J. T.; and de Vaux, O. P. *Discoveries in the Judaean Desert of Jordan*, III: *Les 'Petites Grottes' de Qumrân*. Oxford: Clarendon Press, 1962.

Barthélemy, O. P., and Milik, J. T. *Discoveries in the Judaean Desert*, I: *Qumran Cave I*. Oxford: Clarendon Press, 1955.

Burrows, M., ed. *The Dead Sea Scrolls of St. Mark's Monestary*, Vol. II, Fascicle 2:*Plates and Transcriptions of the Manual of Discipline*. New Haven, 1951.

Fitzmyer J. A., and Harrington, D. J. *A Manual of Palestinian Aramaic Texts*. Biblica et Orientalia, 34. Rome: Biblical Institute Press, 1978.

Habermann, A. M. *מגילות מדבר יהודה* ("The Scrolls from the Judaean Desert." Jerusalem; Machbaroth Lesifrut Publishing House, 1959.

Jongeling, B.; Labuschagne, C. J.; and van der Woude, A. S. *Aramaic Texts from Qumran with Translations and Annotations*. Semitic Studies Series, 4. Leiden: Brill, 1976.

Lohse, E. *Die Texte aus Qumran, Hebräisch und Deutsch mit Masoretischer Punktation,Übersetzung, Einführung und Anmerkungen*. 2nd ed. München: Kösel Verlag, 1971.

Milik, J. T., ed. *The Books of Enoch, Aramaic Fragments of Qumrân Cave 4*. Oxford: Clarendon Press, 1976.

________. "Fragment d'une source du Psautier (4QPs 89) et fragments des Jubilés, du Document de Damas, d'un Phylactère dan la grotte 4 de Qumrân." *Revue Biblique*, 73 (1966), 74-106.
This article is the main source for 4Q266 Da 1 XVII, although it is cited as 4Q226 apparently due to a misprint. Cf. Fitzmyer, *Major Publications*, p. 31.

________. "Milkî-ṣedeq et Milkî-reša' dans les anciens écrits juifs et chrétiens." *Journal of Jewish Studies*, 23 (1972), 95-144.
In this article are found the following sources used in this study: 4Q266, 4Q270, 4Q286, 4Q287 and 11QMelch 3 II.

__________. Review of *The Manual of Dicipline*, by P. Wernberg-Møller. *Revue Biblique*, 67 (1968), 410-416.
In this review Milik lists a number of variant readings for 1QS from Cave 4.

Rabin, C. *The Zadokite Documents*. 2nd ed. Oxford: Clarendon Press, 1958.

Sanders, J. A. *Discoveries in the Judaean Desert of Jordan*,IV: *The Psalms Scroll of Qumran Cave 11*. Oxford: Clarendon Press, 1965.

Strugnell, J. "The Angelic Liturgy at Qumran, 4Q Serek Šîrôt ʿOlat Haššabbāt." Supplements to *Vetus Testamentum*, 7 (1959), 318-345.

________. "Notes en marge du Volume V des 'Discoveries in the Judaean Desert of Jordan'." *Revue de Qumrân*, 7 (1969-1971), 163-276.

In this article Strugnell offers among other things a reconstruction of 4Q177. This differs from the edition offered by J. Allegro as found in Allegro, *Discoveries*, V.

Sukenik, E. L. אוצר המגילות הגנוזות בידי האוניברסיטה העברית ("The Dead Sea Scrolls of the Hebrew University of Jerusalem.") Jerusalem: Bialik Foundation and Hebrew University, 1954.
Among other things, this edition offers transcriptions and photographs of 1QM and 1QH.

Yadin, Y. *The Temple Scroll*, vol. 2: *Text and Commentary*. Jerusalem: Israel Exploration Society, 1983.

3. TRANSLATIONS AND COMMENTARIES

Bardtke, H. *Die Handschriftenfunde am Toten Meer*. 2nd ed. Berlin: Evangelische Haupt-Bibelgesellschaft, 1961.

Brownlee. W. H. "The Dead Sea Manual of Discipline, Translation and Notes." *Bulletin of the Americal Schools of Oriental Research*, supplementary studies, 10-12 (1951).

Carmignac, J. *La Règle de la Guerre, des Fils de Lumière contre les Fils de Ténèbres*. Paris: Letouzey et Ané, 1958.

________, and Guilbert, p. *Les Textes de Qumran, traduits et annotés*. Vol. I: *La Règle de la Communauté, la Règle de la Guerre, les Hymnes*. Autour de la Bible. Paris: Letouze et Ané, 1961.

_______; Cothenet, É.; and Ligné. *Les Textes de Qumran, traduits et annotés*. Vol. II: *Règle de la Congrégation, Recueil de Bénédictions, interprétations de prophètes et de Psaumes, Document de Damas, Apocryphe de la Genèse, fragments des grottes 1 et 4*. Autour de la Bible. Paris: Letouse et Ané, 1963.

Davies, P. R. *The Damascus Covenant, An Interpretation of the "Damascus Document"*. Journal for the Study of the Old Testament Supplement Series, 25. Sheffield: JSOT Press, 1982.

________. 1QM, *The War Scroll from Qumran. Its Structure and History*. Rome: Biblical Institute Press, 1977.

Delcor, M. "La Guerre des fils de lumière contre les fils de tenebres, ou le 'Manuel du parfait combattant' de Qumrân." *La Nouvelle Revue Théologique*, 77 (1955), 372-399.

________. *Les Hymnes de Qumran (Hodayot). Texte hébreu, introduction, traduction, commentaire*. Autour de la Bible. Paris: Letouzey et Ané, 1962.

Dupont-Sommer, A. *Les écrits esséniens découverts près de la Mer Morte*. Bibliothèque Historique. Paris: Payot, 1959

________. "Règlement de la Guerre des fills de lumière. Traduction et notes." *Revue de l'Histoire des Religions*, 7-12 (1955), 25-43 and 141-180.

Fitzmyer, J. A. *The Genesis Apocryphon of Qumran Cave 1, A Commentary*. 2nd ed. Biblical et Orientalia, 18a. Rome: Pontifical Biblical Institute, 1971.

Gaster, T. H. *The Dead Sea Scriptures*. 3rd ed. Garden City: Anchor Books, 1976.

Holm-Nielsen, *Hodayot, Psalms from Qumran*. Aarhus: Universitetsforlaget I, 1960.

Jongeling, B. *Le rouleau de la guerre de manuscrits de Qumrân*. Studia Semitica Neerlandica,4. Assen, 1962.

Lambert, G. "Un 'Genèse apocrypha' trouvée à Qumran." *Recherches Bibliques*, 4. (1959), 85-107.

Leaney, A. R. C. *The Rule of Qumran and its Meaning. Introduction, translation and commentary*. The New Testament Library. Philadelphia: Westminster Press, 1966.

Licht, J. - *מגילת הסרכים ממגילות מדבר יהודה. סרך היחד - סרך העדה - סרך הברכות* ("The Rule Scroll. A Scroll from the Wilderness of Judaea. 1QS, 1QSa, 1QSb. Text, Introduction and Commentary.") Jerusalem: Bialik Institute, 1965.

________. *מגילת ההודיות ממגילות מדבר יהודה* ("The Thanksgiving Scroll. A Scroll from the Wilderness of Judaea. Text, Introduction, Commentary and Glossary.") Jerusalem: Bialik institute, 1957.

Maier, J. *Die Texte vom Toten Meer*. Vol I: *Übersetsung*. Vol. II: *Anmerkungen*. München: Reinhardt Verlag, 1960.

Mansoor, M. *The Thanksgiving Hymns. Translated and Annotated with an Introduction*. Studies on the Texts of the Desert of Judah, 3. Leiden: Brill, 1961.

Medico, H. I. del. *L'énigme des manuscrits de la Mer Morte. Étude sur la date, la provenance et le contenu des manuscrits découverts dans la grotte I de Qumrân*. Paris: Librairie Plon, 1957.

Ploeg, J. van der. "La Règle de la Guerre. Traduction et notes." *Vetus Testamentum*, 4 (1955), 373-420.

________. "Un petit rouleau de psalmes apocryphes (11QPsApa)." *Tradition und Glaube*, Festgabe für K. G. Kuhn. Göttingen: Vandenhoeck & Ruprecht, 1971.

________. *Le Rouleau de la Guerre. Traduit et annoté avec une introduction*. Studies on the Texts of the Desert of Judah, 2. Leiden: Brill, 1959.

Vermes, *The Dead Sea Scrolls in English.* Baltimore: Penguin Books, 1968.

Wernberg-Møller, P. *The Manual of Discipline. Translated and Annotated with an Introduction.* Studies of the Texts of the Desert of Judah, 1. Leiden: Brill, 1957.

Yadin, Y. מגילת מלחמת בני אור בבני חושך ("The Scroll of the War of the Sons of Light against the Sons of Darkness.") Jerusalem: Bialik Institute, 1955. English: *The Scroll of the War of the Sons of Light against the Sons of Darkness.* Translated by Batya and Chaim Rabin; Oxford: Oxford University Press, 1962.

4. RELATED WORKS

Allegro, J. M. *The Dead Sea Scrolls.* Baltimore: Penguin Books, 1956.

Anderson, A. A. "The Use of 'Ruah' in 1QS, 1QH and 1QM." *Journal of Semitic Studies,* 7 (1962), 293-303.

Bardtke, H. "Considerations sur les cantiques de Qumrân." *Revue Biblique,* 63 (1956), 220-233.

Baumbach, G. *Qumrân und das Johannes-Evangelium. Eine vergleichende Untersuchung der dualistischen Aussagen der Ordensregel von Qumrân und des Johannes Evangeliums mit Berücksichtigung der spätjüdischen Apokalypsen.* Aufsätze und vorträge zur Theologie und Religionswissenschaft, 6. Berlin: Evangelishe Varlagsanstalt, 1958.

Beaven, E. L. "Ruah Hakodesh in Some Early Jewish Literature." Unpublished Ph.D. dissertation, Vanderbilt University, 1961.

Bergmeier, R. *Glaube als Gabe nach Johannes. Religions- und theologiegeschichtliche Studien zum prädestinatianischen Dualismus im vierten Evangelium*. Stuttgart: Kohlhammer, 1980.

Becker, J. *Das Heil Gottes. Heils- und Sündenbegriffe in den Qumrantexten und im Neuen Testament* Studien zur Umwelt des Neuen Testaments, 3. Göttingen: Vandenhoeck & Ruprecht, 1964.

Betz, O. *Offenbarung und Schriftforschung in der Qumransekte*. Wissenschaftliche Untersuchungen zum Neuen Testament, 6. Tübingen: Mohr, 1960.

________. "Die Geburt der Gemeinde durch den Lehrer." *New Testament Studies*, 3 (1957), 314-326.

__________. *Der Paraklet, Fürsprecher im häretischen Spätjudentum, im Johannesevangelium und in neu gefundenen gnostischen Schriften*. Leiden: Brill, 1963.

_________. "'To Worship God in Spirit and in Truth': Reflections on John 4:20-26." *Standing before God*. Edited by A. Finkel and L. Frizzel. New York: Ktav. 1981, pp. 53- 72.

Böcher, O. *Der johanneische Dualismus im Zusammenhang des nachbiblischen Judentums*. Güttersloh: Gerd Mohn, 1965.

Brandenburger, E. *Fleisch und Geist. Paulus und die dualistische Weisheit*. Wissenschaftliche Monographien zum Alten und Neuen Testament. Neukirchen: Neukirchener Verlag, 1968.

Braun, F. M. "L'arrière-fond judaïque du Quatrième Évangile et la Communauté de l'Alliance. *Revue Biblique*, 62 (1955), 5-44.

Braun H. *Qumran und das Neue Testament*. Vols. I and II. Tübingen: Mohr, 1966.

Brown, R. "The Qumran Scrolls and the Johannine Gospel and Epistles." *Catholic Biblical Quarterly*, 17 (1955), 183-207.

Brownlee, W. H. "Anthropology and Soteriology in the Dead Sea Scrolls and in the New Testament." *The Use of the Old Testament in the New and Other Essays, Studies in honor of W. F. Stinespring*. Edited by J. E. Efird. Durham, N. C.: Duke University Press, 1972, pp. 210-240.

Bruce, F. F. "Holy Spirit in the Qumran Texts." *The Annual of Leeds University Oriental Society*, 6 (1966-1968), 49-55.

Burrows, M. *The Dead Sea Scrolls*. New York: Viking Press, 1955.

_________. *More Light on the Dead Sea Scrolls*. New York: Viking Press, 1958.

Carmignac, J. *Christ and the Teacher of Righteousness*. Translated by K. Pedley. Baltimore: Helicon Press, 1962.

Charles, R. H., and Cowley, A. "An Early Source of the Testaments of the Patriarchs." *Jewish Quarterly Review*, 19 (April, 1907), 566-583.

_________. *The Greek Versions of the Testaments of the Twelve Patriarchs*. Hildesheim: George Olms Verlagsbuchhandung, 1960 (reprint of the 1908 work).

Charlesworth, J. H., ed. "A Critical Comparison of the Dualism in 1QS 3:13-4:26 and the 'Dualism' contained in the Gospel of John." *John and Qumran*. London, 1972, pp. 76-106.

_________, ed. *The Old Testament Pseudepigrapha*. 2 vols. Garden City: Doubleday, 1983-1985.

Chevallier, M. A. *Souffle de Dieu. Le Saint-Esprit dans le Nouveau Testament*. Vol. I: *Ancient Testament, Hellenisme et Judaisme. La tradition synoptique. L'œvre de Luc*. Paris: Éditions Beauchesne, 1978.

Coppens, J. "Les Documents du Désert de Juda et les Origines du Christianisme." *Analecta Lovaniensia Biblica et Orientalia*. Sér. II, fasc. 39 (1953), 23-39.

________. "Le don de l'Esprit d'après les Textes de Qumrân et le quatrième Évangile."*L'Evangile de Jean. Études et Problèms*, Recherches Bibliques, 3. Louvain: M. E. Boismard, 1958, 209-223.

Cross, F. M., Jr. *The Ancient Library of Qumran and Modern Biblical Studies*. 2nd ed. Garden City: Doubleday and Co., 1961.

Daniélou, J. "Une source d la spiritualité Chrétienne dans le Manuscrits de la Mer Morte: la doctrine des deux esprits." *Dieu Vivant*, 25 (1953), 127-136.

Davies, W. D. "Paul and the Dead Sea Scrolls: Flesh and Spirit." *The Scrolls and the New Testament*. Edited by K. Stendahl. New York: Harper and Brothers, 1957, pp. 157-182.

de Jonge, M. *Studies on the Testaments of the Twelve Patriarchs*, Text and Interpretation. Leiden: Brill, 1975.

_________. *Testamenta XII Patriarchum*. Pseudepigrapha Veteris Testamenti Graece, 1. Leiden: Brill, 1964.

_________. "The Use of the Word 'Anointed' in the Time of Jesus." *NovemTestamentum*, 8 (1966), 132-148.

________, and van der Woude, A. S. "Melchizedek and the New Testament." *New Testament Studies*, 12 (July 1966), 301-326.

Delcor, M. "V. Doctrines des Esseniens." *Supplement au Dictionnaire de la Bible.* Fasc 51. Paris, 1978, col. 960-980.

De Vries, S. J. "Consecutive Constructions in the 1Q Sectarian Scrolls." *Doron Hebraic Studies*, Essays in Honor of Professor Abraham L. Katsch. New York, 1965, pp. 75-87.

________. "The Syntax of Tenses in the Interpretation of the Hodayot." *Revue de Qumrân*, 5 (1965), 375-414.

Dietzel, A. "Beten im Geist. Eine religionsgeschichtliche Parallele aus den Hodajot zum paulinischen Beten im Geist." *Theologische Zeitschrift*, 13 (1957), 12-32.

Dombkowski Hopkins, D. "The Qumran Community and 1QHodayot: a Reassessment." *Revue de Qumrân*, 10 (1981), 323-364.

Driver, G. R. *The Judaean Scrolls. The Problem and a Solution.* Oxford: Basil Blackwell, 1965.

Duhaime, J. L. "L'instruction sur les deux esprits et les interpolations dualistes à Qumran (1QS III, 13 - IV, 26). *Revue Biblique*, 4 (1977), 566-594.

________. "La rédaction de 1QM 13 et l'évolution du dualisme à Qumran." *Revue Biblique*, 2 (1977). 210-238.

Dupont-Sommer, A. "Deux documents horoscopiques esseniens découverts à Qoumrân, près de la Mer Morte." *Académie des Inscriptions & Belles-Lettres, Comptes Redus*. Paris: Librairie C. Klincksieck, 1967, pp. 229-253.

________. "Exorcismes et guérisons dan le écrits de Qoumrân." Supplements to *Vetus Testamentum*, 7. Leiden: Brill, 1960, 246-261.

________. "L'instruction sur les deux Esprits dans le Manuel de Discipline." *Revue de l'Histoire des Religions*, 142 (1952), 5-35.

________. "Le problem des influences etrangeres sur le secte juive de Qoumrân." *Revue d'Histoire et de Philosophie Religieuses*, 35 (1955), 75-94.

Ellis, E. E. "'Spiritual' Gifts in the Pauline Community." *New Testament Studies*, 20 (1974), 128-144.

Flusser, D. "The Dead Sea Scrolls and Pre-Pauline Christianity." *Scripta Hierosolymitana*, IV (1958), 246-252.

________. "The Dualism of 'Flesh and Spirit' in the Dead Sea Scrolls and in the New Testament," (Hebrew). Tarbiş, 27 (1958), 158-65.

________. "Healing through the Laying-on of Hands in a Dead Sea Scroll." *Israel Exploration Journal*, 7 (1957), 107-8.

________. "Qumran and Jewish Apotropaic Prayers." *Israel Exploration Journal*, 16 (1966), 194-205.

Foerster, W. "Der Heilige Geist im Spätjudentum," *New Testament Studies*, 8 (Jan., 1962), 117-134.

Gammie, J. G. "Spatial and Ethical Dualism in Jewish Wisdom and Apocalyptic Literature." *Journal of Biblical Literature*, 93 (1974), 356-385.

Glanzman, G. S. "Sectarian Psalms from the Dead Sea." *Theological Studies*, 13 (1952), 487-524.

Goshen-Gottstein, M. H. "Linguistic Structure and Tradition in the Qumran Documents." *Scripta Hierosolymitana*, IV (1958), 101-137.

Graystone, G. "The Dead Sea Scrolls and the New Testament." *The Irish Theological Quarterly*, vol. 22 (1955), 214-230, 329-346, vol. 23 (1956) 25-48.

Grelot, P. "Sur l'Apocryphe de la Genèse (col. XX, Ligne 26)." *Revue de Qumrân*, 2 (1958), 273-276.

Hauschild, W. D. *Gottes Geist und der Mensch*. Beiträge zur evangelischen Theologie, 63. München: Kaiser Verlag, 1972.

Hempel, J. "Christentum vor Christus? Die Handschriftenfunde vom Toten Meer und das Neue Testament." *Deutsches Pfarrerblatt*, 51 (1951), 480-484.

Hengel, M. "Qumran und der Hellenismus." *Bibliotheca Ephemeridum Theologicarum Lovaniensium*, XLVI (1978), 333-372.

Hill, D. *Greek Words and Hebrew Meanings: Studies in the Semantics of Soteriological Terms*. Society for New Testament Studies Monograph Series, 5. Cambridge, 1967.

Hübner, H. "Anthropologischer Dualismus in den Hodayoth?" *New Testament Studies*, 18 (1972), 268-284.

Huppenbauer, H. W. "Belial in den Qumrantexten." *Theologische Zeitschrift*, 15 (1959), 81-89.

_________. *Der Mensch zwischen zwei Welten. Der Dualismus der Texte von Qumran (Höhle I) und der Damaskusfrag-*

mente. Ein Beitrag zur Vorgeschichte des Evangeliums. Abhandlungen zu Theologie des Alten und Neuen Testaments, 34. Zürich: Zwingli Verlag, 1959.

Hyatt, J. P. "The View of Man in the Qumran 'Hodayot'." *New Testament Studies*, 2 (1956), 276-284.

Imschoot, P. van. *Theology of the Old Testament*, I. Translated by K. Sullivan and F. Buck. New York: Desclee, 1965.

Irwin, A. L. "Conflict Spirit-Dualism in the Qumran Writings and the New Testament." Unpublished Ph.D. dissertation, Hartford Theological Seminary, 1960.

Jaubert, A. *La notion d'alliance dans le Judaïsme aux abords de l'ère chrétienne.* Patristica Sorbonensia, 6. Paris: Éditions du Seuil, 1963.

Jeremias, J. *New Testament Theology, The Proclamation of Jesus.* Translated by J. Bowden. New York: Charles Schribner's Sons, 1971.

Jeremias, G. *Der Lehrer der Gerechtigkeit.* Studien zur Unwelt des Neuen Testaments, 2. Göttingen: Vandenhoeck and Ruprecht, 1963.

Jewett, R. *Paul's Anthropological Terms.* Arbeiten zur Geschichte des antiken Judentums und des Urchristentums, X. Leiden: Brill, 1971.

Johnston, G. "Spirit and Holy Spirit in the Qumran Literature." *New Testament Sidelights.* Essays in Honor of A. C. Purdy. Hartford, 1960, pp. 27-42.

Kamlah, E. *Die Form der katalogischen Paränese im Neuen Testament.* Wissenschaftliche Untersuchungen zum Neuen Testament, 7. Tübingen: Mohr, 1964.

________. "Geist." *Theologisches Begriffslexikon zum Neuen Testament*, vol. 3. Edited by L. Coenen, E. Beyreuther and H. Bietenhard. Wuppertal: Theologischer Verlag Rolf Brockhaus, 1967, 479-487.

Kirchschläger, W. "Exorzismus in Qumran?" *Kairos*, 18 (1976), 135-153.

Kuhn, H. W. *Enderwartung und gegenwärtiges Heil, Untersuchung zu den Gemeindeliedern von Qumran*. Studien zur Umwelt des Neuen Testaments, 4. Göttingen: Vandenhoeck & Ruprecht, 1966.

Kuhn K. G. "Der Epheserbrief im Licht der Qumrantexte." *New Testament Studies*, 7 (July, 1961), 334-346.

________. "Die in Palästina gefundenen Hebräischen Texte und das Neue Testament." *Zeitschrift für Theologie und Kirche*, 47 (1950), 192-211.

________. "Πειρασμός - ἁμαρτία - σάρξ im Neuen Testament und die damit zusammenhängenden Vorstellungen." *Zeitschrift Für theologie und Kirche*, 49 (1952), 200-222.

________. "Qumran." *Die Religion in Geschichte und Gegenwart*. 3rd ed. Vol. V, (1961), col. 745-754.

________. "Die Sektenschriften und der iranische Religion." *Zeitschrift für Theologie und Kirche*, 49 (1952), 296-316.

Laurin, R. B. "The Question of Immortality in the Qumran Hodayot." *Journal of Semitic Studies*, 3 (1958), 344-355.

Licht, J. "An Analysis of the Treatise of the Two Spirits in DSD." *Scripta Hierosolymitana*, IV (1958), 88-100.

________. "The Doctrine of the Thanksgiving Scroll." *Israel Exploration Journal*, 6 (1956), 1-13 and 89-101.

Lichtenberger, H. *Studien zum Menschenbild in Texten der Qumrangemeinde*. Studien zur Umwelt des Neuen Testaments, 15. Göttingen: Vandenhoeck & Ruprecht, 1980.

Lilly, R. E. "The Idea of Man in Qumran Literature." Unpublished Ph.D. dissertation, Boston University Graduate School, 1962.

Lys, D. *"Rûach", le Souffle dans l'Ancient Testament*. Paris: Presses Universitaires de France, 1962.

Maier, G. *Mensch und freier Wille. Nach den Jüdischen Religionsparteien zwischen Ben Sira und Paulus*. Wissenschaftliche Untersuchungen zum Neuen Testament, 12. Tübingen, Mohr, 1971.

Manns, F. *Le symbole eau-esprit dans le Judaisme ancien*. Studium Biblicum Franciscanum, 19. Jerusalem: Franciscan Printing Press, 1983.

May, H. G. "Cosmological Reference in the Qumran Doctrine of the Two Spirits and in Old Testament Imagery."*Journal of Biblical Literature*, 82 (1963), 1-14.

McNamara, M. *The New Testament and the Palestinian Targum to the Pentateuch*. Rome: Pontifical Biblical Institute, 1966.

Merrill, E. H. *Qumran and Predestination, A Theological Study of the Thanksgiving Hymns*. Studies on the Texts of the Desert of Judah, 8. Leiden: Brill, 1975.

Michaud, H. "Un livre apocryphe de la Genèse in Araméen." *Positions Lutheriennes*, 5 (1957), 91-104.

________. "Un myth Zervanite dans un des manuscrits de Qumrân." *Vetus Testamentum*, 5 (1955), 137-147.

Milik, J. T. *Ten Years of Discovery in the Wilderness of Judea*. Translated by J. Strugnell. Studies in Biblical Theology, 26. Naperville, Ill.: Alec R. Allenson, Inc., 1959.

Molin, G. *Die Söhne des Lichtes, Zeit und Stellung der Handschriften vom Toten Meer*. Wien: Verlag Herold, 1954.

Montague, G. T. *The Holy Spirit: Growth of a Biblical Tradition*, New York: Paulist Press. 1976.

Murphy, R. O. *The Dead Sea Scrolls and the Bible*. Westminster, Maryland: Newman Press, 1956.

________. "*Yeṣer* in the Qumran Literature." *Biblica*, 39 (1958), 334-344.

Murphy-O'Connor, J. "La genèse littéraire de la *Règle de la Communauté*." *Revue Biblique*, 76 (1969), 528-549.

Nötscher, F. "Geist und Geister in den Texten von Qumran." *Mélanges Bibliques*. Rédigées en l'honneur de A. Robert. Paris, 1957, pp. 305-315.

________. "Heiligkeit im Qumranschriften." *Revue de Qumran*, 2 (1959-1960), 315-344.

________. *Zur theologischen Terminologie der Qumran-Texte*. Bonner Biblische Beiträge, 10. Bonn: Hanstein, 1956.

Noll, S. F. "Communion of Angels and Men in realized Eschatology in the Dead Sea Scrolls." *Proceedings of the Eighth World Congress of Jewish Studies*, Division A, 1981 (1982), pp. 91-97.

________. "Angelology in the Qumran Texts." Unpublished Ph.D. dissertation, University of Manchester, 1979.

Osten-Sacken, P. von der, *Gott und Belial. Traditionsgeschichtliche Untersuchungen zum Dualismus in den Texten aus Qumran*. Studien zur Umwelt des Neuen Testaments, 6. Göttingen: Vandenhoeck & Ruprecht, 1969.

Otzen, B. "Die neugefundenen hebräischen Sektenschriften und die Testamente der zwölf Patriarchen." *Studia Theologica,* 7 (1953), 125-157.

________. "Old Testament Wisdom Literature and Dualistic Thinking in Late Judaism." Supplements to *Vetus Testamentum,* 28 (1975), 146-157.

Ploeg, J. van der. "The Belief in Immortality in the Writings of Qumran. *Bibliotheca Orientalis,* 18 (1961), 118-124.

________. *The Excavations at Qumran, A Survey of the Judaean Brotherhood and its Ideas*. Translated by K Smyth. London: Longmans Green and Co., 1958.

Pryke, J. "'Spirit' and 'Flesh' in the Qumran Documents and some New Testament Texts. *Revue de Qumrân,* 5 (1965), 345-360.

Ringgren, H. *The Faith of Qumran, Theology of the Dead Sea Scrolls*. Translated by E.T. Sander. Philadelphia: Fortress Press, 1963.

Russell, D. S. *The Method and Message of Jewish Apocalyptic.* Old Testament Library. London: SCM Press, 1964.

Schnackenburg, R. "Die 'Anbetung in Geist und Wahrheit' (John 4:23) im Lichte von QumrânTexten." *Biblische Zeitschrift,* 3 (1959), 88-94.

Schubert, K. *The Dead Sea Community. Its Origin and Teachings*. Translated by J. W. Doberstein. London: Adam & Charles Black, 1959.

________. "Der Sektenkanon von En Feshcha und die Anfänge der jüdischen Gnosis." *Theologische Literaturzeitung*, 78 (1953), 495-506.

Schreiner, J. "Geistbegabung in der Gemeinde von Qumran." *Biblische Zeitschrift*, 9 (1965), 161-180.

Schweizer, E. "Gegenwart des Geistes und eschatologische Hoffnung bei Zarathustra, spätjüdischen Gruppen, Gnostikern und den Zeugen des Neuen Testaments." *The Background of the New Testament and its Eschatology*. Essays in Honor of C. H. Dodd. Cambridge, 1956, pp. 481-508.

________. *Heiliger Geist*. Bibliothek Themen der Theologie Ergänzungsband. Stuggart: Kreuz Verlag, 1978.

________. "πνεῦμα, πνευματικός κτλ." *Theological Dictionary of the New Testament*, 6. Translated and edited by G. W. Bromiley. Grand Rapids, 1961, 389-452.

________. "Die sieben Geister in der Apokalypse." *Evangelische Theologie*, 11 (1951-1952) 502-512.

Seitz, O. "Two Spirits in Man: An Essay in Biblical Exegesis." *New Testament Studies*, 6 (1959-1960), 82-95.

Shaked, S. "Qumran and Iran: Further Considerstions." *Israel Oriental Studies*, II (1972), 433-446.

Sjöberg, E. "Neuschöpfung in den Toten-Meer-Rollen." *Studia Theologica*, IX (1955), 131-7.

________. "πνεῦμα, πνευματικός κτλ." *Theological Dictionary of the New Testament*, 6. Translated and edited by G. W. Bromiley. Grand Rapids, 1961, 375-389.

________. "Wiedergeburt und Neuschöpfung in palästinischen Judentum." *Studia Theologica*, IV (1950 [51-52]), 44-85.

Stone, M. E., ed. *Jewish Writings of the Second Temple Period*. Philadelphia: Fortress Press, 1984.

Teicher, J. L. "The Teaching of the Pre-Pauline Church in the Dead Sea Scrolls." *Journal of Jewish Studies*, vol. 3 (1952), 111-118, vol. 4 (1953), 1-13.

Trautmann, C. "'L'instruction sur les deux Esprits': Le dualisme dans la doctrine et la pratique des Esséniens." *Foi et Vie*, 80 (1981), 26-40.

Treves, M. "The Two Spirits of the Rule of the Community." *Revue de Qumrân*, 3 (1961-1962), 449-452.

VanderKam, J. C. *Textual and Historical Studies in the Book of Jubilees*. Harvard Semitic Museum Monographs, 14. Missoula, Montana: Scholars Press, 1977.

Vermes, G. *The Dead Sea Scrolls - Qumran in Perspective*. Cleveland: Collins World, 1978.

Wernberg-Møller, P. "A Reconsideration of the Two Spirits in the Rule of the Community (1 QSerek III,3 - IV,26)." *Revue de Qumrân*, 11 (1961), 413-441.

Wildberger, H. "Der Dualismus in den Qumran Schriften." *Asiatische Studien*, 1-4 (1954), 163-177.

Winston, D. "The Iranian Component in the Bible, Apocrypha, and Qumran: A Review of the Evidence." *History of Religions*, 5 (1966), 183-216.

Wolverton, W. I. "The Double Minded Man in the Light of Essene Psychology." *Anglican Theological Review,* 38 (1956), 166-175.